Fionnua

A Simulation Framework for the Teaching and Learning of Distributed Algorithms

Fionnuala O'Donnell

A Simulation Framework for the Teaching and Learning of Distributed Algorithms

VDM Verlag Dr. Müller

Impressum/Imprint (nur für Deutschland/ only for Germany)

Bibliografische Information der Deutschen Nationalbibliothek: Die Deutsche Nationalbibliothek verzeichnet diese Publikation in der Deutschen Nationalbibliografie; detaillierte bibliografische Daten sind im Internet über http://dnb.d-nb.de abrufbar.

Alle in diesem Buch genannten Marken und Produktnamen unterliegen warenzeichen-, marken- oder patentrechtlichem Schutz bzw. sind Warenzeichen oder eingetragene Warenzeichen der jeweiligen Inhaber. Die Wiedergabe von Marken, Produktnamen, Gebrauchsnamen, Handelsnamen, Warenbezeichnungen u.s.w. in diesem Werk berechtigt auch ohne besondere Kennzeichnung nicht zu der Annahme, dass solche Namen im Sinne der Warenzeichen- und Markenschutzgesetzgebung als frei zu betrachten wären und daher von jedermann benutzt werden dürften.

Coverbild: www.purestockx.com

Verlag: VDM Verlag Dr. Müller Aktiengesellschaft & Co. KG
Dudweiler Landstr. 99, 66123 Saarbrücken, Deutschland
Telefon +49 681 9100-698, Telefax +49 681 9100-988, Email: info@vdm-verlag.de
Zugl.: Dublin, Trinity College Dublin, 2006

Herstellung in Deutschland:
Schaltungsdienst Lange o.H.G., Berlin
Books on Demand GmbH, Norderstedt
Reha GmbH, Saarbrücken
Amazon Distribution GmbH, Leipzig
ISBN: 978-3-639-12298-5

Imprint (only for USA, GB)

Bibliographic information published by the Deutsche Nationalbibliothek: The Deutsche Nationalbibliothek lists this publication in the Deutsche Nationalbibliografie; detailed bibliographic data are available in the Internet at http://dnb.d-nb.de.

Any brand names and product names mentioned in this book are subject to trademark, brand or patent protection and are trademarks or registered trademarks of their respective holders. The use of brand names, product names, common names, trade names, product descriptions etc. even without a particular marking in this works is in no way to be construed to mean that such names may be regarded as unrestricted in respect of trademark and brand protection legislation and could thus be used by anyone.

Cover image: www.purestockx.com

Publisher:
VDM Verlag Dr. Müller Aktiengesellschaft & Co. KG
Dudweiler Landstr. 99, 66123 Saarbrücken, Germany
Phone +49 681 9100-698, Fax +49 681 9100-988, Email: info@vdm-publishing.com
Dublin, Trinity College Dublin, 2006

Copyright © 2009 by the author and VDM Verlag Dr. Müller Aktiengesellschaft & Co. KG and licensors
All rights reserved. Saarbrücken 2009

Printed in the U.S.A.
Printed in the U.K. by (see last page)
ISBN: 978-3-639-12298-5

DEDICATION

For Dad

"A Dhaidí, mór an trua nach bhfuil tú anseo anois. Nach ort a bheadh an bród!
Ach, a Dhaidí, bhí tú liom, ta tú liom, is beidh tú liom i gcónaí.
Míle Buíochas!"

ACKNOWLEDGEMENTS

Firstly, to my supervisor, Brendan Tangney, I thank you for your support, encouragement and patience throughout this endeavour. We have travelled a long and at times rocky road together but somehow have managed to come out the other end!

Secondly, to the members of the CRITE research group, both past and present, I say thank you for your endless hours of support, encouragement and cheerful banter which always seemed to brighten up even the dullest of days! A special word of thanks to my good friend, James, without whom this project would simply have floundered!

Thirdly, I would like to extend my appreciation to Stephen Barrett, Björn Franke and Damian Gordon who took time out of their busy schedules as lecturers to assist me in evaluating FADA. I am deeply grateful.

Lastly, a special word of thanks to my family and friends. To my brothers, Pauric and Kevin, I say thank you for your continuous support and advice. You will be glad to know my days of doing things the "hard way" are finally at an end. To my sisters, Yvonne and Emer, thanks for being you and for keeping me grounded. To Yvonne, especially, thanks for listening to what must have seemed like an eternity of endless moans and for providing me with many a delightful distraction! To my mum, thanks for never loosing faith in me and for simply being there when ever I've needed you. To Alice, thanks for your prayers and kind ear but above all, thanks for the homemade bread and cheese, it was like rocket fuel to the brain!!

Finally, to all those people, I now call dear friends, who I had the good fortune to meet along my academic travels, I say *'buíochas'* and *'Lets party as I have finally made it…well to the finishing line at least!'*

ABSTRACT

Teaching and learning about distributed algorithms is difficult. This is because distributed algorithms are made up of multiple independent elements, each with their own state and control, who interact through the exchange of messages. Such a configuration results in a large amount of data which describes not only the local state information of each element within the distributed algorithm but also, their complex interactions. Thus, the use of traditional teaching methodologies, for example pseudo code descriptions, execution traces, chalk and talk do not lend themselves well to the easy disclosure of material which is highly concurrent in nature and which may suffer from partial failure that is, the loss or failure of one or more of its elements.

Consequently, animation was put forward as one means of capturing the temporal evolution of a distributed algorithm's behaviour. However, creating an animation for each and every distributed algorithm that an instructor wishes to teach is a very time consuming process and one which instructors cannot readily commit to due to time constraints. Moreover, educational researchers have questioned the educational value of such systems as they may not engage learners in the high order thinking skills of analysis, synthesis and evaluation. As a result of this, researchers within the field of algorithm animation have looked for ways to expand the 'communicative expressiveness of algorithm animation systems' by building algorithm simulation systems. These are systems which allow a learner to interact with, manipulate or change the behaviour of an algorithm while it executes by, for example, changing the state of its variables or by causing a message to fail.

However, like algorithm animation systems, building algorithm simulation systems is a very time consuming and difficult process as, not only, must an instructor implement the logic of the distributed algorithm that he is intending to animate but he must also define how it is to be animated. Moreover, he must define which components of an algorithm's process that a learner can interact with, modify or change as it executes. Thus, researchers within the field of algorithm animation have looked for ways to combat the problem of building algorithm simulations by reanalyzing the educational benefit of algorithm animation systems. Informed by findings from constructionist educationalists, which show that learners who generate their own representations of an entity have a deeper understanding of that entity and better recall abilities than those who do not, researchers have developed systems to facilitate the easy creation of algorithm animations.

Drawing upon practices within software engineering of developing a framework whenever several or (partly) similar applications within a particular domain need to be developed, researchers have developed animation frameworks, which a learner can use to define the behaviour of an algorithm. These frameworks provide a set of prefabricated software building blocks that a learner can use to customise or build his own animation of an algorithm's behaviour. However, whilst these systems allow a learner to construct an animation of a distributed algorithm's behaviour in a timely manner, they do not allow him to exercise his higher order thinking skills by enabling him to manipulate the algorithm as it evolves.

Thus, informed by the strengths of algorithm simulation systems and algorithm construction systems, this thesis presents a simulation framework named FADA for the teaching and learning of distributed algorithms. The engagement model of FADA is that of a highly interactive simulation. Its underlying pedagogy is based on theories of constructionism and social constructivism. The design is also informed by the theories of dual coding and epistemic fidelity. Simulations are written in a conventional programming language, in this case JAVA, with a wrapper class making transparent calls to the underlying visualization API. The development environment contains an editor, a wizard and a debugger as typified by modern programming environments. To overcome the cost, in terms of development time, for creating new simulations, a framework for common message passing algorithms has been developed. Of particular note is that this framework also acts as a basis for scaffolding learners in the process of constructing their own simulations, à la the theory of constructionism.

As a consequence of its design, FADA can be attributed two modes of use. It can be used by instructors and learners as an interactive presentation tool. FADA provides an instructor or learner with a collection of pre-canned simulations that he can use to present to a class for discussion, exploration and feedback. The latter is informed by theory of social constructivism. FADA can also be used as a tool to allow instructors and learners to create their own simulations of an algorithm's behaviour. These can then be added to the aforementioned collection of simulations provided by FADA in order to create a repository of algorithm simulations.

A number of exploratory case studies were carried to investigate both the pedagogical and operational effectiveness of FADA. The aim of the case studies was twofold; to investigate to what extent the ability to view an algorithm's behaviour, interact with its behaviour in real time, customize or build its implementation facilitates learners in acquiring a deep understanding of its process and facilitates instructors in their teachings. From a pedagogical perspective, results suggest that learners engage with and are motivated by such systems and as a consequence, are challenged to test their understanding of an algorithm's behaviour in a deep way. Equally, results suggest that instructors find such systems an effective, intuitive and concrete means by which to demonstrate and convey the dynamic and concurrent behaviour of an algorithm. From an operational perspective, results suggest that instructors find such systems easy to use and assist them in creating active simulations for use in their own teachings in a timely and efficient manner. In summary the main contributions of this research are:

- The development of an algorithm animation system that engages learners in higher order thinking with an algorithm's behaviour.
- The development of a novel framework to facilitate the easy and quick creation of an active algorithm simulation.
- Results from exploratory case studies as to the effectiveness of active simulation systems in engaging and motivating learners to experiment with their understanding of an algorithm's behaviour in a deep manner.

TABLE OF CONTENTS

LIST OF FIGURES

LIST OF TABLES

CHAPTER 1
INTRODUCTION

1.1 Motivation

Learning about computer algorithms, the building blocks of computer software [1], is difficult. This is because algorithms are, in general, by their nature abstract and understanding how the myriad of variables in an algorithm are used and how control flows in an algorithm can be quite a challenge [2]. This is particularly true of distributed algorithms, which are made up of multiple independent elements, each with their own state and control, who interact through the exchange of messages [3]. Traditional teaching methodologies, like for example 'chalk and talk', use of transparencies slides, whiteboards, pseudo code descriptions, execution traces, etc., do not lend themselves well to the easy disclosure of material which is dynamic and concurrent in nature, and which may suffer from partial failure (that is, the loss or failure of one or more of its components). Such difficulties have prompted researchers to investigate tools and approaches to ease the difficulty of teaching and learning distributed algorithms. The author's own experiences of learning distributed algorithms as a postgraduate student have prompted her to investigate ways in which to enhance the teaching and learning of these algorithms.

   This chapter documents the manner by which this research was carried out. It describes current approaches taken by researchers to ameliorate the teaching and learning of distributed algorithms and documents problems inherent in these approaches. It puts forward the design and implementation of a new approach for the teaching and learning of distributed algorithms, one which addresses the challenges faced by current approaches through the provision of a simulation framework. Lastly, it describes a number of exploratory case studies conducted with the artefact to investigate its pedagogical effectiveness and its ease of use.

1.2 Current Approaches and their Inherent Problems

Animation has long since been put forward as one means of capturing the temporal evolution of a distributed algorithm's behaviour. By giving concrete depictions of the abstractions and operations of a distributed algorithm's behaviour, algorithm animation was thought to make distributed algorithms more meaningful [2]. As a consequence of this

1

belief, a spectrum of algorithm animation systems has evolved. These have ranged from *passive animation systems*, which provide prepared continuous animations of an algorithm's behaviour for a learner to view, through *active simulation systems*, which enable a learner to view a prepared algorithm animation and manipulate its behaviour in real time by altering the behaviour of its nodes or messages, to *algorithm construction systems*, which enable a learner to create his own visualisation of an algorithm's behaviour.

However, despite this proliferation of algorithm animation systems, these systems have failed to catch on in mainstream computer science education [1]. The majority of educators still prefer to use the traditional pedagogical aids of blackboards, whiteboards and over head projectors. This begs the question as to why? A number of researchers have postulated that their lack of adoption is due to shortcomings in their designs. Each of the aforementioned types of systems suffers from one or more of the following failings. These are:

- *Lack of real time interactivity with an algorithm's content,*

  In order for a learner to acquire an appreciation for and a deep understanding of the operations of an algorithm's behaviour, the learner must be able to manipulate the behaviour of its variables, nodes and messages in real time, that is, while the algorithm executes. However, most algorithm animation systems provide offline interaction [3], that is, they require a learner to specify prior to the execution of an algorithm's behaviour which property or mode of its behaviour that they would like to modify and observe. As a consequence, learners are rendered passive in their interactions with an algorithm's content while it executes and as a result, are unable to determine its level of fault tolerance.

  An algorithm is said to be fault tolerant if it continues to function despite the loss or failure of one or more of its components like, for example, nodes or messages. However, whilst active simulation systems facilitate real time interaction, they present an expert's mental model of an algorithm's behaviour and not that of the learner's. According to current thinking in education, knowledge is not merely a commodity to be transmitted, encoded, retained and reapplied but a personal experience to be constructed [4]. Thus, there is need of an algorithm animation system which enables a learner to present his own representation of an algorithm's behaviour and enables him to experiment with it in real time.

- *Time and effort required to build an algorithm simulation [1],*

  Building an active simulation is a very difficult and time consuming task and one which instructors cannot readily commit to. In constructing an active simulation, an instructor must not only implement the logic of the algorithm process but also, define how it is to be visualised and in turn, designate which sections of its process a learner can interact with, modify or change. Thus, there is need of a mechanism to reduce the complexity and time associated with creating an active simulation of an algorithm's behaviour.

- *The pedagogical value of algorithm animation systems has not been substantiated [5-8].*

  To date many empirical evaluations have been carried out to determine the educational effectiveness of algorithm animation systems in general. However, the results of these evaluations have been mixed [9-12]. Some have indicated that the use of algorithm animation technology does lead to a beneficial effect on learning, (e.g. [6, 13]), whilst others have found no beneficial effect (e.g. [7]) or have found a beneficial effect that can only be partially attributed to the technology itself (e.g. [5]). Some researchers have postulated that the problem of under-utilized algorithm animation technology has its roots in the pedagogical theory of learning guiding their design [1]. To date, the design of algorithm animation systems has been informed by one of four different theories of learning [9]. These are:

  o *Epistemic fidelity* [9, 14], which assumes that graphics have an excellent ability to encode an expert's mental model of an algorithm's behaviour leading to the robust, efficient transfer of that mental model to the viewer,

  o *Dual coding* [15], which assumes that cognition consists largely of the activity of two partly interconnected, but functionally independent and distinct symbolic systems. One encodes verbal events such as words or audio; the other encodes non-verbal events such as pictures, kinesthetic

3

actions or sounds in the environment. The two subsystems are said to be functionally independent in that one system can be active without the other or both can be active in parallel. One important implication of this is that verbal and non-verbal codes corresponding to the same object can have additive effects on recall. The interconnections between the two systems are one to many in both directions, and activation is probabilistically determined by the strength of different interconnections interacting with the stimulus context. Thus, the theory hypothesizes that visualizations that encode knowledge in both verbal and non-verbal modes allow learners to build dual representations in the mind and referential connections between those representations [16]. As a consequence, such visualisations facilitate the transfer of target knowledge more efficiently and robustly than do visualizations that do not employ dual encoding [9]. This hypothesis is supported by findings from over sixty empirical studies [17], all of which show that information which is encoded both visually and verbally is better learned than information which is encoded using text only, audio only, combined text and audio or pictures only [18].

o   *Individual differences* [19], which assumes that learners learn differently from each other, process and represent knowledge in different ways and prefer to use different types of resources [20]. It assumes that learners learn best when the style of instruction is matched to their preferred learning style. Learning style can be defined as the habitual manner in which a learner approaches learning tasks that is consistent over long periods of time and across many activities [20]. A battery of instruments has been developed to rate and classify an individual's learning style along a number of different dimensions. These include; Vark's learning style inventory [119] and the MIDAS questionnaire [21], to name but a few. The former inventory rates a learner's learning style with respect to one of four different preferences for the intake of information. These include a preference for obtaining information through the read-write modality, the auditory modality, the kinaesthetic modality and the visual modality. The

MIDAS questionnaire classifies an individual's learning style with respect to Gardner's theory of multiple intelligences [22]. This is a theory which proposes that there are eight different ways to demonstrate intelligence with each having its own unique characteristics, tools and processes that represent a different way of thinking, solving problems and learning. These eight intelligences are described as the linguistic/verbal, musical/rhythmic, spatial/visual, logical/mathematical, interpersonal, intrapersonal and naturalistic intelligences [23].

> 'The functional role of individual difference variables, like those of stimulus and contextual variables, can be expressed in probabilistic terms: They influence the probability with which verbal and non-verbal representations will be aroused (and used successfully) in a given task' [24] (p. 68).

The theory of individual differences asserts that measurable differences in human abilities and styles will lead to measurable performance differences in scenarios of algorithm animation use [9]. However, the preponderance of evidence from the realm of adaptive educational systems has not proved this to be true [25]. Adaptive educational systems are predicated on the assumption that if one dynamically adapts learning content to suit an individual's learning style that greater learning will occur. However, evidence with respect to this had been inconclusive. One reason for this, is because it is difficult to match learning characteristics with instructional environments and it is not clear how the matching should take place, that is, it is unclear which model or test of individual differences one should use to characterise an individual's learning style and act as the basis for adapting the presentation of learning content [23]. However, of note to this thesis are findings from the work of Kelly [23], which suggest that learning gain increases when learners are provided with resources not normally preferred. This would suggest that what motivates a learner to learn is challenge that is, the challenge to learn and understand resources not normally preferred.

o *Cognitive constructivism* [26] which assumes that learning is the active process of constructing knowledge rather than of acquiring knowledge. It hypotheses that learners do not stand to benefit from algorithm animation systems by merely passively viewing the animations, no matter how high the level of epistemic fidelity. Instead, learners must become actively engaged with the animation in order to benefit from it.

However of these theories, a meta analysis of twenty four experimental studies found that systems informed by the theory of cognitive constructivism were the most successful in yielding a learning outcome [9]. This would suggest that it is what learners do, not what they see, that significantly impacts upon their understanding of an algorithm's behaviour [9]. This raises the question as to which mode of interactivity is the most effective in returning a learning gain.

1.2.1 Current Modes of Engagement and their Educational Effectiveness

To date algorithm animation systems, in general, have permitted learners to engage with the behaviour of an algorithm in one of three different ways. These are: by creating and inputting their own data sets and observing their effects on the algorithm's behaviour, by making future predictions about the behaviour of the algorithm and lastly, by building their own visual representations of an algorithm's behaviour [9]. However, findings in relation to the effectiveness of each of the aforementioned modes of interaction have been mixed [8, 9, 27].

Byrne [5] found that learners who orally predicted future frames of an algorithm's animation performed significantly better than learners who only viewed an animation of an algorithm's behaviour without making predictions about its future behaviour. However, the individual effects of prediction and animation could not be disentangled statistically. In contrast, Jarc [28] did not find a significant difference between learners who made predictions about an algorithm's behaviour and those who did not. He postulated that the reason for this finding was because poorer learners treated the automated prediction as a game. When they became lost in the animation, they completed the questions by making guesses. However, he did note that with increased proper use of prediction learners' performance on post tests improved [29].

6

Lawrence [6] found that learners who were allowed to change the input to an algorithm's behaviour performed significantly better than those who passively watched an algorithm driven by data supplied by the experimenter. Stasko [12] found that learners who created their own implementation of an algorithm's behaviour using the Samba system had a better understanding of that algorithm's behaviour than learners who watched a visualisation constructed for them. However, Hundhausen and Douglas [8] found no significant difference between learners who created their own visualisation of an algorithm's behaviour ('the self construct group') and those who interacted with one created by an expert ('the view active group').

This finding can be attributed to the manner in which the experiment was carried out. Learners in the 'self construct group' had to create their own visualisations using simple art supplies such as pens, paper, crayons and so on. Such art supplies mirror the capacity of traditional pedagogical aids, which are known not to lend themselves well to the easy disclosure of material which is dynamic in nature.   Moreover, learners in the 'self construct' group were prohibited from discussing their creations with their instructor, thus, they were provided with no information which was dissonant to their current understandings of the algorithm's behaviour. This may have accounted for the high number of incorrect visualisations received by Hundhausen and Douglas.

According to Piaget [30], a learner learns by struggling to absorb dissonant information into his existing mental models and the resulting cognitive uncertainty results in a modification of his previous understanding. Consequently, if one removes cognitive struggle, one stultifies the learning environment [31]. Findings in relation to the 'view active group', echo those of Stasko's [7], who found that

'for a student to benefit from an animation, the student must understand both the mapping (from the algorithm to the graphic) and the underlying algorithm on which it is based. Students just learning about an algorithm do not have a foundation of understanding upon which to construct the visualisation mapping.' (p.61) [7].

Thus, this finding would suggest that in order for learners to truly understand the behaviour of an algorithm, they must attempt to build their own representations of the algorithm's behaviour. This is an assumption upheld by findings from educational research in general, which show that material is better remembered if it is actually generated by the learner rather than merely presented to the learner [26]. Such findings are further reinforced by evidence from empirical studies carried out by Jarc [29], who found that learners were unable to replicate the behaviour of an algorithm, despite stating emphatically that they understood the algorithm, after viewing and engaging with a visualisation of its behaviour. Such findings accord with a branch of cognitive constructivism known as constructionism.

Constructionists believe that the structuring phase of learning builds the framework of understanding upon which subsequent knowledge in the domain is based. There is plenty of evidence to suggest that this constructive process is facilitated during the conduct of tasks which require an inspectable output [32]. As Papert [33] put it, 'this happens felicitously when the learner is engaged in the construction of something external or at least sharable...a sand castle, a machine, a computer program, a book. This leads us to a model using a cycle of internalization of what is outside, then externalization of what is inside and so on" (p.10). Thus, the theory of cognitive constructionism provides a promising pedagogical framework from which one can base the design of a new algorithm animation system, one which is designed to overcome the lack of deep interaction associated with current systems, by enabling learners to exert their high order thinking skills of analysis, synthesis and evaluation through experimentation with an algorithm's behaviour while it executes, through building their own algorithm simulations and through presenting their findings to peers or instructors for discussion and feedback. Such predications accord with findings from Grissom [35] who found that as a learner's level of engagement increased so did his understanding. This would suggest that more deeply involved a learner is with an algorithm's behaviour and the more opportunities he has to involve himself with the algorithm, the greater his understanding of that algorithm will be.

1.3 Research Goal

Taking all of the above findings into consideration, the research goal of this thesis was to design and develop a new algorithm animation system (FADA) which addresses the following research questions. These were:

- *How can one design an algorithm animation system which facilitates the easy creation of active simulations by both learners and instructors?*

8

This was informed by the author's own experiences of building an active simulation of the token ring algorithm from scratch and by the examination of ways in which current algorithm construction systems facilitate the creation of algorithm visualisations. This led to the design of a novel framework which not only provides a collection of prefabricated software building blocks for the easy implementation of an algorithm's behaviour but also automates the drawing of the latter and the level of interactivity associated with it. The ease by which the framework facilitates the creation of an active algorithm simulation was validated through its use by three different instructors from the realm of distributed systems teaching. Each deployed FADA to build active simulations of set algorithms for use within their own teachings. The ease of use by learners was validated through the use of a multiple case study methodology.

- *To what extent does the algorithm animation approach adopted in this thesis enhance the teaching and learning of distributed algorithms?*

    Concomitant with this question were a number of sub questions.

    o   *To what extent does it facilitate learners to engage in higher order thinking when learning about an algorithm's behaviour?*

    o   *To what extent does the software tool under examination facilitate higher order dialogues about an algorithm's behaviour between learners and between learners and instructors?*

    o   *To what extent does the embodiment of the dual coding theory within the user interface design of the software tool under examination aid in the algorithmic problem solving process?*

    o   *To what extent does the software tool under examination engage learners in an iterative cycle of learning?*

These questions were answered by carrying out a number of exploratory case studies involving one of three different participant groups. Each group was given, in the first instance, a lecture which availed of the use of the algorithm animation system to introduce participants to the behaviour of an algorithm in an interactive and exploratory manner. Next, each group was asked to complete a task whereby they had to amend the behaviour of the algorithm to overcome one or more failure scenarios or concepts encountered within the aforementioned lecture setting. With respect to the question as to what extent the algorithm animation approach adopted within this thesis enhanced the teaching of distributed algorithms; this was answered by having the three aforementioned instructors deploy FADA within their own teachings.

1.4 Framework Animations of Distributed Algorithms (FADA)

FADA was designed to differ from other categories of algorithm animation systems on two levels. These were on a pedagogical level and on an operational level. On a pedagogical level, FADA was designed to emulate that of an active simulation by enabling both an instructor and a learner to engage with the behaviour of an algorithm in real time. FADA enables a user, in the simple case, to change the state of an algorithm's variables or, in the more sophisticated case, to cause one or more of its components to fail. Moreover, FADA was designed to reinforce a user's understanding of an algorithm's behaviour through the provision of dual representations of its behaviour. FADA provides a learner with both a visual representation of an algorithm's behaviour and a textual representation of its implementation. Thus, FADA enables users to map the graphical representation of an algorithm's behaviour to that of its implementation. FADA was also designed to differ from passive animation systems and active simulation systems by enabling a user to create his own algorithm implementation. This was facilitated through the provision of a framework for common message passing distributed algorithms.

The framework was also designed to distinguish FADA operationally from passive animation systems and active simulation systems. This was achieved through the provision of a set of generic function calls that a user can quickly customise and invoke to reflect the behaviour of the algorithm that he is implementing. These function calls are written in a conventional programming language, namely Java, and as a result were designed to mirror the manner by which an algorithm's behaviour is implemented in the real world. Equally, FADA was designed to facilitate the easy construction of algorithm animations through the provision of a built-in visualisation API. Unlike current algorithm construction systems, this API was designed to define the manner by which components of an algorithm's behaviour are visualised and also, the manner by which a user interacts with them in real time. Simulations written using the aforementioned function calls were designed to make transparent calls to the underlying visualisation API. This automates the drawing of the simulations and further reduces the cost, in terms of development time in creating the simulations. FADA scaffolds the algorithm implementation process by providing a development environment that includes both an editor and a debugger as typified by modern programming environments. Moreover, FADA's development environment includes a wizard which is designed to enable a user through the selection and customisation of simple menu items to quickly generate code relating to the messages that a node will receive, the content of those messages and the type of variables that the node is to hold. As a result of its design, FADA can be attributed two modes of use.

- *It can be used as an interactive presentation tool.*

   FADA provides a collection of prepared algorithm simulations which an instructor can use to present to a class for active exploration, discussion and feedback. FADA is designed to scaffold the algorithm learning process by presenting learners with dual representations of the algorithm's behaviour. This is informed by findings from the theory of dual coding, which assert that the provision of dual representations of an algorithm's behaviour reinforces a learner's understanding of that algorithm's behaviour by enabling him to form referential connections between the two representations. The latter is facilitated through the design of FADA as a split pane interface. This is subdivided into two frames, the code frame, which contains a textual description of the algorithm's behaviour and the animation frame, which contains its corresponding visual representation.

- *It can be used both by instructors and learners to create their own active simulations of an algorithm's behaviour.*

   This is facilitated through the provision of a framework which cuts down on the time and complexity associated with creating an algorithm simulation by providing a set of prefabricated software building blocks for the easy implementation of an algorithm's behaviour, by automating the drawing of the algorithm's implementation and the level of interactivity associated with it. By automating the drawing of an algorithm's behaviour and its level of interactivity, FADA enables a user to concentrate solely on the implementation of the algorithm's logic and not on the implementation of its drawing or its level of interactivity.

In achieving its research goals, the main contributions of this thesis can be summarised as:

- The development of an algorithm animation system that engages learners in higher order thinking with an algorithm's behaviour.
- The development of a novel framework to facilitate the easy and quick creation of an active algorithm simulation.
- Results from exploratory case studies that support the effectiveness of active simulations in engaging and motivating learners to question and experiment with their understanding of an algorithm's behaviour in a deep manner.

1.5 Thesis Structure

In constructing an algorithm animation system like FADA a number of key issues needed to be addressed. These were:

- The development of a model of engagement that enables learners when interacting with the behaviour of an algorithm to engage their high order thinking skills of analysis, synthesis and evaluation.
- The development of a framework that facilitates the quick and easy implementation of an algorithm simulation.
- The analysis of results from a number of exploratory case studies as to the effectiveness of FADA in terms of pedagogy and ease of use. One of the central arguments underpinning this thesis is that entities which are dynamic and concurrent in nature do not lend themselves well to representation by text and static imagery. Hence, in order to assist the reader in interpreting the data derived from the use of FADA in each of the case study settings analysed, a CD is included containing sample movies from each setting. These movies provide the reader with a real world snap shot of the manner by which learners and instructors interacted with FADA in each instance and the effects that

such interactions had on the behaviour of the algorithm being investigated and on their understanding of it.

The following chapters describe in detail each of these different stages:

- *Chapter 2* provides an overview of the current direction in algorithm animation in general. It documents the pedagogy informing researchers' design decisions and the results from empirical studies as to the effectiveness of such decisions. It also presents a critique of algorithm animation systems designed specifically for the teaching and learning of distributed algorithms. This is in order to inform the architecture design and implementation of FADA.

- *Chapter 3* describes the manner by which the level of engagement afforded by FADA over an algorithm's behaviour is informed by the theory of constructionism. It also describes the manner by which the author's own preliminary experience of building a highly interactive algorithm simulation together with findings from the literature review inform the design of FADA's framework architecture.

- *Chapter 4* describes the manner by which FADA was implemented

- *Chapter 5* describes the exploratory case studies conducted in order to explore FADA's pedagogical and operational effectiveness.

- *Chapter 6* presents an analysis and presentation of the case study findings.

- *Chapter 7* concludes with an overview, summary and directions for future work.

Chapter 2
Literature Review

2.1 Introduction

Scientists have always resorted to illustrations, figures and diagrams to elucidate the difficult concepts that they are trying to explain and understand, and computer scientists are no different. 'With the advent of powerful graphical workstations in the 1980s, illuminating diagrams in computer science moved from paper to computer screen, as a new era of computer science – algorithm visualisation (AV) - emerged as a way to perceive computer programs in execution' [36] (p.3). Beginning with the development of Brown's Balsa system during the 1980s [36], algorithm visualisation systems (AVs) have evolved from batch oriented software that enable instructors to construct animated films [37], 'to highly interactive systems that enable students to explore dynamically configurable animations of algorithms on their own (e.g. [37, 38]); to interactive programming environments that enable students to quickly construct their own visualisations (e.g. [39])' [9] (p. 259). Yet despite their intuitive appeal, AVs, in general, have failed to catch on in main stream computer science education [9]. The reasons for this are three fold. Instructors claim that AVs require too much time to learn how to use, require too much time to create a visualisation of an algorithm's behaviour and are not educationally effective [9]. Of these three claims, the third is the most worrying, as it questions one of the basic theoretical assumptions upon which the field of algorithm visualisation is based, that is, the premise that in learning, pictures are superior to words [36]. This raises a number of questions for review. The first of which is; what historical evidence exists to support the claim that in learning pictures are superior to words [36]? Second, has such evidence informed the design of AVs in general and in particular, the design of AVs for the teaching and learning of distributed algorithms? Third, have such systems been subjected to empirical evaluations and if so, what has been the outcome of these evaluations in terms of learning gain? Fourth, how have algorithm visualisation systems been designed to facilitate the creation of an algorithm visualisation? In answering these questions, the author hopes to shed light on possible reasons why AVs have failed to gain wide spread popular use in computer science education and in particular, in the teaching of distributed algorithms, and based on such findings, to put forward requirements for the design of a new algorithm visualisation system for the teaching and learning of distributed algorithms.

This chapter is structured as follows:

Section 2.2 reviews the historical evidence to support the claim that in learning pictures are superior to words [36].

Section 2.3 explores the extent to which Paivio's dual coding theory, Nelson's sensory semantic model, Anderson's tri code theory and Larkin and Simon's empirical evidence (these are theories and evidence arising from the review carried out in section 2.2), have directly or indirectly informed the design of AVs in general and in particular, AVs designed primarily for the teaching and learning of distributed algorithms. This section also documents evidence from empirical studies as to the educational effectiveness of the aforementioned systems.

Section 2.4 documents and critiques the manner by which AVs have been designed to facilitate the creation of algorithm visualisations by both learners and instructors.

Section 2.5 outlines the shortcomings in the design of current algorithm visualisation systems for teaching and learning of distributed algorithms and identifies the need for a new algorithm visualisation system, one which is informed by the pedagogical theories of cognitive constructivism, social constructivism, constructionism, dual coding and epistemic fidelity.

Section 2.6 concludes and summarises the chapter.

2.2 Picture Superiority Effect

Before one can document empirical evidence to support the claim that, in learning, pictures are superior to words, one needs to define, what one means by 'superior'? How is a picture superior to words? [36]. This is in order to lend the aforementioned assumption to scientific analysis. For a picture to be superior to words, a picture must be more easily remembered and understood than words. That is, given a picture and a textual description of the same concept, both of which are semantically equivalent representations, the picture should facilitate recall of the concept better than the textual description. If one remembers the picture more readily and easily than the words, then 'the act of viewing algorithms through pictures that are semantically equivalent to conventionally used words should afford students a better memory of the algorithm's behaviour' [36] (p. 10). Another means by which a picture may be superior to words is, if a picture facilitates the encoding of information more efficiently than words. The latter is alluded to by the ancient Chinese proverb 'a picture is worth 10,000 words'. From a picture, one can infer a wealth of information, in order to infer the same amount of information from text; one requires a great number of words [36]. The following section will document evidence in support of such claims.

2.2.1 Historical Evidence

1894 is the earliest known year in which an experimental study was carried out to test humans' recall ability of pictures and words [36]. Kirkpatrick [40] presented 329 subjects with two lists of items, both in picture and word format. He asked subjects to recall the objects on both lists at two different time intervals. These were immediately and seventy two hours later. Kirkpatrick's results showed that subjects had higher retention levels for objects presented visually than for objects presented textually. These findings were replicated by large scale empirical studies carried out during the 1960s and early 1970s (e.g. [41, 42]). An example of which is an experimental study carried out by Standing [43], who presented subjects with between 10 to 10,000 complex pictures. He found that subjects were able to recall subsets of these pictures with 95% accuracy [36].

Such findings prompted cognitive psychologists in the late 1970s and 1980s to investigate ways to explain the observed differences in humans' recall abilities of pictures and words. This led to the formation of two distinct strands of research, both of which were predicated on the assumption that one could explain the differences in humans' recall abilities by the manner in which pictures and words were internally represented in the brain or by the cognitive processes (operators) available to apply to the internal representation. As a result of this research activity, a number of theories evolved [36]. The next section will document, from each line of research, two representative samples of theories put forward. It will begin with theories put forth by Paivio [44] and Nelson [45] in favour of the internal representation argument and will move to theories put forth by Anderson [46] and Larkin [47] in favour of the process-oriented argument [36]. This section ends with a discussion as to the applicability of these theories to the teaching and learning of algorithms and in particular, distributed algorithms.

16

2.2.1.1 Paivio's dual coding theory

This theory assumes

> 'an orthogonal relation between symbolic systems and specific sensorimotor systems. Verbal and non-verbal systems symbolically represent the structural and functional properties of language and the non-linguistic world, respectively. However, both classes of events come in different modalities– visual (printed words versus visual objects), auditory (spoken words versus environmental sounds), haptic (tactual and motor feedback from writing versus manipulation of objects) and the internal symbolic systems presumably retain these distinctions' [17] (p. 257-258).

The representational units of the verbal and non-verbal systems were initially referred to as verbal representations and imaginal representations but later, Paivio borrowed from Morton [48] the terms *logogen* (word generator) and *imagen* (image generator) to distinguish the underlying structural representations from their expression as consciously experienced images and inner speech.

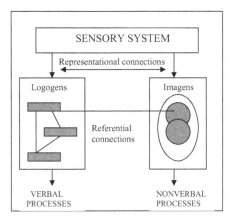

Figure 2.1: A representational diagram of Paivio's dual coding theory (adapted from [24]).

These two systems are assumed to be functionally independent in that one system can be active without the other or both can be active in parallel. One important implication of this assumption is that verbal and nonverbal codes corresponding to the same object (e.g. pictures and their names) can have additive effects on recall [17].

'Interconnectedness of the codes implies that one code can be transformed into the other. The assumption means simply that, [for example,] pictures can be named, words can evoke non verbal images, and similar transformations can occur entirely at the cognitive level – an object name, covertly aroused, can arouse an image of such an object; conversely, the name of the object presumably can be retrieved from its memory image. Pictures are remembered better than words because pictures are more likely to be encoded both as images and as verbal traces. The codes must be at least partially independent, so that encoding could be in terms of one or the other, or both; if it is both, one code presumably could be forgotten and the verbal response could still be retrieved from the other' [44] (p. 23).

The multiple sensorimotor side of the theory has often been overlooked. This is perhaps because dual coding research has emphasised visual imagery more than other modalities, just as other imagery researchers have done [17]. This is predicated on evidence which suggests that in normal sighted individuals the visual system is dominant that is, the transfer of discriminative responding from sight to touch or vice versa is guided or mediated by the visual system. However, the degree to which the visual system dominates in normal sighted individuals varies [24].

Thus, 'the overall probability of the activation and use of verbal and nonverbal representations is a function of the combined effects of stimulus attributes (e.g. word concreteness, meaningfulness and familiarity), instructions and other contextual stimuli and individual differences (e.g. imagery or verbal ability). The precise nature of the combination (whether additive or interactive, for example) is an empirical question' [24] (p.68-69).

However, to date, there exists evidence from over sixty empirical studies which show that the 'presentation of a pictorial representation of an item and [the] presentation of a verbal representation of the same concept have independent and additive effects on recall, unlike picture-picture or word- word representations ' [49] (p.80).

2.2.1.2 Nelson's sensory-semantic model

Nelson sensory-semantic model is based on three assumptions. The first of which is that 'both pictures and words access a common semantic code' [50] (p.785) and that pictures access this information more directly than words [36]. Second, it assumes that 'pictures access phonemic information about their verbal labels after semantic access' [50] (p.785) and that words access phonemic information prior to semantic access [36]. Third, it assumes that pictures and words differ in their sensory and physical features and that pictures are more discernible and distinctive than words [36]. One study which verifies Nelson's theory is that carried out by Nelson, Reed and Walling [45]. They showed subjects pictures of objects with similar shape but low conceptual similarity. They predicated that the pictures would no longer act as better recall cues than words [36]. Results showed that 'pictures were no better as [recall] cues than words at a relatively slow rate of presentation (2.1 sec) and that they were actually less efficient [recall] cues at a faster rate of presentation (1.1 sec)' [50] (p.785).

2.2.1.3 Anderson's tri-code theory

Whilst Paivio's theory of dual coding [17] assumes the existence of two types of mental encoding, Anderson [51] postulates the existence of 'three codes or representation types' [51] (p.45). These are 'a temporal code, which encodes the order of a set of items; a spatial image, which encodes spatial configuration; and an abstract proposition, which encodes meaning' [51] (p.45). Anderson [51] claims that 'it is impossible to identify whether a particular notation correctly expresses the structure of a representation or whether different knowledge structures are encoded according to different notations' [51] (p.46). However, 'it is possible', he claims 'to decide that different knowledge structures have different processes defined upon them' [51] (p.46). Hence, Anderson [51] believes that the mental representation of pictures and words can only be determined by the processes that act upon them. He argues that the value of a certain representation will always depend on issues of processing efficiency, and not on the representation itself [36].

2.2.1.4 Larkin and Simon's analysis of sentential and diagrammatic representations
Rather than focus their research efforts on identifying the different internal representations that pictures and words can take in the brain [36], Larkin and Simon [47] compared the role that diagrammatic representations and sentential representations play in three cognitive processes. These were search, recognition and inference [52]. They defined sentential representations as expressions which form 'a sequence corresponding, on a one-to-one basis, to the sentences in a natural language description of a problem' [47] (p. 66). They defined diagrammatic representations as expressions that 'correspond, on a one to one basis, to the components of a diagram describing the problem' [47] (p. 66). Larkin and Simon [47] compared diagrammatic representations and sentential representations based upon their informational and computational equivalence. The two representations were said to be informationally equivalent 'if all the information in the one is also inferable from the other, and vice versa' [47] (p. 67). Likewise, the two representations were said to be computationally equivalent, 'if they were informationally equivalent, and, in addition, any inference that could be drawn easily and quickly from the information given explicitly in the one could also be drawn easily and quickly from the information given explicitly in the other and vice versa' [47] (p. 67).

Larkin and Simon [47] found that diagrams made it easier to find relevant information as one could scan from one element to another nearby much more rapidly than one could with a list of numbers or verbal assertions. In searching a verbal assertion, a linear search down the data structure is required to find each informational item. In contrast, since related information is most often grouped together in a diagrammatic representation, all required information can often be obtained 'for free' by finding the first informational item [36]. Diagrams were also found to make it easier to identify instances of a concept. An iconic representation can be recognised much faster than a verbal description [52]. This is because diagrams preserve explicitly 'the information about the topological and geometric relations among the components of a problem' [47] (p. 66). This results in fewer (explicit) inferences needing to be drawn from diagrammatic representations than from sentential representations, resulting in more efficient computation [36].

However, about inference, Larkin and Simon [47] wrote 'in view of the dramatic effects that alternative representations may produce on search and recognition processes, it may seem surprising that the differential effects on inference appear less strong. Inference is largely independent of representation if the information content of the two sets of inference rules [one operating on diagrams and the other operating on verbal statements] is equivalent – that is the sets are isomorphs' [47] (p. 70). However, in a later experiment, Bauer and Laird [52] found that diagrams aid inference by making alternative possibilities more explicit. They found that the ability to bypass the construction of meanings from verbal premises and to manipulate visual images appeared to reduce the load on working memory and to speed up the process of inference. Subjects were found to respond faster and to draw many more valid conclusions from the diagrams than from the verbal premises [52].

2.2.1.5 Discussion

From the above sample studies, there is much empirical evidence to suggest that people remember pictures more readily and easily than words, and that, pictures are a more efficient means of encoding information than words [36]. However, in accepting such claims, a word of caution must be aired. Much of the empirical evidence in support of these claims comes from testing them with 'concrete' everyday pictures and words. Algorithms are not concrete entities. They are abstract entities and as such, have no real world equivalents. However, if one were to concretise an algorithm's behaviour that is, provide both a visual and textual representation of its behaviour, one may, as evidenced by the dual coding theory [15], facilitate its recall from memory more easily and efficiently than if one had not deployed dual encoding [9]. Equally, if one were to render the visual representation of an algorithm's behaviour manipulable, one may, as informed by Baird and Laird's analysis [52], lend to the learner's process of inference. Such an analysis has important implications for the teaching and learning of distributed algorithms, as it suggests, that given the dynamic and concurrent nature of the aforementioned algorithms that the use of static imagery may not lend itself well to the easy disclosure of their behaviours. This is something which Anderson [51] alluded to in his tri-code theory, when he asserted that the value of a certain representation is not in and of itself, but dependent upon the processes that a learner can enact upon it. Thus, this raises the question as to whether any of the aforementioned theories or empirical evidence has informed the design of algorithm visualisation systems (AVs) in general or the design of AVs for the teaching and learning of distributed algorithms, either directly or indirectly. If the answer is yes, have these systems been subjected to empirical evaluations and if so, what has been their outcome in terms of learning gain? By carrying out such an analysis, one may begin to identify reasons as to why instructors have failed to embrace AVs in general and in particular, AVs for the teaching and learning of distributed algorithms. However, in order to begin such analysis, one must first identify the theories of learning that have informed the design of algorithm visualisation systems to date.

2.3 Theories of learning informing the design of algorithm visualisation systems (AVs)
To date the design of AVs has been in general informed by one of four different theories of learning [9]; epistemic fidelity [9, 53], dual coding [15], individual differences [19] and cognitive constructivism [120].

Epistemic fidelity (See figure 2-2) assumes that 'graphical representations, like, for example, AVs, are endowed with an excellent ability to support representations that closely match an expert's mental model of an algorithm's process' [1] (p. 16). It assumes that the higher the 'fidelity' of the match between the visualisation and the expert's mental model, the more robust and efficient is the transfer of that mental model to the viewer of the visualisation, who decodes and internalises the target knowledge [9].

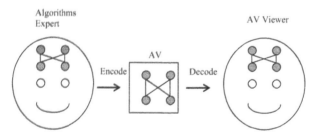

Figure 2-2: A schematic diagram of knowledge flow according to the theory of epistemic fidelity (adapted from [1]).

Dual coding as defined earlier in section 2.2.1.1 assumes that 'visualisations that encode knowledge in both verbal and non-verbal modes allow learners to build dual representations in the brain, and referential connections between those representations. As a consequence, such visualisations facilitate the transfer of target knowledge more efficiently and robustly than do visualisations that do not employ dual encoding' [9] (p. 272).

Individual differences, as defined previously in chapter 1, section 1.2, posits that learners reflecting their own individual traits process and represent knowledge in different ways, prefer to use different types of resources and exhibit consistent and observable patterns of behaviour [20]. It assumes that learners learn more effectively when the style of instruction is adapted to their individual learning traits [54]. Traits are the psychological constructs that describe how individuals generally behave over the long term [55] and include concepts of intellectual ability and learning styles. Abilities refer to the things that one can do such as execute skills or strategies, whereas styles refer to individual preferences in the use of abilities [56]. The concept of a learning style reflects a person's style of behaviour when learning and lies in the area of psychology at the interface between abilities and personalities [57]. A battery of instruments has been developed to rate and classify a learner's individual learning style along a number of different dimensions [9]. These include Vark's learning style inventory [119] and the MIDAS questionnaire [21]. Vark's inventory rates an individual's learning style in accordance with one of four different preferences for the way in which information is acquired. These include a read write preference, an auditory preference, a kinesthetic preference and a visual preference. The MIDAS questionnaire rates an individual's learning style in accordance with one or more relatively independent abilities as classified by Gardner's eight multiple intelligences [22]. These include the verbal/linguistic intelligence, which is the ability to use language in pragmatic ways such as rhetoric (using language to convince others to take a specific course of action), mnemonics (using language to remember information), explanation (using language to inform) and meta language (using language to talk about itself), logical/mathematical intelligence, which is the ability to detect patterns, reason deductively and think logically, visual/spatial intelligence, which is the ability to perceive the visual-spatial world accurately, to perform transformations on those perceptions and to create visual expressions, the musical/rhythmic intelligence, which is the ability to recognise and compose musical pitches, tones and rhythms, bodily/kinaesthetic intelligence, which is the ability to learn by doing and by using one's mental ability to coordinate bodily movements, interpersonal intelligence, which is the ability to work and communicate with others, intrapersonal intelligence, which is the ability to have an accurate picture of oneself, one's strengths and limitations and the ability to act adaptively based on that knowledge and naturalist intelligence, which is the ability to comprehend, discern and appreciate the world of nature [23]. The theory of individual differences asserts that measurable differences in human abilities and learning styles will lead to measurable performance differences in scenarios of AVs use [9]. However, the preponderance of evidence has not proved this to be true [58]. Such findings replicate those from the realm of adaptive educational systems, which are predicated on the assumption that if one dynamically adapts the presentation of content to suit an individual's learning style then this leads to demonstrable learning gains in that individual's understanding of the content. However, evidence in support of such an assumption is inconclusive [23]. Some studies have found that learning improves when individual differences are taken into account (e.g. [54]), whilst others have found no differences (e.g. [59]). One reason for this is because, in practice, it is difficult to match learning characteristics with instructional environments and it is not clear how the matching should take place that is, it is unclear as to which pedagogical model (e.g. Gardner's theory of multiple intelligences), one should use to characterise an individual's learning style and to act as the basis for adapting the presentation of content [23]. Of special interest to this thesis, however, are findings from the work of Kelly [23] which suggest that learning gain increases when learners are provided with resources not normally preferred. This would suggest that what motivates a learner to learn is challenge that is, the challenge to understand resources not normally preferred.

Cognitive constructivism assumes that learning is an active process of constructing rather than of acquiring knowledge. 'Instead of presupposing that knowledge is a representation of what exists, knowledge is a mapping in the light of human experience of what is feasible' [60] (p. 162). By learners becoming actively engaged with their learning environments, learners actively construct new understandings by interpreting new experiences within the context of what they already know. Thus, it hypothesises that learners do not stand to benefit from AVs by merely passively viewing visualisations, no matter how high their level of epistemic fidelity. Instead learners must become actively engaged with the technology in order to benefit from it [9].

Of these four theories, three share the same basic theoretical assumption that is, that 'knowledge exists independently of humans and can be instantiated as symbolic structures in humans' brains' [1] (p.16). Such an assumption adheres to the internal representation argument documented earlier in section 2.2.1.1. The three theories which comply with the aforementioned assumption are the theory of epistemic fidelity, the theory of dual coding and the theory of individual differences. The theory of cognitive constructivism adheres to the process oriented argument (See section 2.2.1.3). It assumes that the value of an algorithm visualisation system lies not in the visual representation of the algorithm's behaviour that it presents, but in the level of engagement that it affords a learner over the representation. It believes that knowledge does not flow from expert to AV to learner [1], but is constructed by the learner through experimentation with the representation. The next section will document the manner by which the design of AVs in general has evolved in accordance with the aforementioned learning theories.

2.3.1 Linking learning theories to the evolving design of algorithm visualisation systems in general

Historically, AVs in general have been informed by the theory of epistemic fidelity and as such, have been designed to encode and present to a learner an expert's mental model of an algorithm's behaviour. The first known attempt at such a construction was Brown's Balsa system [61], which was designed not only to present learners with multiple graphical representations of an algorithm's behaviour but also, to 'expose properties of the [algorithm] that might otherwise be difficult to understand or remain unnoticed' [61] (p. 1). This system heralded the dyadic user model (See figure 2-3) as the way forward for building algorithm visualisation systems and for encoding and acquiring an expert's understanding of the algorithm's behaviour. According to this model, an algorithm visualisation system provides an algorithm animation system for the algorithm expert and an end user environment for the learner. These two interfaces are not only conceptually distinct, but technologically distinct [1]. 'The algorithm animation system is the code with which [the algorithm expert] interfaces, and the algorithm animation environment is the run time environment that [the learner] sees. It is the result of compiling the code that [the algorithm expert] implements with the algorithm animation system' [61] (p. 6-7).

25

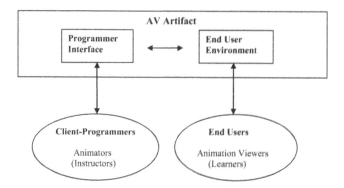

Figure 2-3: Brown's dyad user model [61] for AV software development (adapted from [1]).

With the advent of increased computational power and the arrival of more sophisticated graphical technologies, algorithm visualisation researchers looked to increase the amount of knowledge that they could encode in an algorithm visualisation. This was based on the epistemic premise that the more knowledge one could encode within an algorithm visualisation, the more knowledge one could transfer to the viewer of the visualisation, the learner [1]. Thus, algorithm visualisation systems evolved from facilitating multiple concurrent views of an algorithm's behaviour (e.g. [62]), to providing smooth animations of the latter (e.g. [63, 64]). This was in order to reduce the cognitive load on the learner and to enable the learner to view the state changes in an algorithm's behaviour more readily and easily. Colour was next added to the animations to focus learners' attentions on specific changes in an algorithm's state behaviour (e.g. [38, 65]). This was similarly followed by the use of sound (e.g. [65]), two dimensional graphics and even three dimensional graphics (e.g. [66, 67]). This culminated in the addition of VCR-like controls which were designed to enable learners to control the rate at which the algorithm visualisation system presented the algorithm behaviour to the learner and to enable the learner to step through the visualisation and to reverse it, if need be (e.g. [68]).

However, the use of passive animation systems was found not to lead to significant improvements in a learner's understanding of an algorithm's behaviour [69]. This was due to two reasons. The first was that the beneficial effects of the visualisations were lost unless accompanied by teacher provided explanations [69]. Such findings accord with the theory of dual coding theory, which holds that in order for an animation to be educationally effective it must be encoded both visually and textually to allow learners to build dual representations in their minds, and to form referential connections between these representations [9]. The second problem associated with passive animation systems was as a result of their inability to permit learners to exercise their higher order thinking skills by enabling them to interact with the behaviour of the algorithm. Higher order thinking can be defined as 'thinking that requires learners to manipulate information and ideas in ways that transform their meaning and implications such as, when learners combine facts and ideas in order to synthesise, generalise, explain, hypothesise or arrive at some conclusion or interpretation' [70] (p. 20).

Higher order thinking skills is another means by which one refers to Bloom's taxonomy of educational objectives. The latter was designed to provide instructors with explicit formulations of the ways in which learners are expected to be changed by the educative process. Its aim was to identify what learners do when they really understand which they do not do when they do not understand [71]. Bloom's taxonomy structures a learner's depth of understanding along a linear progression of six increasingly sophisticated levels [72]. These are *knowledge*, which is the ability to bring to mind the appropriate material, *comprehension*, which is the ability to discern meaning, *application*, which is the ability to apply an appropriate abstraction to a problem without having to be prompted to do so, *analysis*, which is the ability to break down material into its constituent parts, to identify or classify elements of the communication, *synthesis*, which is the ability to work with elements to combine them in such a way as to constitute a pattern or structure not clearly there before and *evaluation*, which is the ability to make judgements about the value for some purpose of ideas, works, solutions, methods, materials and so on [71] .

Level in Bloom's Taxonomy	What a learner can do at this level	Sample tasks and Assignments
1. Knowledge	Recognise and informally define specific concepts in algorithmics like for example, Quicksort	List three different sorting algorithms
2. Comprehension	Understand the general principle behind an algorithm and explain how it works using words and figures	Trace your chosen algorithm using the following input set 25, 7, 38, 15, 32, 8, 27, 12
3. Application	Adapt a previously studied algorithm for some specific application, environment or representation of data.	Implement a program that sorts a linked list of strings using insertion sort and demonstrate that it works.
4. Analysis	Understand the relation of the algorithm with other algorithms solving the same or related problems.	Compare the performances of the Quicksort to the HeapSort.
5. Synthesis	Design solutions to complex problems where several different data structures, algorithms and techniques are needed.	Design the data structures and algorithms needed by a car navigation system.
6. Evaluation	Discuss the pros and cons of different algorithms that solve the same or similar problems.	Discuss the design of a solution, and argue why it is better or worse than a different solution.

Table 2-1: An over view of Bloom's taxonomy and the depth of understanding expected at each level within the taxonomy together with a depiction of sample exercises designed to engage learners at each level of the taxonomy (adapted from [72]).

Passive animation systems facilitate the attainment of the first two levels of this taxonomy. These are knowledge and comprehension. They enable learners to recall basic facts about an algorithm's behaviour like for example, the manner by which a selection sort algorithm 'sorts' a list of elements based on the value of the smallest element with in that list. They also enable learners to discern meaning that is, when confronted with a visualisation of a selection sort algorithm they enable learners to recognise it as a sort algorithm. However, such levels of comprehension represent the lowest levels of understanding. 'It relates to the type of understanding or apprehension such that an individual knows what is being communicated without necessarily relating it to other material or seeing its fullest implications' [71] (p. 89). In order to achieve higher levels of understanding that is, application, analysis, synthesis and evaluation, there was need of systems which enabled learners to analyse the behaviour of an algorithm in order to identify its constituent parts and their relevance to one another. Moreover, there was need of systems to aid learners in the process of inference, by enabling them to formulate and execute hypotheses. Such interactivity was needed in order to enable learners to draw conclusions about an algorithm's behaviour and to judge its suitability to different problem domains.

Consequently, researchers developed systems, which were designed to overcome the problems inherent in passive animation systems by enabling learners to augment the process of viewing an algorithm's behaviour [9] by inputting their own data sets (e.g. [73]), by predicting future frames of an algorithm's behaviour (e.g. [5, 28, 74]) and by answering strategic questions about the state of the algorithm's behaviour (e.g. [69, 75]). Such developments constituted a move away from the traditional pedagogy of epistemic fidelity to the theory of cognitive constructivism. This was based on the assumption that if one increased the level of learner involvement with an algorithm visualisation, one would increase the learner's understanding of that algorithm's behaviour. However, whilst these systems did facilitate increased learner involvement with an algorithm's behaviour in line with the theory of cognitive constructivism, results from empirical studies (which shall be more closely examined in section 2.3.3), as to their educational effectiveness were mixed [9]. This is because learners, who are just beginning to learn about an algorithm's behaviour, may not have a foundation of understanding upon which to map the logic of an algorithm's implementation to that of its graphical counterpart [2].

Thus, researchers developed ways by which learners could create their own understanding of an algorithm's behaviour as a visualisation. Such a move aligned more with the branch of cognitive constructivism known as constructionism. Constructionists claim that the structuring phase of learning builds the framework of understanding upon which subsequent knowledge in a domain is based. There is plenty of evidence to suggest that this constructive process is facilitated during the conduct of tasks that require an inspectable output [32]. Hence, the building of what the author terms as algorithm construction systems represented an end to the strong hold which the dyadic user model had on algorithm visualisation development, as now learners were no longer seen just as end users but as algorithm experts. Now, the question that seemed to enthral researchers and to eclipse the question of how to facilitate and sustain higher order thinking was how to facilitate the easy creation of an algorithm visualisation?

To this end, a number of systems were developed; each deployed one of four different methodologies for the easy creation of an algorithm visualisation. These were *annotation* (e.g. [61, 76, 77]), which is a process of manually annotating the source code of an algorithm's behaviour to include calls to functions of an animation library that as far as possible hide the productions of graphics connected with the visual from the learner, *non-invasive annotation* (e.g. [78]), which is a process of automating the aforementioned manual annotation process [79], *scripting* (e.g. [12, 80, 81]), which is an alternative approach to manual annotation which tries to combine the flexibility of function calls with a modest amount of programming knowledge [82], and *animation frameworks* [38, 83], which is the provision of a set of generic reference data types for a given algorithm domain including a control flow that performs interaction among the object instantiated from it. Frameworks hail from the domain of software engineering and are widely used as it is easier to modify and customise a framework than to write an application from scratch [79]. However, despite enabling learners to concretise their own understanding of an algorithm's behaviour as a visualisation, findings in relation to their educational effectiveness have been mixed [84]. One reason for this is because learners become distracted by the process of implementing an algorithm's behaviour and fail to acquire an understanding for all necessary concepts relating to that algorithm's behaviour [1]. This may be due, as some have claimed, to the inadequacies or complexities of the tools provided by such systems for the creation of an algorithm visualisation (See section 2.4) [9] or, as the author postulates, to the failure of these systems to enable learners to build upon their current levels of understanding of an algorithm's behaviour. By enabling learners to manipulate the behaviours of their algorithm representations in real time, that is, while they execute, one enables them to encounter information which is dissonant to their current understanding. Only by enabling learners to absorb such dissonant information will deeper understanding of an algorithm's behaviour prevail. As Piaget [121] defined, one learns by struggling to

30

absorb dissonant information into one's existing mental models, and the resulting cognitive uncertainty, results in a modification of one's previous understanding.

The ability for a learner to interact with his own representation of an algorithm's behaviour in real time is crucial for a learner to obtain a deep understanding of a distributed algorithm's behaviour, in particular. This is because there are episodes of behaviour which occur in the real world, like, for example, the loss of a communication channel, that can, if not accounted lead, to that algorithm malfunctioning or terminating. Thus, in order to ensure that a learner gains an appreciation for and an understanding of such scenarios of behaviour, the learner must be able to re-enact such scenarios and observe their effects on his cognitive representation of the algorithm's behaviour. Thus, the question arises, have algorithm visualisation systems for the teaching and learning of distributed algorithms been designed to facilitate such deep levels of engagement?

2.3.2 Design of algorithm visualisation systems (AVs) for the teaching and learning of distributed algorithms

AVs for the teaching and learning of distributed algorithms have evolved in a similar manner to AVs in general, in that, their design has initially been informed by the theory of epistemic fidelity and, as a result of attempts to engage learners in the high order thinking skills of analysis, synthesis and evaluation, moved to the theory of cognitive constructivism. As a consequence, these systems have evolved from systems, which present learners with prepared multiple views of an algorithm's behaviour (e.g. [85]), to systems, which augment the viewing process, by enabling learners to directly manipulate the behaviour of an algorithm's components in real time that is while it executes (e.g. [86]), to systems, which facilitate the easy creation of an algorithm's visualisation (e.g. [3, 87-91]). Of interest to this thesis, is the manner by which these systems have facilitated real time interactivity with an algorithm's behaviour and enabled learners to create their own visualisation of an algorithm's behaviour. These two areas are of relevance as the author believes that it is the inability of currently available algorithm visualisation systems to enable learners to build and experiment with their own visual representations of an algorithm's behaviour in real time that has led to their mixed performance in evaluation studies and to their lack of adoption in computer science education.

Real time interactivity can be defined as the ability to influence the execution of an algorithm's behaviour as it evolves [3]. This can be achieved by enabling learners to, in the simple case, change the state of an algorithm's variables or, in the more sophisticated case, to cause one or more of its components to fail. To date the only known system to facilitate real time interaction is HiSAP (Highly Interactive Simulations of Algorithms and Protocols) [86]. In HiSAP, a learner can change the order in which operations are carried out by an algorithm by, for example, clicking on a node and causing it to fail. As a result of such interaction, the learner is able to explore the degree to which the algorithm is fault tolerant. An algorithm is said to be fault tolerant if it continues to function despite the presence of one or more failed components.

However, HiSAP presents an expert's mental model of an algorithm's behaviour and not that of the learner. As such, it does not provide facilities to enable learners to make explicit their own cognitive representations of an algorithm's behaviour as defined by the branch of cognitive constructivism known as constructionism. Constructionists believe that one learns by first making explicit their own cognitive understandings of an entity and that this provides the platform from which all subsequent knowledge is built. Moreover, HiSAP does not enable learners to modify the underlying implementation logic of an algorithm's behaviour. Indeed, it hides the implementation code from the learner. As a consequence HiSAP only provides learners with one mode of representation that is a visual representation. This is counter to the theory of dual coding which posits that in order for instruction to be successful, a learner must be able to encode knowledge in both verbal and non verbal modes in order to allow him to build dual representations in his mind, and referential connections between those representations. This is in order to facilitate the efficient transfer of knowledge [9]. One application which has successfully emulated the theoretical underpinnings of the dual coding theory, but which falls outside the domain of distributed system algorithms, is an application known as Jeliot [92, 93]. This is an application which has been designed to aid learners in understanding basic programming concepts by visualising the behaviour of a program while it executes. Jeliot provides a spilt pane interface, which is subdivided into two interchangeable halves. In one half of the interface is the code relating to the program's implementation and, in the other, is the visualisation of its implementation while it executes. The former is known as the code frame, whilst the latter is known as the animation frame.

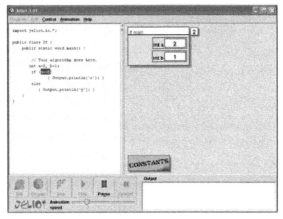

Figure 2-4: A screenshot of Jeliot's user interface dynamically illustrating the behaviour of an 'If' statement. To the right hand side is the code frame and to the left hand side is the animation frame. The code frame contains code relating to the manner by which the 'If' statement is implemented in Java, whilst the animation frame displays a visual representation of the aforementioned code in action.

One reason for the lack of AVs offering real time interactivity may be due to the difficulty in developing such systems. In creating active simulation systems, one must not only define the logic of the algorithm's behaviour that one is intending to animate, but also, the manner by which it is to be animated. Moreover, one must define what components of the algorithm's behaviour that a learner can engage with and modify. As a result of such development difficulty, researchers have looked for alternative ways to engage learners with algorithm visualisations. This has been achieved by designing systems to enable learners to create their own algorithm visualisations. Like AVs in general, these systems have deployed one of three different methodologies to facilitate the creation of an algorithm visualisation. These are annotation (e.g. [88, 94]), the use of a formal scripting language (e.g. [87, 91]) and the provision of animation frameworks (e.g. [89, 90]). However, whilst providing learners with tools to make explicit their own current cognitive understandings of an algorithm's behaviour, these systems have failed to enable learners to build upon that understanding by enabling them to experiment with the behaviour of their representations in real time. An upshot of this has been that learners have had no means of determining the degree to which their cognitive representations of an algorithm's behaviour have been fault tolerant. This raises the question as to what degree has algorithm visualisation systems in general and those designed primarily for the teaching of distributed algorithms been found to be educationally effective, that is, led to a significant improvement in a learner's understanding of an algorithm's behaviour?

2.3.3 Educational effectiveness of algorithm visualisation (AV) technology, in general

To date a number of empirical studies have been carried out to substantiate the educational effectiveness of algorithm visualisation (AV) technology in general. However, results from these studies have been markedly mixed [10]. Some have indicated that the use of AV technology does lead to a beneficial effect on learning (e.g. [6, 13]), whilst other have found no beneficial effect (e.g. [7]), or have found a beneficial effect that can only be partially attributed to the technology itself (e.g. [5] [9]). However, of interest to this thesis, are findings from a meta-analysis of twenty four experimental studies which suggest that how learners use AV technology has a greater impact on educational effectiveness than what an algorithm visualisation shows them. Out of fourteen studies that varied the level of learner involvement with the algorithm visualisation, ten (71%) of these returned a significant learning outcome. Whilst, out of ten studies which varied the representational characteristics of the learning material, by showing text or animation or by showing animation first or text first or by varying the various graphical attributes of the animation, only three (33%) of these returned a significant learning outcome. This would suggest that the most successful uses of AV technologies are those in which the technology is used as a vehicle for actively engaging learners in the process of learning algorithms [9]. This alignes well with cognitive constructivism.

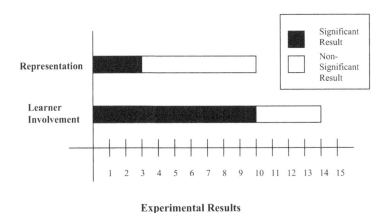

Experimental Results

Figure 2-5: Summary of results from a meta-analysis of 24 visualisation effectiveness experiments broadly classified by their independent variables (adapted from [72]). Total number of experiments in each classification is delineated by the height of each hollow bar. Number of experiments yielding significant results is indicated by the proportion of each hollow bar that is filled in.

To date AV technology has actively engaged learners by enabling them to predict future frames of an algorithm's visualisation, to input their own data sets, to answer questions about the algorithm's behaviour and to construct their own algorithm visualisations [9]. Such varying modes of engagement have prompted researchers to question their effects upon learning. This has resulted in a number of empirical studies, the results of which have been at best mixed ([8, 9]).

Lawrence [6] found that enabling learners to create and input their own data sets to an algorithm visualisation led to higher accuracy on post test examination of understanding of the algorithm when compared to students who viewed prepared examples. She found that the ability to enable learners to input their own data sets significantly impacted upon their conceptual understanding of the algorithm's behaviour. Learners in the 'active lab' group scored higher on questions requiring conceptual knowledge than on questions requiring recognition of individual steps of the algorithm (procedural knowledge) [6]. Conceptual knowledge can be defined as an understanding of the abstract properties of an algorithm, for example, its range of output or its limits on input data that it can process. Procedural knowledge can be defined as an understanding of the procedural, step-by-step behaviour of an algorithm [9].

Byrne [5] found that one way in which animations may aid learning of procedural knowledge of an algorithm's behaviour is by encouraging learners to orally predict the algorithm's behaviour. However, such a learning improvement was also found when learners made predictions about an algorithm's behaviour from static diagrams. This suggests that prediction, rather than animation per se, may have been the key factor in aiding learning [5].

Jarc [28] automated the aforementioned prediction process in his web based algorithm visualisations and found no significant differences between learners who made predictions about an algorithm's behaviour and learners who did not. He postulated that the reason for this was because poorer learners treated the automated prediction as a game. When they became lost in the animation, they completed the questions by simply making guesses. However, he did note that with increased proper use of prediction, learners' performances on post tests improved [29].

Findings from Grissom [35] echo those of Byrne [5]; however, he did caution that in order to expect relatively naïve learners to benefit from AVs, one must carefully guide them in their explorations with the tool. This would suggest that AV technology is best suited to a scaffolded learning environment that is, one which allows learners to correct their misunderstandings through discussion and interaction with instructors or fellow learners. This accords with findings from a qualitative study carried out by Hubscher-Younger [95], who found that learners learn algorithms by employing informal and collaborative meaning building activities. These include studying in small groups, solving home work problems together and explaining and helping each other with different concepts. Such a mode of learning concurs with the branch of cognitive constructivism known as social constructivism. According to social constructivism, learning is inherently social. What one learns is a function of social norms and interpretations and knowledge is simply not constructed by the individual, but by social groups [1].

With respect to the ability to create one's own algorithm visualisation, one would expect learners who construct their own visualisations to have a greater understanding of the algorithm's behaviour. However, evidence in support of such an assumption is as yet unclear. Stasko [12] found that learners who constructed their own understanding of an algorithm's behaviour using his Samba system had a better understanding of the algorithm than students who viewed a visualisation created by an expert. Findings from Hundhausen and Douglas [8] contradicted those of Stasko's. He found no significant differences between learners who constructed a visualisation ('the self construct group') and those who watched and interacted with an expert constructed visualisation ('the view active group').

However, these findings can be attributed to the manner in which Hundhausen's experiment was carried out. Learners in the 'self construct' group had to create their own visualisations using simple art supplies such as pens, crayons and so on. Such art supplies are known not to lend themselves well to the easy disclosure of material which is dynamic in nature. Moreover, learners in the 'self construct' group were prohibited from discussing their creations with their instructors, thus, they were provided with no information which is dissonant to their current understanding of the algorithm's behaviour and as a result, were unable to modify or build upon their understanding. This may have accounted for the large number of incorrect visualisations received by Hundhausen and Douglas. Findings in relation to the 'view active' group echo those of Stasko's [7], who found that for students to benefit from AV, they must understand not only the concepts underlying the algorithm, but also, the manner in which those concepts are mapped to the animated computer graphics domain [96]. Thus, this finding would suggest that in order for learners to truly understand an algorithm's behaviour, they must attempt to build their own representations of the algorithm. This is an assumption upheld by Jarc [29], who found that learners were unable to replicate the behaviour of an algorithm, despite stating emphatically that they understood the algorithm, after viewing an interactive visualisation of its behaviour.

Perhaps the most interesting findings come from the work of Grissom [35], who found that as a learner's level of engagement with an algorithm visualisation increased so did his understanding. This suggests that it is the accumulative effect of different modes of engagement that significantly impact upon learning than any one individual mode. Essentially the more effort that is required to engage with the algorithm, the more robust one's understanding of that algorithm will be [9].

Study	Independent Variable	Dependent Variable	Key Results
Lawrence (Chapter 6) [6]	*Level of learner involvement* 1. Study text + passively view animation 2. Study text + actively view animation by constructing own input data sets.	Post test accuracy. Time to take post test.	Participants who actively viewed animation scored significantly higher than students who passively viewed animation.
Byrne, Catrambone & Stasko [5]	*Learning medium* 1. Study text only 2. Study text + make predictions 3. Study text + view animation 4. Study text + view animation + make predictions	Post-test accuracy Prediction accuracy	Participants who viewed animation and/or made predictions scored significantly higher on 'hard questions than participants who did neither
Jarc, Feldman & Heller [28]	*Interactive prediction* (Use of animation software that enables prediction of next algorithm step vs. use of animation software with no prediction)	Post-test at end of three weekly lab sessions. Learning time	No significant differences were detected on post test. The prediction group spent significantly more time using the animation software than the no-prediction group
Grissom, McNally & Naps [35]	*Level of learner involvement* 1. Lecture only 2. Lecture + passively view animation 3. Lecture + view animation + actively engage with animation by responding to interactive questions posed	Post test accuracy	Participants who viewed the animation and responded to interactive questions posed about the algorithm's behaviour significantly outperformed participants who passively viewed the animation or who learned through the lecture only. Participants who received the lecture accompanied by the use of the non interactive use of the animation significantly outperformed those who received the lecture without the use of the animation.

Stasko [12]	*Level of learner involvement* 1. Self construct visualizations 2. View predefined visualization	Post test accuracy	Participants who actively constructed their own algorithm visualizations using Stasko's Samba system significantly outperformed participants who viewed an algorithm visualisation created for them by an expert
Hundhause n and Douglas [8]	*Level of learner involvement* 1. Self construct visualizations 2. Actively view predefined visualizations.	Accuracy and time on tracing and programming tasks.	No significant differences detected.

Table 2-2: Summary of controlled experiments that consider algorithm visualisation effectiveness (adapted from [1, 9]).

As a consequence of this analysis, two questions remain.

1   To what extent have AVs for the teaching and learning of distributed algorithms been subjected to empirical evaluations?

2   To what extent have techniques used by algorithm construction systems hindered or assisted learners in creating their own algorithm visualisations?

2.3.4 Educational effectiveness of algorithm visualisation systems (AVs) for the teaching and learning of distributed algorithms

Although a number of AVs have been developed for the teaching and learning of distributed algorithms, little is known about their educational impact or how instructors and learners use them in class [97]. After an extensive trawl of the literature and at the time of writing, the author could only uncover empirical evidence as to the deployment and educational effectiveness of two systems, namely HiSAP [98] and Lydian [3].

HiSAP consists of a framework to build simulations and generate applets from formally specified algorithms or protocols [98]. As defined earlier in section 2.3.2, all applets rendered by HiSAP enable learners to directly manipulate the behaviour of components of the visualisation as they evolve, that is, in real time. HiSAP was deployed for use by three different instructors across three different modules in three different computer science graduate courses. Each instructor used HiSAP to teach one of three different algorithms. These were the token ring algorithm, the asymmetric two-way authentication algorithm and the adaptive synchronisation protocol. These algorithms were prepared and created by a third party (i.e. a programmer) and not by the instructor himself or the learners. Each instructor used HiSAP to introduce a particular algorithm to the class. Learners were then asked to individually complete questions based on the algorithm's behaviour. For this, each learner was given access and freedom to play with the relevant HiSAP derived applet [98].

Researchers compared learners' understanding of the protocols and algorithms with and without the use of the applets. They found that learners who had worked with the applets really understood the behaviour of the algorithms or protocols and stated that the applets had been crucial to their understanding [98]. However, on questions of self estimation of learning, in each of the three cases, the majority of learners answered that they were 'unsure' as to their level of understanding. Such findings echo those of Stasko's who found that for a learner to understand an algorithm's behaviour, the learner must be able to understand the algorithm implementation and the mapping from the implementation to the graphics [7]. This suggests that in order to instil confidence in a learner, one must provide facilities to enable him to make explicit his own cognitive representations of the algorithm's behaviour and to enable him to present the latter to an audience for feedback and discussion.

Unlike HiSAP, Lydian was used by learners to build their own implementation of an algorithm's behaviour. Each learner was set a task to use Lydian to implement the behaviour of one of three different algorithms. These were leader election based on the echo broadcast algorithm, leader election based on a voting approach and resource allocation based on logical clocks. Learners were given the option to create a visualisation of their algorithm implementations if they so wished. This was facilitated through the design of Lydian. In Lydian, the implementation of an algorithm's behaviour is held separate from that of its visualisation. In order to create a visualisation of an algorithm's behaviour, one must first implement the behaviour of the algorithm using a language based on a C syntax and then manually annotate the latter with calls to functions of a built in visualisation library known as Polka [97].

Findings from the study showed that the majority of learners thought the implementation experience helped them to understand the algorithm better. Although some learners experienced difficulties in using specific parts of the Lydian environment, the overall impression was that it was helpful or relatively helpful to their understanding. However, of note was that learners who had tested the animation part of the algorithm had a better insight into the algorithm's behaviour than those who had not [97]. This accords with the theory of dual coding and suggests that the building of dual representations of an algorithm's behaviour facilitates one's understanding of it. However, over 60% of learners did not experience any behaviours of the algorithm that they had not thought of prior to implementation. This suggests that perhaps these learners did not experiment with the behaviour of their visualisations once created. This may be due to the mode of interactivity afforded by Lydian over an algorithm's behaviour while it executes. Lydian affords offline interaction [3], that is, a learner must specify prior to execution the properties of the algorithm that he wishes to observe, change or modify. However, in many cases, it is desirable to receive feedback and change the behaviour of the algorithm by failing links or processes as the execution evolves [3]. This is particularly important if a learner wishes to demonstrate to a class or instructor the degree to which his cognitive representations of an algorithm's behaviour are fault tolerant. Further research is needed for the promise of algorithm visualisation in the teaching and learning of distributed algorithms to be realised. It stills remains a challenge to identify which of the following modes of engagement with an algorithm's behaviour significantly impact upon one's understanding of it. These are: (1) the ability to view an algorithm's behaviour, (2) the ability to interact with an algorithm's behaviour in real time, or (3) the ability to customise or create one's own algorithm visualisation.

2.4 Techniques deployed by algorithm construction systems to facilitate the creation of algorithm visualisations by learners or instructors

As documented in section 2.3.1 and section 2.3.2, algorithm construction systems deploy one of four different techniques to facilitate the creation of an algorithm visualisation. These are manual annotation (e.g. [61, 76, 77]), which is the process of manually transforming or annotating the source code of an algorithm's behaviour to include calls to functions of a visualisation library [79], (non-invasive) automated annotation (e.g. [78]), which is the process of automatically adding the aforementioned animation calls to the algorithm's source code [79], scripting languages (e.g. [12, 80, 81]), which is an alternative approach to manual annotation which tries to combine the flexibility of function calls with a modest amount of programming knowledge [82] and animated frameworks (e.g. [89, 90]), which is the provision of a set of generic reference types for a given algorithm domain including a control flow system that performs interaction among the objects instantiated from it [79]. Hence, the question of concern to this thesis is which of the aforementioned techniques lends itself more favourably to the easy creation of an algorithm visualisation? Such a question can be answered by analysing the strengths and weaknesses of current approaches.

The main strength of the manual annotation approach lies in the ease with which it generates an animation 'on the fly'. This is achieved once the given algorithm source code has been annotated with the corresponding visualisation function. Such functions are usually assembled together in function libraries more commonly referred to as APIs (Application Programming Interfaces) [82]. However, the main drawback of this approach lies in the need for instructors and learners to be familiar with the function calls of the API and also with programming. The API calls are usually embedded directly in the algorithm source code. This may prevent instructors or learners with little or no knowledge of the underlying programming language from using this approach. Furthermore, the approach is only helpful if the learner or instructor uses the same programming language for the algorithm as used by the API, as calling functions in a library written in a different programming language remains difficult [82]. Moreover, such an approach requires learners and instructors to have an in depth knowledge of the interesting events associated with an algorithm's behaviour in order for them to be able to visualise it. This is something which naïve learners may not be able to comply with.

Automated annotation frees the instructor or learner from having to define animation commands or doing extra work to generate the animations as it directly generates the animation from the source code. As a result, the animation is consistent with the underlying source code. By being based directly on the source code, new animations can usually be generated by simply exchanging algorithm parameters and restarting the algorithm [82].

However, there are drawbacks with this approach. First, instructors or learners must implement the behaviour of the algorithm in the programming language supported by the system. If they do not, then the system is rendered unusable. Moreover, the animation effects are hard coded into the underlying source code interpreter. Consequently, instructors or learners are unable to change the view of the animation if they so wish [82].

Unlike APIs, scripting languages provide a set of easy to use programming commands that are normally devoid of programming structures, such as conditional statements or loops, to specify the algorithm visualisation in. These commands can be generated and edited using any text editor and usually consist of a single command per line. However, whilst each single line of the generated animation may be easily read, it is often rather difficult to get a feeling for what the animation might look like. While experimenting with the code lines is easy, generalising the desired effects and putting them into an algorithm's source code can be difficult [82].

An animation framework, on the other hand, provides a set of prefabricated software building blocks that learners or instructors can quickly customise to build their own implementation of an algorithm's behaviour. This is then automatically outputted as a visualisation. Thus, frameworks free learners or instructors to concentrate solely on the implementation of the algorithm's logic and not on its visualisation [82]. However, like automated annotation, animation frameworks are closely tied to the programs that they are visualising.

From this analysis, it is clear that both automated annotation and animation frameworks offer the easiest means to generate an animation as this is done by the animation system itself. Moreover, both facilitate the generation of multiple animations without much effort [82]. However, animation frameworks outweigh automated annotation through the provision of a generic library for the easy implementation of an algorithm's behaviour. Such a library together with the automation of the animation process reduces the time required and the level of difficulty associated with creating an algorithm animation by an order of magnitude. However, such an approach does not render its animated visualisations open to interactive influences, that is, it does not create visualisations which a learner can engage with or modify in real time that is, while they execute. In order to achieve this level of engagement, an instructor or programmer has to manually annotate the code to specify which components or sections of an algorithm's behaviour that a learner could interact with and change. As a consequence, animation frameworks as they currently stand do not permit the automatic creation of active algorithm simulations.

2.5 Discussion

As evidenced by the literature review, algorithm visualisation systems (AVs) for the teaching and learning of distributed algorithms can be defined as falling into one of three different categories. These are *passive animation systems*, which provide multiple prepared views of an algorithm's behaviour for a learner to view, stop, pause, reset, step through or rewind, *active simulation systems*, which enable a learner to investigate issues of partial failure by permitting him to change the state of an algorithm's variables or to cause one or more of its components (e.g. nodes or messages) to fail during execution and *algorithm construction systems*, which provide tools to facilitate the easy creation of an algorithm visualisation. However, despite this spectrum of systems, each of them suffers from one or more of the following short comings.

These are:

- *A lack of a deep model of engagement with an algorithm's behaviour in real time.*
  In the real world, distributed algorithms suffer from partial failure, that is, the loss or failure of one or more its components, for example, nodes or messages. If such behaviours are not accounted for, that is, if services are not provided to enable the algorithm to continue functioning despite their presence, the algorithm will terminate or malfunction. Thus, in order to enable a learner to develop an appreciation for and an understanding of such episodes of behaviour, there is need for him to be able to re-enact these behaviours while the algorithm executes. This is achieved by enabling the learner to cause one or more of an algorithm's components to fail during execution. By so doing, the learner is able to decipher the degree to which the algorithm is fault tolerant. An algorithm is said to be fault tolerant, if it can continue to function despite the presence of failed components. Currently, the only algorithm visualisation system which enables learners to investigate issues of partial failure is active simulations. However, these systems hide the implementation details of the algorithm's behaviour from the learner and as a result,

do not enable him to amend the algorithm's implementation code to put interventions in place to enable it to handle certain partial failure issues, if need be.

- *An underdeveloped model of pedagogy.*

Current AVs for the teaching and learning of distributed algorithms have been informed by one of four different theories of learning. These are epistemic fidelity, dual coding, individual differences and cognitive constructivism. Of these four, a meta analysis found that systems informed by the theory of cognitive constructivism were the most successful in returning a learning gain. This would suggest that it is what learners do with the technology and not what they see that has the greatest impact upon their learning. This also implies that active simulation systems and algorithm construction systems offer the greatest potential in returning a learning gain as both actively engage the learner with the learning content. Active simulations actively engage the learner by enabling him to change the state of an algorithm's variables and to cause one or more of its components to fail. Algorithm construction systems actively engage the learner by enabling him to build his own representation of an algorithm's behaviour. However, whilst active simulation systems enable learners to engage with the behaviour of an algorithm in a deep way, they do not enable him to modify or amend its underling implementation code. Consequently, learners are not provided with any opportunity to build dual representations of an algorithm's behaviour or to map the graphical representation to its underlying implementation. This may explain why learners have been found not to be able to replicate the behaviour of an algorithm despite stating emphatically that they understood it after engaging with an active simulation of its behaviour.

Unlike active simulations, algorithm construction systems enable learners to make explicit their own cognitive representations of an algorithm's behaviour. However, once built, they do not afford the learner the ability to experiment with the representation created in a deep way. A learner is unable to change the state of an algorithm's variables or to cause components to fail during execution. Hence, learners are not provided with any information which is dissonant to their current understandings of the algorithm's behaviour and are provided with no means to build upon that understanding or to modify it. Constructionists believe that it is the structuring phase of learning that builds the framework of understanding upon which subsequent knowledge is built. It is this 'subsequent knowledge' that is of interest to this thesis, and is believed to be greatly facilitated through the provision of a deep model of engagement with the algorithm's behaviour and through interaction with others.

- *Level of difficulty and time associated with creating an algorithm visualisation.*
  Many algorithm construction systems require instructors and learners to learn how to use two systems in order to create an algorithm animation. These are: the development environment (to create the algorithm implementation) and the visualisation library (to create its corresponding animation). Moreover, some require a user to manually annotate the algorithm implementation code with calls to functions of a built in visualisation library in order to render the animation. Hence, such systems require users to have in-depth knowledge of the interesting events associated with the algorithm's behaviour in order to return an animation of it. Other systems automate the annotation process, but require the user to implement the algorithm in a given specification language. Such languages are recognised as non intuitive and difficult for novices to learn [90]. Furthermore, there is a lack of an easy to use and universally accessible platform for implementing the algorithms' behaviour and for investigating their dynamic behaviours [90]. To create an active simulation, a user must, not only, implement the algorithm logic, but also, its corresponding visualisation and its interactive components. Such overheads in terms of development time serve only to deflate the user's motivation and to cause him to shy away from the use of the technology.

- *Lack of empirical evidence to substantiate their educational effectiveness.*
  At the time of writing this thesis, the author could only gather empirical evidence relating to the educational effectiveness of two AVs for the teaching and learning of distributed algorithms. These were HiSAP, which is an active simulation system and Lydian, which is an algorithm construction system. (See section 2.3.4). However, neither study gave any true insight into the learning benefits to be derived from enabling learners to create their own algorithm visualisations as both studies did not set such a task as a core requirement. In HiSAP, learners were presented

with prepared simulations of an algorithm's behaviour, whilst in Lydian, learners were only required to implement the algorithm's behaviour; the requirement to create its visualisation was left optional. Moreover, both studies evaluated the educational effectiveness of the technology solely from the perspective of the learner and not from that of the instructor. Thus, neither study gave insight into how the technology assists instructors in their teachings or how easy it is for them to use. This is surprising given that the basis for the technology rests on the need to assist instructors in capturing and conveying to learners the dynamic and concurrent behaviour of a distributed algorithm. Hence, there is need of further study to determine what impact the ability to (1) view an algorithm's behaviour, (2) interact with an algorithm's behaviour in real time, or (3) customise or build an algorithm visualisation has on a learner's understanding of an algorithm's process. Equally, there is need of evidence to ascertain to what extent instructors find such functionality to be educationally beneficial.

Thus, the research challenge posed in this thesis is to design and implement an algorithm visualisation system which will enable one to overcome the aforementioned shortcomings. In order to address such shortcomings, there is need of a system which is easy to use and which also:

- Provides visualisations that support the theory of dual coding that is, provide both a graphical and textual representation of an algorithm's behaviour,
- Provides visualisation that enable one to engage with the behaviour of an algorithm in a deep way, in accordance with the theory of cognitive constructivism, by changing the state of algorithm's variables or by causing one or more of its components to fail during execution,
- Scaffolds the algorithm implementation process,
- Automatically executes each algorithm implementation as a highly interactive visualisation,
- Permits one to easily amend, modify the behaviour of an algorithm.

Thus, in order to create an algorithm visualisation system for the teaching and learning of distributed algorithms, which satisfies each of the above design requirements, there is need of a framework. A framework can be defined as a partial design and implementation for an application in a given problem domain [99]. It can be tailored to create complete applications or in this case, to return active simulations. Frameworks are generally developed when several or (partly) similar applications need to be developed. A framework implements the commonalities between applications and as a consequence, reduces the effort needed to build them [100]. However, unlike current animation frameworks (See section 2.4), the framework proposed here, must be designed, not only, to provide a set of prefabricated software building blocks for the easy implementation of an algorithm's behaviour, but also, must be designed to make transparent calls to an underlying visualisation library and to functions specifying which components of the algorithm's behaviour are to be rendered manipulable during execution. This is necessary in order to reduce the cost, in terms of development time, in creating the simulation and to enable learners to concentrate solely on the implementation of the algorithm's behaviour and not on its visualisation or its level of real time interactivity. In designing and implementing such a framework, this thesis proposes that the FADA algorithm visualisation system addresses the shortcomings in currently available algorithm visualisation systems in one of two novel ways. These are through:

- The development of a model of engagement that enables the learner when interacting with the behaviour of an algorithm to engage his higher order thinking skills of analysis, synthesis and evaluation,
- The development of a framework which facilitates the quick and easy creation of highly interactive algorithm simulations.

In deploying FADA, it is possible to explore different educational issues such as the impact which different modes of engagement with an algorithm's behaviour have on a learner's understanding of it and the pedagogical benefits to be derived from using an application like FADA within a lecture setting. More specifically, this research, through the use of exploratory case studies, examines two research questions. These are:

- To what extent does the algorithm animation approach adopted by FADA enhance the teaching and learning of distributed algorithms?
- To what extent is FADA easy to use?

2.6 Summary

This chapter has briefly outlined the current state of play in algorithm visualisation development. It has argued that despite the current failure to substantiate its educational effectiveness, algorithm visualisation still holds much potential for both instructors and learners. It offers instructors the potential to assist them in capturing and conveying the dynamic and concurrent behaviour of a distributed algorithm's process. Moreover, it offers learners the potential to gain a deeper understanding of distributed algorithms. In order to realise this potential, this chapter has identified the need for a new algorithm visualisation system for the teaching and learning of distributed algorithms, one which is easy to use, deploys a model of engagement with an algorithm's behaviour which is informed by the theory of cognitive constructivism and social constructivism, enables learners, in accordance with the theory of constructionism, to create their own algorithm implementations in a timely and intuitive manner through the use of a framework and renders each implementation automatically as a highly interactive simulation through the use of automated annotation. The next chapter defines the manner by which this algorithm visualisation system was designed in accordance with design principles set out in section 2.5

Chapter 3
Design

3.1   Introduction

This chapter documents the manner by which FADA was designed in accordance with a set of design principles derived from the literature review (See section 2.5). It can be subdivided into four main sections. The first section provides an overview of FADA's design. The second section delineates the deep model of engagement that FADA affords a user over an algorithm's behaviour while it executes. The third section documents the manner by which FADA was designed to support the theory of dual coding and to scaffold the algorithm implementation process. The fourth section describes the manner by which FADA was designed to facilitate the easy implementation of an algorithm's behaviour and the automatic rendering of the latter as a highly interactive simulation. This was achieved through the provision of a framework which makes transparent calls to an underlying visualisation API. The design of the framework and the API were informed by findings arising, not only, from the literature review, but also, from the author's own experiences of building an active simulation of the token ring algorithm. This chapter concludes with an overview and summary.

3.2   Overview of FADA's design

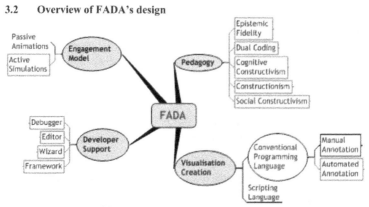

Figure 3-1: A graphical overview and breakdown of the engagement model, the pedagogical model, the developer support and the visualisation support which FADA was designed to provide. (These are highlighted in red).

FADA was designed to overcome shortcomings posed by existing algorithm visualisation systems for the teaching and learning of distributed algorithms and as such, was designed to facilitate each of the following requirements. These were:

- *Ease of use,*

This was achieved through the provision of a framework for common message passing distributed algorithms and through the design of FADA's development environment. The framework was designed to scaffold the user in implementing the behaviour of an algorithm through the provision of a library of generic function calls, which a user could quickly and easily customise to reflect the behaviour of an algorithm that he is implementing. These calls were implemented in JAVA. This is the most commonly taught language to date in third level institutes [101, 102] and as such, was not thought to impose a steep learning curve on users. Moreover, JAVA is platform independent and thus, renders FADA amenable to a number of different learning settings. All implementations created using the framework were designed to be automatically rendered as highly interactive simulations. This was achieved through the design and encapsulation of a predefined visualisation API and through a process of automated annotation. Consequently, as a result of its design, FADA enables users to concentrate solely on the implementation of an algorithm's logic and not on that of its visualisation or level of interactivity.

The development environment was designed to assist in the algorithm implementation process through the granting of an editor, a debugger and a wizard as typified by any standard programming environment. The wizard was designed to assist novices in implementing the behaviour of an algorithm by enabling them through the selection and customisation of simple menu items to automatically generate code relating to the messages that a node is to receive, the content of those messages and the type of variables that a node is to hold.

- *To provide a deep model of engagement with an algorithm's behaviour while it executes,*

This was procured by enabling users to change the state of an algorithm's variables or to cause one or more of its components (e.g. message, nodes) to fail while it executes. By affording users such deep levels of real time interaction with an algorithm's behaviour, FADA enables them to encounter information which may be dissonant to their current understandings of an algorithm's behaviour and enables them to absorb such information so as to modify their understanding.

- *To provide a rich pedagogical model,*

This was in order to render FADA amenable to a number of different uses by instructors. This was realised by designing FADA to accord with the theoretical underpinnings of five different theories of learning. These were: cognitive constructivism, constructionism, dual coding, epistemic fidelity and social constructivism. In the first instance, FADA was designed, to accord with the theory of cognitive constructivism and as such, was designed to actively engage users by enabling them to change the state of an algorithm's variables or to cause one or more of its components (e.g. nodes or messages) to fail. Secondly, FADA was designed, to accord with the theory of constructionism, by enabling users to create their own algorithm simulations. This was achieved through the provision of a framework for common message passing distributed algorithms and through the use of automated annotation. Thirdly, FADA was designed, to accord with the theory of dual coding, and as such, was designed to provide users with dual representations of an algorithm's behaviour. This was in order to enable them to reinforce their understanding of an algorithm's behaviour through mapping its graphical representation to that of its implementation. The dual representations of an algorithm's behaviour were afforded by sub dividing FADA's interface into two separate but inter-changeable halves similar to that created by Jeliot (See section 2.3.2). These were the code frame and the animation frame. The code frame was designed to display a textual representation of the algorithm's implementation whilst the animation frame was designed to display its corresponding visualisation. Fourthly, all visualisations rendered by FADA were designed to accord with the theory of epistemic fidelity and as such, were designed to present users with visualisations of an algorithm's behaviour akin to those presented by standard text books. Lastly, FADA was designed, to accord with the theory of social constructivism, and as such was designed to enable users to present their own simulations to an audience for feedback and discussion. This was facilitated, not only, through the model of engagement afforded by FADA over an algorithm's behaviour, but also, through the provision of a set of controls, which enables a user to control the pace at which he presents his simulation content.

- *To reduce the time and complexity associated with creating an active simulation.*

FADA was informed by the author's own experiences of building an active simulation (See section 3.5.1) and, as a result, was designed as a modular architecture (See figure 3-2).

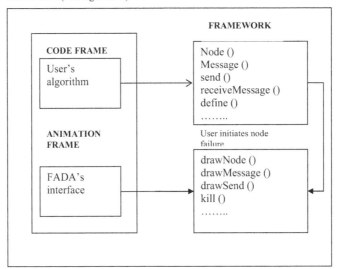

Figure 3-2: Overview of FADA's modular architecture design.

This architecture was designed to reduce the complexity associated with creating an active simulation by subdividing the problem of creating it into three separate independent sub problems. These were: the creation of the algorithm implementation, the creation of its corresponding visualisation and the creation of its interactive components. FADA was designed to automate the solution to the visualisation of an algorithm's behaviour and to that of its real time interaction. This was achieved through the design and encapsulation of a built-in visualisation API and through the use of automated annotation. FADA was designed to provide a framework and a heavily scaffolded development environment so as to enable users to quickly implement the behaviour of an algorithm.

3.3 Model of Engagement

FADA was designed to provide a deep model of engagement with an algorithm's behaviour and as such, was designed to enable a user to engage with an algorithm in one of two ways. These were by controlling the pace of its execution or by manipulating its behaviour during run time. The first was achieved through the provision of a set of controls that enable a user to stop, pause, reset or change the pace of an algorithm's execution.

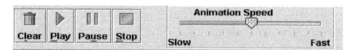

Figure 3-3: Controls provided by FADA to control the simulation execution.

The latter was achieved by designing FADA to enable a user to change the state of an algorithm's behaviour during run time and by enabling him to cause one or more of its components to fail.

Partial failure can occur in one of two different modes. These are omission failures or arbitrary failures. Omission failures occur when nodes or communication channels fail to perform actions that they are suppose to. This can result in a node crashing that is halting and failing to execute further steps of its program. Moreover, it can result in a message getting lost that is, being dropped by the communication channel. Arbitrary failures result in a node or communication channel exhibiting any type of failure. An arbitrary failure of a node is one which arbitrarily omits intended processing steps or takes unintended steps. Thus, in order for a user to be able to investigate the effects of each of the aforementioned failure modes, he must be able to replicate their behaviours during run time either through changing the state of an algorithm's behaviour or by causing one or more of its components to fail. This is in order to enable the user to determine whether the algorithm can continue to function despite their loss. A service masks a failure by hiding it altogether or by converting it into a more acceptable type of failure. Failure is hidden using a protocol which retransmits messages that do not arrive at their destinations. It is normally used in association with a timeout scheme [103].

Consequently, FADA was designed to enable a user to cause a node to fail during the execution of an algorithm's behaviour by enabling him to click on the node's visual representation and, from the menu of behaviours displayed, to select the command 'kill'. This action was designed to automatically result in the node failing to respond to any further messages sent to it.

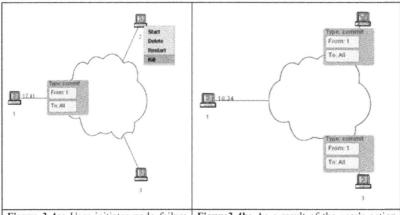

Figure 3-4a: User initiates node failure within the *two phase commit algorithm* by right clicking on node 2 and selecting 'Kill' from the menu options displayed.	**Figure3-4b:** As a result of the user's action in Figure 3-4a, node 2 does not send a reply to node 1's 'commit' message.

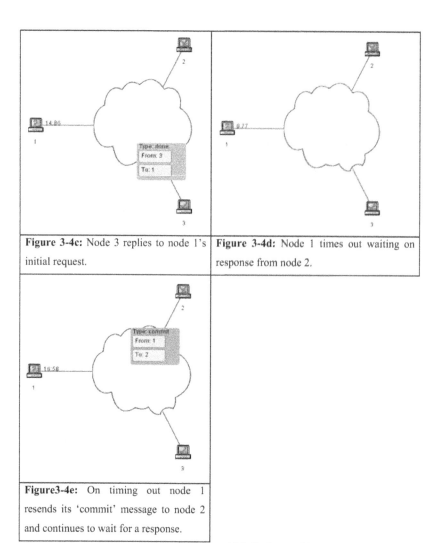

Figure 3-4c: Node 3 replies to node 1's initial request.

Figure 3-4d: Node 1 times out waiting on response from node 2.

Figure3-4e: On timing out node 1 resends its 'commit' message to node 2 and continues to wait for a response.

Figure 3-4: A depiction of the manner by which FADA enables a user to initiate node failure during an algorithm's execution.

Equally, FADA was designed to enable a user to cause a message to fail by enabling him to right click on its visual representation during transit. This action was designed to cause the message to disappear from screen, signifying its loss in transmission.

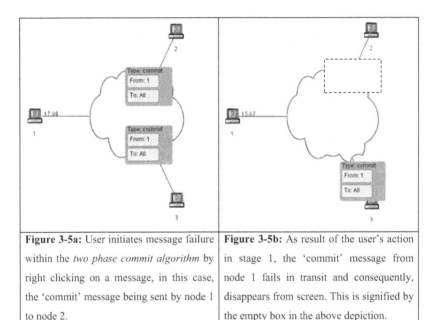

Figure 3-5a: User initiates message failure within the *two phase commit algorithm* by right clicking on a message, in this case, the 'commit' message being sent by node 1 to node 2.	**Figure 3-5b:** As result of the user's action in stage 1, the 'commit' message from node 1 fails in transit and consequently, disappears from screen. This is signified by the empty box in the above depiction.

Figure 3-5: A depiction of the manner by which FADA enables a user to initiate message failure during an algorithm's execution.

Furthermore, FADA was designed to enable a user to change the state of an algorithm's variables by enabling him to right click on the visual representation of a node. This action was designed to depict on screen a panel displaying all local variables belonging to that node instant and their current state values. These values were designed to be modified by the user at run time, so as to enable him to determine what effects, if any, such state changes would have on the algorithm's behaviour.

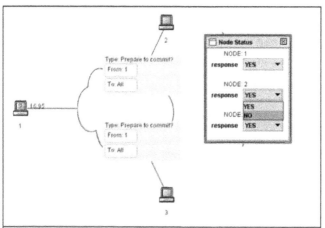

Figure 3.6a: User initiates state changes within the *two phase commit algorithm* by clicking on a node icon, in this case, node 2, and by changing the value of its local response variable from 'YES' to 'NO'.

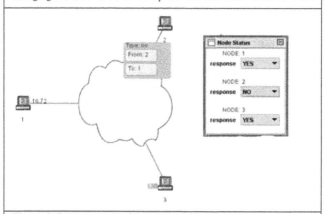

Figure 3.6b: As a result of the user's action in stage 1, node 2 replies 'NO' to the 'Prepare to commit' message sent by node 1.

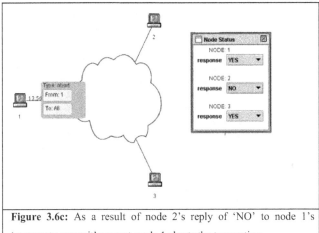

Figure 3.6c: As a result of node 2's reply of 'NO' to node 1's
'prepare to commit' request, node 1 aborts the transaction.

Figure 3.6: A depiction of the manner by which FADA enables a user to initiate state
changes within an algorithm's behaviour in real time that is, during its execution.

3.4   FADA's Development Environment

Informed by the theory of dual coding, FADA's development environment was designed to
enable a user to reinforce his understanding of an algorithm's behaviour through building
referential connections between the visual representation of an algorithm's behaviour and
its underlying implementation code. This was achieved through the design of a split pane
interface. The interface was subdivided into two interchangeable halves. These were the
code frame and the animation frame. The code frame was designed to house the
implementation code of an algorithm's behaviour, whilst the animation frame was designed
to house its corresponding visualisation.

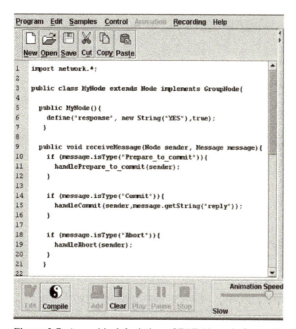

Figure 3-7: A graphical depiction of FADA's code frame. It contains code relating to the implementation of the *two phase commit* algorithm.

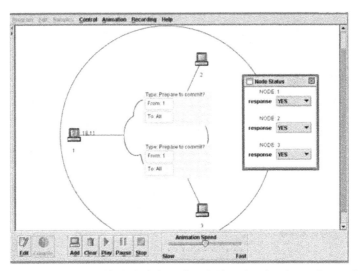

Figure 3-8: A graphical depiction of FADA's animation frame. It contains a graphical representation of the algorithm code contained within Figure 3-7.

Moreover, the code frame was designed to scaffold a user in the construction of an algorithm's implementation through the provision of an editor, a debugger and a wizard. The editor was designed to enable a user to edit, cut, copy, paste, save the algorithm implementation code whilst, the debugger was designed to alert users to logical or syntactical errors in their implementations. These were visualised to the user through FADA's built in console window.

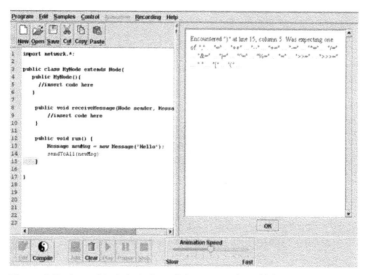

Figure 3-9: A graphical depiction of the manner by which FADA automatically alerts users to syntax errors in their algorithm implementation code. In the above example, the user has forgotten to close the statement in line 14 with a semi colon.

The wizard was designed to further scaffold the algorithm implementation process by enabling users through the selection of simple menu items to automatically generate code relating to the messages that a node is to receive, the type of content that the messages are to contain and the variables that the node is to hold.

62

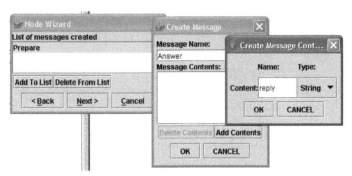

Figure 3-10: A graphical depiction of the manner by which a user deploys the wizard to create a message called 'Answer' and to associate with that message a parameter called 'reply'. 'Reply' holds the value of a node's response to the 'Prepare to commit' message in the *two phase commit algorithm*. The code generated from such an action is depicted in Figure 3-11.

```
import network.*;

public class MyNode extends Node{

  public MyNode(){}

  public void receiveMessage(Node sender, Message message){
    if (message.isType("Answer")){
      handleAnswer(sender,message.getString("reply"));
    }
  }

  public void handleAnswer(Node sender,String reply){
    //Insert code to handle message
  }

  public void run(){
    //Insert code here
  }
}
```

Figure 3-11: A depiction of the code automatically generated by the wizard in Figure 3-10. This code is outputted to the code frame within FADA.

3.5   FADA's Framework Design

FADA was designed to cut down on the time required to create an implementation of a distributed algorithm's behaviour through the provision of a framework for common message passing distributed algorithms. These algorithms were chosen as all communication within a distributed system is message-based and dictated by the aforementioned types of algorithms [103]. Thus, in order, for one to begin to understand how a distributed system functions, one must first develop an appreciation for the manner by which communication between the software components of that system is performed. To this end, the framework was designed to provide a set of prefabricated software building blocks which a user could quickly customise to reflect the behaviour of a message passing distributed algorithm. This was achieved by designing the framework to accord with guidelines set out by Booch [104]. However, given that the author was not an expert within the proposed framework domain, it was necessary for her to acquire such expertise by building an active simulation of an algorithm from that domain. This was in order to enable her to gain insight into the complexities associated with such an implementation and to enable her on comparison against other algorithm behaviours to identify key abstractions and areas of variable functionality which would form part of the framework core. Section 3.5.1 describes the manner by which the author designed and implemented an active simulation of the token ring algorithm [122]. It also documents difficulties encountered in the implementation process and offers solutions to overcome each. These solutions together with data realised from the literature review inform the overall architectural design of FADA as depicted in section 3.2. Section 3.5.2 documents the representative classes of message passing distributed algorithms which were analysed in order to derive the abstractions which formed the design of the framework core.

3.5.1   The Token Ring Simulation

This simulation was designed to espouse both an epistemic fidelity and a cognitive constructivist approach to the teaching and learning of the token ring algorithm. As such, it was designed to provide a learner with an expert's mental model of the algorithm's behaviour which he could directly manipulate in real time and in multiple ways. This was in order to enable the learner to build his own conceptual understanding of the algorithm's behaviour through a process of experimentation with the expert's representation. To this end, the token ring simulation was designed to enable the learner to vary the size of the network and to create different network configurations such as include or exclude a monitor. The simulation was also designed to enable the learner, through the provision of a set of predefined controls, to analyse and observe the effects of different network configurations on the ability of a node to send a message, to cope with token failure, packet failure, monitor failure and or node failure. With respect to node failure, a learner was able to cause a node to fail at any time during the execution of the algorithm. This was achieved through the provision of a set of radio controls which were designed to turn the behaviour of a node 'on' or 'off' during the algorithm's execution. The same applied to packets, monitors and tokens in that, a learner could turn their behaviours off at any time during the algorithm's execution by selecting the appropriate radio control function (See Figure 3-12).

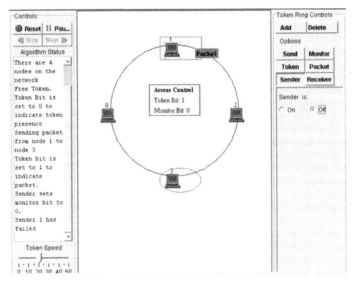

Figure 3-12: A screen shot of the token ring simulation in which the user has selected via the controls to the left hand side of the screen node 1 (the sender of the

packet) to fail. Such an action has resulted in all remaining nodes being prevented from gaining access to the token as node 1 has not release it.

Additional features included the ability to enable the learner to control the pace at which the simulation executed and to enable him to stop, pause, reset or step through its contents whenever he so wished. However, the underlying implementation code of the algorithm's behaviour was kept hidden from the learner. Thus, he was provided with no opportunity to build dual representations of the token ring's behaviour.

A significant amount of development time was required to create the above simulation (fifty plus hours). This was because, not only, had the author to implement the behaviour of the algorithm, but also, she had to specify how it was to be visualised. Moreover, she had to identify areas in the token ring's behaviour which, if rendered manipulable, would lend to a learner's understanding of it. This development process was further complicated from the outset by the author's failure to adopt a modular architecture. Such an architecture subdivides a problem into a number of sub-problems and solves each independently of each other. A solution to the original problem is realised through the amalgamation of the solutions to the sub-problems.

By adopting a modular architecture, the author could have subdivided the problem of creating the token ring simulation into three isolated sub-problems. These were: the creation of the algorithm's implementation, the creation of its corresponding visualisation and lastly, the creation of its interactive components. Each of these sub-problems could then have been solved independently of each other. Moreover, through a process of manual annotation, the author could have quickly outputted the active simulation. However, such a process is only suited to someone who has expert knowledge of the algorithm's behaviour as it requires one to have detailed knowledge of the interesting events associated with it in order to enable one to render them manipulable at run time. The use of a modular architecture would have also permitted the author to simulate further consensus algorithms, for example, the election algorithm, more quickly, as all that would have needed to be re-implemented would have been the algorithm implementation code. The implementation of its visualisation would have remained relatively unchanged. Furthermore, it was also noted that there was need of mechanisms to scaffold the algorithm implementation process in order to facilitate a user in creating the latter and in debugging it.

3.5.2   Design of the framework core.

In order to design the framework, one first had to examine the behaviours of a number of representative classes of message passing algorithms in order to abstract out their commonality. Such abstractions formed the basis of the building blocks' design.

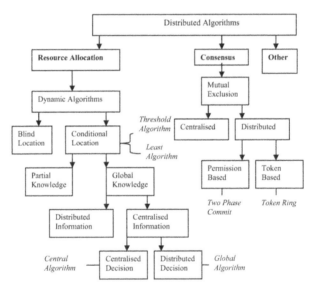

Figure 3-13: A breakdown of the representative classes of message passing distributed algorithms that were analysed in order to identify the abstractions which would form the basis of the framework core.

In its initial design, FADA was designed to focus upon the following representative classes. These were load balancing algorithms and consensus algorithms. Load balancing algorithms deal with performance issues in distributed systems. They distribute work around the system in accordance with some criteria, such as; no node should remain idle while other nodes are waiting for access to another node in the system [105]. Consensus algorithms dictate that a collection of nodes must agree on some value like for example, access to a shared resource [106].

In each of the aforementioned classes, the following algorithms were analysed. In load balancing, these were the threshold algorithm, the centralised algorithm and the global algorithm. These algorithms were chosen as they are representative of dynamic algorithms whose decisions are based on no a-priori knowledge of system state [105]. All knowledge of system state is gathered during execution through a process of message passing. Centralised and global algorithms are examples of algorithms which base their decision to offload work to another node on the basis of global knowledge of system state. This is either held centrally by a single node or stored across a number of different nodes. With respect to consensus algorithms, the following algorithms were analysed. These were the token ring algorithm and the two phase commit algorithm. These were chosen as they are examples of mutual exclusion algorithms, which are algorithms which dictate the manner by which access to a shared resource is controlled within a distributed system. The token ring algorithm was chosen as it dictates access to a shared resource based on the possession of a token whilst, the two phase commit algorithm dictates access to a shared resource based on permission gained from all other members within the distributed system. Unless all members agree, no access to the shared resource is granted. However, despite their different methodologies, all algorithms were found to share the same basic set of primitive operations.

These were to enable a node to:

- Create a message and to associate with that message a unique identifier.
- Place content of any data type inside a message.
- Retrieve content of any data type from a message.
- Send a message either to another node, to a subset of nodes or to all remaining nodes.
- Receive a message.

- Distinguish between different messages that it receives.
- Set or change the value of one or more variables.
- Retrieve the value of a state variable.
- Associate a time out with a message.
- Schedule a timer for 'once off' execution or for repeated execution.

Each of these operations was encapsulated in a number of Java classes in order to realise their behaviours (See chapter 4 for more details).

In order to automatically visualise the behaviour of an algorithm, each of the aforementioned operations were designed to make transparent calls to methods which were designed to visualise their behaviours. Separate depictions were provided for each of the following components of an algorithm's behaviour. These were nodes, messages, variables and timers. Equally, visualisations were provided for the each of the following aspects of an algorithm's behaviour. These were the queue of messages waiting to be sent by a node, the transfer of messages between nodes, the loss of a message, the failure of a node and the count down of the timer. The use of separate visualisations was necessitated in order to enable the author to designate the behaviour of a node, a message or variable editable during run time and to enable their behaviours once changed to be updated and repainted to the animation frame.

3.6   Summary

This chapter has documented the manner by which FADA was designed to address the initial research challenge put forward in section 1.3 of how to facilitate the easy creation of active simulations by both learners and instructors. This was achieved by designing FADA in accordance with a set of design requirements derived from the literature review and in accordance with insights gained from the author's own experiences of building an active simulation. First, this chapter described the manner by which FADA was designed to facilitate ease of use through the provision of a framework for common message passing algorithms and through the provision of a heavily scaffolded development environment. Next, it outlined the manner by which FADA was designed to enable a user to engage with and experiment with the behaviour of an algorithm in real time. Lastly, it documented the manner by which FADA was designed to reduce the time and complexity associated with creating an active simulation through the provision of a modular architecture, a framework and automatic annotation. The next chapter describes the manner by which FADA's overall design was implemented.

Chapter 4
Implementation

4.1 Introduction

This chapter documents the manner by which FADA's design was implemented. In the main, it delineates the manner by which FADA was implemented as a modular architecture in order to reduce the time and complexity associated with creating an active simulation. A modular architecture, as previously stated, is one, which divides a problem into a number of sub problems and solves each independently of each other. A solution to the original problem is realised through the amalgamation of solutions to the sub problems.

FADA was designed to subdivide the problem of creating an active simulation into three separate sub problems. These were: the creation of an algorithm's implementation, its corresponding visualisation and its real time interactivity. FADA was implemented to provide a framework for common message passing distributed algorithms which a user could easily customise to reflect the behaviour of a particular algorithm. The methods of the framework were implemented to make transparent calls to a set of predefined visualisation methods in order to automatically render the algorithm's behaviour upon execution as an interactive visualisation. This was in order to enable a user to modify the behaviour of an algorithm in real time by manipulating the behaviour of one or more of its components like, for example, its nodes, variables or messages.

In order to realise this implementation, it was necessary to create two modules. These were the Network module and the GUI module. A module can be likened to a physical container in which one stores all classes or objects relating to a particular aspect of the overall design of the application. The GUI module was created to house classes relating to the depiction of an algorithm's behaviour as an interactive visualisation. It was also implemented to house classes relating to FADA's implementation as a split pane interface. FADA was designed to be subdivided into two frames. These were the code frame and the animation frame. The subdivision was necessary in order to enable FADA to provide dual representations of an algorithm's behaviour in accordance with the theory of dual coding. The code frame was implemented to house the user's description of an algorithm's behaviour together with tools to assist and scaffold in implementing the algorithm. The animation frame was implemented to house the interactive visualisation of an algorithm's behaviour together with controls to control its presentation. The Network module was created to house classes relating to the implementation of an algorithm's behaviour.

Section 4.2 describes how classes within the Network module were implemented to provide FADA's framework methods. These methods were implemented to realise the behaviour of the abstractions noted in section 3.5.2. Section 4.3 describes how classes within the GUI module were implemented to graphically depict the behaviour of a user defined algorithm as an interactive visualisation. This was achieved through the creation of a set of predefined visualisation methods. These methods were automatically invoked by the FADA's framework methods. This was in order to automate the drawing of an algorithm's behaviour upon execution. Section 4.4 defines the manner by which FADA was implemented as a split pane interface in order to encapsulate the algorithm's description and its interactive visualisation in one window. Equally, it delineates the manner by which FADA's code editor was implemented together with its wizard to assist users in implementing the algorithm's behaviour. Section 4.5 concludes with a summary of the chapter.

4.2 Network Module

Classes within the Network module were primarily implemented to realise the behaviour of the abstractions noted in chapter 3, section 3.5.2 and to enable a user to quickly customise their behaviours to reflect the behaviour of a set algorithm. In order to achieve this, it was necessary to implement all classes to support composition. This enables a user to easily adapt the behaviour of a class through parameterisation. A user customises the behaviour of a class by filling in parameters, which provide some required functionality. As a consequence, users do not have to have in depth knowledge of how these components operate in order for him to achieve customisation. In all three classes were implemented to realise the generic behaviour of a distributed algorithm. These were the Node class, the Message class and the Variable class.

The Node class (See Figure 4-1) was implemented to replicate the behaviour of a node within a distributed system.

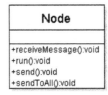

Figure 4-1: Node class

It was initially created to provide methods, which a user could invoke to enable a node:

1   To receive a message from another node within a distributed system.

This method (See Figure 3-2) was implemented to accept two parameters. These were: the name of the node sending the message and the reference to the message object being sent. The behaviour of this method was left undefined within the framework so as to enable a user to customise its behaviour to reflect that of the algorithm that he is implementing.

```
public void receiveMessage(Node sender, Message m){
      .....................
      .....................
}
```

Figure 4-2: A depiction of the *receiveMessage()* method provided by the Node class which a node instance invokes on receipt of a message.

2   To start the execution of the algorithm's behaviour.

Like the *receiveMessage()* method, this method was also left undefined. This was in order to enable a user to customise its behaviour in accordance with how the algorithm dictates a node should initiate it.

```
public void run(){
      .....................
      .....................
}
```

Figure 4-3: The *run()* method provided by the Node class which a user overwrites to enable a node instance to initiate the algorithm's behaviour.

3   To send a message to another node or to all other nodes within the distributed
     system.

     In order to invoke the functionality of a send operation, each send method (See
     Figure 4-4) was implemented to accept one parameter that is, a reference to the
     message object that the node instance wishes to send. Both methods were designed
     to replicate the communication behaviour of an algorithm whose underlying
     topology reflects that of a bus topology, that is, where all nodes within the system
     are independent of one another. In a bus topology, a node can communicate by
     sending a message to another individual node or by broadcasting a message to all
     other nodes currently within the system. In order to facilitate a pattern of
     communication which reflects that of a ring topology (that is, where all nodes know
     of each others' identity) or that of a star topology (that is, where all nodes
     communicate with each other via a centralised node), it was necessary to augment
     the behaviour of the Node class (See section 4.2.1 for more details). In a ring
     topology, a node communicates by sending a message to another node or by
     multicasting a message to all nodes within the group. In a star topology, all nodes
     communicate with each other via a centralised node known as a server node. This
     node accepts requests from a sending node known as a client node, executes that
     request and returns a reply. A server node can send a message to an individual client
     node or can multicast a message to all client nodes.

```
public void send(Message m){}
public void sendToAll(Message m){}
```

Figure 4-4: The default communication methods provided by the Node class.

The Message class (See Figure 4-5) was designed to replicate the behaviour of a message
within a distributed system.

74

```
┌─────────────────────────┐
│        Message          │
├─────────────────────────┤
│                         │
├─────────────────────────┤
│ +Message():void         │
│ +put():void             │
│ +putInt():void          │
│ +putDouble():void       │
│ +putBoolean():void      │
│ +putString():void       │
│ +get():Object           │
│ +getInt():int           │
│ +getDouble():double     │
│ +getBoolean():boolean   │
│ +getString():String     │
└─────────────────────────┘
```

Figure 4-5: Message Class

It was designed to provide methods to enable an instance of the Node class:

- To create a message and to associate with that message an unique identity.

  Each message was designed to accept an unique identity consisting of an unique name as opposed to an unique sequence of numbers. This was in order to enable a user to quickly differentiate the meaning of a message once visualised. This method was designed to be overloaded. This was in order to enable a user to associate with a message object further information like for example, the name of the node sending the message or the name of the node to which the message is destined. This was achieved by implementing multiple definitions of the constructor method of the Message class. Thus, in order to enable an instance of the node class to create one or more message objects, a user invokes one of the following constructor methods (See Figure 4-6) and passes to it, one or more of the following values in order to initialise its arguments. These are: the unique identity of that message, the name of node to whom the message is destined and/or the name of the node sending the message.

75

```
public Message(String messageID){}
public Message(Node destination, String messageID){}
public Message(Node destination, Node sender, String messageID){}
```

Figure 4-6: A depiction of the different types of constructor methods provided by the Message class that a node invokes to create one of three different types of message objects. These are: a message object which is addressed to all nodes within the system, a message object which is addressed to a particular node and, finally, a message object which is not only addressed to a particular node, but also, carries the address of the node sending the message.

- To place content of any data type inside a message and to associate with that content an identifier or name.

   In all five methods were implemented. These were created to enable an instance of the Node class to place content of type Object, int, double, boolean or String in side a message and to associate with that content a name.

```
public void put(String paraName, Object value){}
public void putInt(String paraName, int value){}
public void putDouble(String paraName, double value){}
public void putString(String paraName, String value){}
public void putBoolean(String paraName, boolean value){}
```

Figure 4-7: An outline of the methods provided by the Message class to enable a user to associate with a message object content of a particular data type.

- To retrieve content of any data type from a message.

   Five methods were implemented to enable an instance of the node class to retrieve content of a particular named type from a message.

```
public Object get(String paraName){}
public int getInt(String paraName){}
public double getDouble(String paraName){}
public String putString(String paraName){}
public Boolean putBoolean(String paraName){}
```

Figure 4-8: Methods provided by the Message class to enable an instance of the Node class to retrieve content of type Object, int, double, boolean or String from a message object.

The Variable class (See Figure 4-9) was implemented to replicate the behaviour of a state variable within a distributed system.

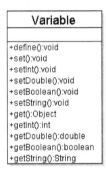

Figure 4-9: Variable Class

It was implemented to provide methods, which an instance of the Node class could invoke:

- To declare a state variable of any data type.

  In total two methods (See Figure 4-10) were implemented. The first method was implemented to enable an instance of the Node class to declare a variable to be of any data type, to associate with that variable a unique identifier and to enable a user to change its value during run time, that is, during the execution of the algorithm's behaviour. The second method was designed to augment the behaviour of the first by enabling one to associate with a variable a default list of values. These are a finite list of values that a variable can store like for example, in response to a question, the values 'yes' or 'no'.

```
public void define(String variable, Object defaultValue,
                   boolean editable){}

public void define(String variable, Object defaultValue,
                   boolean editable, String valueList[]){}
```

Figure 4-10: A description of the two methods provided by the Variable class which an instance of the Node class can invoke to declare a state variable to hold a value of a set data type or to hold a value taken from a predefined range of values of a set data type.

- To change or set the value of a state variable.

  Five methods were implemented in order to enable an instance of the Node class to set the value of a named variable to be of type Object, int, double, boolean or String.

```
public void set(String varName, Object value){}
public void setInt(String varName, int value){}
public void setDouble(String varName, double value){}
public void setString(String varName, String value){}
public void setBoolean(String varName, boolean value){}
```

Figure 4-11: An outline of the methods provided by the Variable class to enable an instance of the Node class to set the value of a variable of a given data type.

- To retrieve the value of a state variable.

  Equally, five methods were implemented to enable an instance of the Node class to retrieve the value of a variable of type Object, int, double, boolean or String.

```
public Object get(String varName, Object value){}
public int getInt(String varName, int value){}
public double getDouble(String varName, double value){}
public String getString(String varName, String value){}
public boolean getBoolean(String varName, boolean value){}
```

Figure 4-12: A depiction of the methods provided by the Variable class to enable an instance of the Node class to retrieve the value of a named variable.

Thus, in order to define the behaviour of an algorithm using the methods provided by the above classes, a user creates a subclass of the Node class and overrides the behaviour of its *run()* method and its *receiveMessage()* method. This is in order to enable a user to customise their behaviours to reflect that of the algorithm that he is implementing. This is achieved through invoking methods of the Message class and the Variable class (See Figure 4-13).

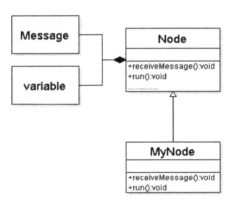

Figure 4-13: A depiction of the classes a user deploys to create his own algorithm implementation in FADA.

79

For example, in order to enable a node to initiate an algorithm's behaviour by sending a 'hello' message to all other nodes within the system, a user invokes the constructor method of the Message class to create the message and then invokes the *sendToAll()* method of the Node class to send that message to each node within the system (See Figure 4-14 for a break down of sample code).

```
public class myNode extends Node
{
     public void receiveMessage(Node sender, Message m){}

     public void run(){
        Message newMsg= new Message("Hello");
        sendToAll(newMsg);
     }

}
```

Figure 4-14: Sample customisation of the MyNode class to enable a node instance to broadcast a message to all nodes with in the system.

4.2.1 Inter-node communication

However, as noted earlier in section 4.2, the manner by which a node can send a message to another node is dictated by the underlying topology of the algorithm's behaviour. In its initial design, the Node class was implemented to replicate the communication behaviour of a bus topology. In order to facilitate the communication behaviour dictated by a star topology or a ring topology, it was necessary to implement methods which when called, would override the communication methods of the Node class. This was achieved by implementing two additional classes, each of which the Node class could inherit. These were the ServerNode class and the GroupNode class. Each was implemented as an interface so as to enable a user when defining the behaviour of an algorithm to create a subclass of the Node class and to inherit the methods of the GroupNode class and the ServerNode class, if need be (See Figure 3-15).

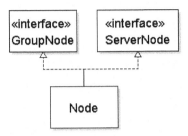

Figure 4-15: Inter-node communication classes

4.2.1.1 ServerNode class

The ServerNode class was implemented to replicate the behaviour of a server node within a star topology. A server node executes a request sent to it by a client node and then, returns a reply to that client or multicasts the reply to all clients. Thus, in order to capture the behaviour of a server node, two new methods were implemented and encapsulated inside the ServerNode class. These were *sendToClient()* method and *sendToAllClients()* method. The former was designed to enable an instance of the ServerNode class to send a message to a specific client node. The latter was designed to enable an instance of the ServerNode class to multicast a message to all clients. However, in order for a server node to be able to send or multicast a message to its clients, it needed to know how many clients it had registered to it at any one time. Thus, a method was implemented to dynamically inform an instance of the ServerNode class each time a new client node registers for its services. This method was called the *registerClient()* method (See Figure 4-16).

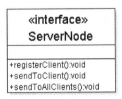

Figure 4-16: ServerNode class

Equally, in order to enable a client node to send a message to a server node, it was necessary to augment the behaviour of the default Node class to allow an instance of that class to send a message to the server. The behaviour of the default Node class was deemed to equate to that of a client node.

4.2.1.2 GroupNode class

The GroupNode class was implemented to replicate the ability of a node within a ring topology to multicast a message, that is, to send a message to all nodes within the topology. However, before the author could implement the latter behaviour, it was necessary to implement methods to define the group node structure. This was in order to allow an instance of the Node class to know when it had joined a group, when another node had decided to leave the group or when a new node instance had decided to join the group. In all three methods were implemented to realise the aforementioned behaviours. These were the *memberAdded()* method, the *memberLeft()* method and *joinGroup()* method. To realise the behaviour of the multicast operation, the *sendToGroup()* method was implemented. To invoke its functionality a user passes to it the reference to the message object that the node instance wishes to send (See Figure 4-17).

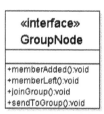

Figure 4-17: GroupNode class

4.2.2 Facilitating fault tolerant behaviour

As defined in section 3.5.2, FADA was designed to enable a node to detect the failure of a node and/or loss of a message through the use of a time out scheme. This can be defined as the length of time a node will wait for in order to receive a reply to its requests. In order to implement the latter functionality, it was necessary to import into the Network module two predefined classes provided by Java's API. These were the Timer class and the TimerTask class. Together these classes provided methods, which an instance of the Node class could deploy to schedule a task for execution in a background thread. The TimerTask class provided a means for a node to define a task for execution when a timer elapses. This is realised in FADA by associating with the myNode class an inner class of the TimerTask class (See Figure 4-18 for an example implementation).

```
import network.*;

public class myNode extends Node
{
    public void receiveMessage(Node sender, Message m){}
    public void run(){}

    public class ExampleTimer extends TimerTask
    {
        public void run(){}
    };

}
```

Figure 4-18: Sample implementation of the manner by which a user associates a timer with a node's behaviour.

Such an implementation gives the node access to the TimerTask's *run()* method. The timer invokes this method when it elapses. Equally, the Timer class provides a node with methods to invoke a timer task to execute once or at repeated intervals. This is achieved by calling one of two different schedule methods and passing to each the TimerTask instance and the time in milliseconds a user wants a node to wait for.

```
public void schedule(TimerTask task, long delay, long period){}
public void schedule(TimerTask task, long delay){}
```

Figure 4-19: A break down of the schedule methods provided by the Timer class which a node instance can invoke to schedule an instance of the TimerTask class for repeated activation at regular intervals or for 'once off' activation.

4.3 GUI Module

As previously stated, classes within the GUI module were implemented to enable a user to automatically execute his algorithm definition code as an interactive visualisation. This was achieved through a process of automated annotation whereby the methods provided by FADA's framework were implemented to make transparent calls to predefined visualisation methods. These visualisation methods were implemented, not only, to visualise the behaviour of the algorithm, but also, to render set components of its behaviour interactive. This was in order to enable the user to be able to manipulate the behaviour of an algorithm as it executes. However, before one could achieve the latter functionality, it was necessary to augment the behaviour of the Node class, the Message class and the Variable class to enable them to create separate depictions on instantiation. Equally, it was necessary to implement additional classes in order to arrange each depiction on screen in a manner which reflects the underlying topology of the algorithm's behaviour. Three separate classes were created to visualise three different topologies. These were the Network class, the GroupNetwork class and the ClientServerNetwork class.

Section 4.3.1 describes the manner by which the implementation of the Node class, the Variable class and the Message class were augmented to provide separate visual depictions for each of their instances. This was in order to enable the author to render them manipulable at run time. Section 4.3.2 describes the implementation of classes to depict the underlying topology of an algorithm's behaviour. Section 4.3.3 describes the manner by which the NetworkCanvas class was implemented, not only, to invoke the drawNetwork() method of each topology class in order to display its graphical representation with in the animation frame, but also, to enable a user to interact with components of the latter representation in real time.

4.3.1 Visualising a node object, a variable object and a messages object

The behaviour of the Node class was augmented to provide a visual representation for each node object created by the user. This was achieved by associating with the Node class a *drawNode()* method. This method is invoked each time the aforementioned class is

84

instantiated. The Node class was also implemented to visualise each state variable that a node creates. This was achieved by associating with the Node class two functions. These were the *showState()* function and *rebuildState()* function. The *showState()* function was implemented to invoke the *display()* function of the Variable class. This function associates with each variable object created a JComponent object, like for example, a text field. This was required in order to enable the user to change the value of a variable at run time. The *rebuildState()* function was created to repaint the panel containing the variables each time a new variable instance is created. The behaviour of the Message class was augmented to graphically depict a message object. This was achieved by associating with the Message class a *draw()* method. This method is invoked each time a user creates a new message object. A message was visualised as consisting of four pieces of information. These were: the name of the message, the unique identifier of the node sending the message, the unique identifier of the node receiving the message and the message contents. Each piece of information was depicted in one of four different boxes stored inside an overall container (See Figure 4-20).

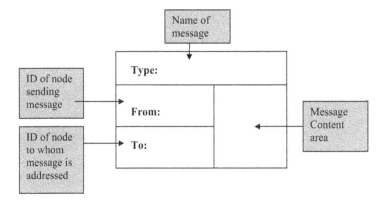

Figure 4-20: A depiction of the information visualised within a message object.

4.3.2. Visualising the underlying topology of an algorithm's behaviour

In total three classes were created. These were the Network class, the GroupNetwork class and the ClientServerNetwork class. These classes were designed to enable a user to visually differentiate between nodes whose communication behaviour is governed by an algorithm informed by a bus topology, a ring topology or a star topology (See Figure 4-21).

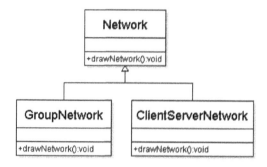

Figure 4-21: Algorithm topology classes.

The Network class was implemented to depict how nodes of the default node type (i.e. the Node class) are interconnected. This was achieved by creating a *drawNetwork()* method which invokes the *drawNode()* method of the Node class. This method was implemented to depict how nodes of the default node type (i.e. Node class) are arranged on screen in a circular fashion around an empty space. The empty space was deployed to give the illusion of autonomous nodes dispersed across a distributed system.

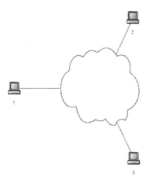

Figure 4-22: Default node topology.

The GroupNetwork class was implemented to inherit the visualisation methods of the Network class and to overwrite them to depict how nodes of the GroupNode type are interconnected. In order to reinforce the group node membership, these nodes were depicted on screen dispersed in a circular fashion around an empty space, which, itself, is enclosed inside a larger circle. The outer circle was deployed to visually reinforce the group node membership.

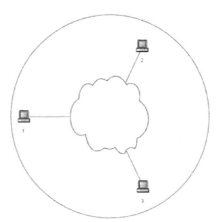

Figure 4-23: Group node topology.

87

In order to depict the behaviour of an algorithm informed by the client server topology, the ClientServerNetwork class was implemented. Again, it was designed to inherit and overwrite the visualisation methods of the Network class. The latter topology was designed to be depicted on screen as an inverted tree structure with the server node residing at the root and the client nodes residing a level below.

Figure 4-24: Client/Server topology.

4.3.3 NetworkCanvas class

The above class was implemented not only to depict the aforementioned topologies within the code frame but also, to detect when the user had interacted with one or more of their components, like for example, a node or a message object. This was in order to enable the NetworkCanvas class to update the behaviour of the algorithm to accord with changes made by the user to its state and behaviour (See Figure 4-25).

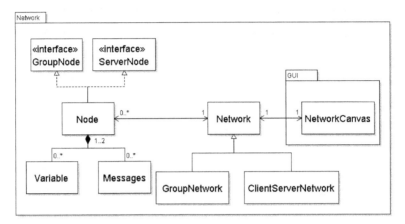

Figure 4-25: Overview of the classes that are invoked in order to enable the NetworkCanvas class to visualise and monitor changes in an algorithm's behaviour at run time.

In order to achieve this, it was necessary, in the first instance, for the NetworkCanvas class to invoke the behaviour of the *drawNetwork()* method of the Network class. This was in order to enable it to display the algorithm topology within the animation frame. At any one time, the animation frame can hold at most one topology. Next, it was necessary to implement the NetworkCanvas class as a mouse listener class so that it could listen for user interactions and in response to those interactions invoke the appropriate mouse event handling method.

In response to a user clicking on a node image, the NetworkCanvas class was implemented to invoke the functionality of two functions provided by the Node class. These were the *click()* function and the *showState()* function. These functions were designed to work in unison such that, if the *click()* function returned true, the NetworkCanvas class would invoke the *showState()* function. This function was implemented to return a panel depicting a list of state variables and their values belonging to that particular node instance. This was outputted to the code frame by the NetworkCanvas in an internal frame. Depending on the data type of the state variable

89

created, a number of different instances of Java's JComponent classes were instantiated to enable the current value of that variable to be displayed and to enable the user to edit its value during run time that is, during the execution of the algorithm's behaviour. For example, if the data type of the variable created was of type Integer, an instance of Java's JTextField class was created to enable a user to enter a new value for the variable. However, the ability to edit the value of a state variable at run time was implemented to be dependent upon the value of a boolean variable called 'editable'. This variable together with the data type of the state variable are defined when the user invokes the *define()* method of the Variable class (See section 4.2 for more details). This method creates a new variable object. If the value of editable is set to true then the JComponent object is rendered active at run time other wise, it is rendered inactive and as a result, does not allow changes to be made to the state of the variable.

The NetworkCanvas class was also implemented to detect when a user had right clicked on a node's image and in response to such an action to display a pop up menu containing a list of predefined behaviours that a user could invoke on that node instance. These were: to start the algorithm's execution, to kill a node, that is, to cause the node to fail to respond to any messages sent to it, to reset the latter behaviour and to delete the node from the underlying node configuration. In order to enable each node instance to have the ability to start the execution of an algorithm's behaviour, it was necessary to amend the Node class such that it inherited Java's Thread class. This was in order to enable each node instance to initiate its own separate thread of execution. This was achieved by the NetworkCanvas class invoking the *startSim()* method. This method was implemented to create a new instance of the Thread class and to pass to it a reference to the node instance. This in turn had the knock on effect of invoking the *run()* method of the Node class. This is the method that a user defines to initiate the algorithm's behaviour (See section 4.2).   The customisation is achieved by invoking the methods of the Message class and the Variable class.

However, in order to enable the NetworkCanvas to animate the sending of a message, it was necessary to modify the behaviour of that class to extend that of a Thread class. This was in order to enable it to animate the sending of a message one at a time. A data structure was implemented to record each message instance as it is created. These instances are then queued and eventually sent in the order in which they were queued. This is depicted on screen using a series of graphical building blocks, each of which is numbered to reflect the order in which each message is to be sent. To kill a message, the NetworkCanvas class was implemented to detect when the user had right clicked on the object. In response to that action, it invoked the *clicked()* function of the Message class. If this returned true, the message instance was set to null. This resulted in the message disappearing from screen.

In order to kill a node, that is, to stop it from responding to any messages sent to it, a boolean variable was created called '*imAlive*'. If this boolean variable was set to false, the node instance would not respond to any messages sent to it. The action of selecting 'kill' from the pop up menu set this value to false. However, the action of selecting 'reset' from the same pop up menu was implemented to reset this value to true. Within the overall *kill()* method invoked by the NetworkCanvas class, there was placed a call to a method which was left undefined. This method was called *die()*. The purpose of this method was to enable the user to override the method to add extra functionality to the kill response. Before animating the transfer of a message, the NetworkCanvas class would check the value of '*imAlive*', if it returned false, then it would not animate or deliver the message object to its destination as it signalled that the node object trying to send the message had failed.

4.4 Split Pane Interface

In order to create FADA as a split pane interface, it was necessary, in the first instance, to create two separate classes to define the structure of the code frame and the animation frame. These were the CodeEditor class and the SimulationWindow class. It was then necessary to create a third class, called MainWindow, to act as a container class, which when invoked, would create instances of the latter two classes and instantiate the split pane with their objects. On instantiation the SimulationWindow class was implemented to invoke an instance of the NetworkCanvas class. This was in order to display the graphical representation of the algorithm's topology within the animation frame. On executing FADA, this frame is initially empty as no node instances exist. These are created when the user compiles and executes his algorithm description.

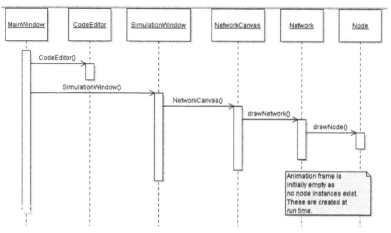

Figure 4-26: A sequence diagram depicting the invocation of calls to set up FADA's split pane interface.

The MainWindow class served two purposes. These were: to create the split pane interface and to provide controls to enable a user to compile his algorithm description code and to execute it as a simulation. It also provided controls to enable the user to control the presentation of content within the animation frame. In order to facilitate the compilation process, it was necessary to import into FADA the interpreter classes of Koala's dynamic Java library. These included its Launcher class and its Interpreter class. Dynamic java is a Java source interpreter which is freely available and whose source files can be downloaded from the following url (http://koala.ilog.fr/djava) These interpreter classes enabled one to convert a user's definition of an algorithm's behaviour into byte code and to return an instance of the Node class. This was achieved by first retrieving the string representation of an algorithm's behaviour from the code editor's text pane and then by passing it as a parameter to the *compile()* method of Koala's Launcher class. This in turn invokes the *interpret()* method of the associated Interpreter class which converts the algorithm description to byte code before creating a new node instance. Any compilation errors detected by koala's interpret() method were implemented to be flagged and outputted as strings to an internal console window.

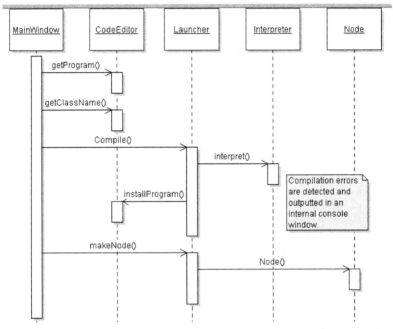

Figure 4-27: A sequence diagram depicting the methods of koala's interpreter classes which are invoked to compile a user's description of an algorithm's behaviour. These methods are invoked by selecting compile from the controls provided by FADA's MainWindow class.

The add button was implemented to visualise a node instance by adding it to the animation frame. Multiple selections of the add button was implemented to visualise and add a corresponding number of node instances to the animation frame. Right clicking on each visualised node instance and selecting '*start*' was implemented to execute the algorithm's behaviour by invoking the run() method of that node instance (See Section 4.2).

4.4.1 CodeEditor class

The above class was implemented to contain a text pane into which a user could load a text file containing a description of an algorithm's behaviour. This was achieved by implementing a method called *loadProgram()* which accepted as a parameter a reference to the file object. This file was then buffered so that its contents could be read and then displayed in the text area of the pane. Before displaying it, the text pane was first cleared of all contents. The text pane was initially implemented to display skeleton code relating to the behaviour of the default node type, that is, a node whose governing algorithm's communication topology mirrors that of a bus topology. This was achieved by implementing a method called *initDocument()* which, when invoked, inserted into the text pane a string definition of that node type's Java class definition. Associated with the contents of the pane was a document listener. This was implemented in order to notify the editor every time a user modified or inserted text with in the text pane. The editor was notified when ever a user inserted a new string, removed a string or changed certain characters within the text pane. This listener was necessary in order to enable the editor to update the contents of the text pane in response to changes made by the user.

Running along the top of the editor was a number of controls. These were implemented to enable a user not only, to load a text file into the text pane as defined earlier but also, to save the contents of the text pane to a file and to cut, copy and paste content to the text pane. All of these controls were implemented as action listeners so as to enable the user to invoke their functionality when ever he so pleased. In order to save the contents of the text pane to a file, a method was created which enabled a user to write the contents to a new file object and to save that file object under a new user defined name to a directory of his own choosing. This was implemented by manipulating and customising the predefined methods of Java's FileWriter class. In order to enable a user to cut, copy and paste text to the editor's text pane, it was necessary to invoke the predefined methods of Java's JTextComponent class of which JTextPane is a child. These methods were *cut()*, *paste()* and *copy()*. The method cut was invoked to enable a user to transfer the currently selected range in the associated text model (i.e. the text pane) to the system clipboard. This action results in the content being removed from the model. Similarly, paste was invoked to

94

enable a user to transfer the contents of the system clipboard into the associated text model. If there is a selection made in the associated view, it replaces the contents of the clipboard. If there is no selection, the clipboard contents are inserted in front of the current insert position in the text pane. If the clipboard is empty, nothing happens.

Also, methods were implemented to enable a user to highlight all content within the text pane or to highlight a segment of content. Both were achieved by invoking the predefined *select()* methods of the JTextComponent class. However, in order to achieve the latter select functionality, it was necessary to decipher the beginning and end of the user's selection. This was in order to enable the editor to highlight only that selection and not the whole content of the text pane. This was achieved by manipulating set methods of Java's inbuilt JTextArea class and JavaCharStream class. The use of these methods enabled the editor to decipher in what line of the text area the selection was made, what the position of the first character selected in that line was and the last character's position. This was achieved, by invoking and passing to the predefined function *getLineStartOffset()* the function *getBeginLine()*. This returned the position of the first character. A similar strategy was deployed to find the end character selected by the user albeit different functions were invoked. Each line of text within the text pane was numbered and highlighted in accordance with the standard format used by current Java development environments.

Associated with the control panel running along the top of the editor was an additional control known as '*New*'. On selecting this control, the code editor was implemented to create a new instance of the NodeBuilder class. This class was implemented to encapsulate the behaviour of the wizard. The wizard as defined in chapter 3 was designed to enable a user to quickly generate skeleton code relating to the underlying topology of an algorithm's behaviour, the messages that a node is to receive and the state variables that a node is to hold. This was implemented by building a class which inherits Java's JDialog class and implements Java's actionListener interface.

The NodeBuilder class was implemented as a JDialog window so as to create a window which was modal, that is, one which prohibits users from activating any other windows while it is active. This was in order to ensure that a user creates or defines completely an algorithm's skeleton functionality prior to compiling it. Such a process was facilitated through the creation of a separate panel for each of the three main parts of an algorithm's definition. These were; the identification of the algorithm's underlying topology, the messages that it permits nodes to receive and the local variables that a node is to store. Each panel was implemented to provide a series of JComponents, like for example text fields, list boxes etc, which a user can customise by inserting data. On completion of the customisation of all panels, a string definition relating to the behaviour of the algorithm is outputted to the code editor's text pane. This was implemented to be written in accordance with the format of a standard Java class definition file (See Figure 4-28 for sample output).

```
1    import network.*;
2
3    public class MyNode extends Node{
4
5      public MyNode(){
6        define("accBalance", new Integer(1000),true);
7      }
8
9      public void receiveMessage(Node sender, Message message){
10       if (message.isType("Transfer")){
11         handleTransfer(sender,message.getInt("amount"));
12       }
13     }
14
15     public void handleTransfer(Node sender,int amount){
16       //Insert code to handle message
17     }
18
19     public void run(){
20       //Insert code here
21     }
22 }
```

Figure 4-28: Sample Java class code generated by the wizard to assist users in defining the manner by which transactions are completed by a distributed banking system.

4.5 Summary

This chapter has delineated the manner by which FADA was implemented as a modular architecture in order to reduce the time and complexity associated with creating an active simulation. First, it outlined the manner by which FADA subdivided the process of creating an active simulation into three separate concerns, two of which it automated. These were:

96

the implementation of an algorithm's behaviour, the creation of its graphical representation and the provision of its real time interactivity. Next, it documented the implementation of a framework to assist users in defining the behaviour of an algorithm. The framework was implemented to provide a set of methods which a user could quickly customise, through the use of parameterisation, to reflect the behaviour of a set algorithm. This chapter also documented the manner by which a graphical representation for an algorithm's behaviour was derived and how components of the latter representation were rendered manipulable in real time. This was in order to enable a user to modify the behaviour of an algorithm while it executes. Furthermore, it delineated the manner by which FADA was implemented to automate the creation of an algorithm's graphical representation upon execution through a process of automated annotation. Lastly, it described the implementation of developer tools to further assist users and to scaffold them in the algorithm implementation process. The next chapter will document the methodology undertaken to investigate the educational effectiveness of FADA.

Chapter 5
Evaluation Methodology

5.1 Introduction

As previously stated FADA differs from other algorithm visualisation (AV) approaches both on a pedagogical level and on an operational level (See Figure 5-1). In terms of pedagogy, FADA, like active simulation systems but unlike algorithm construction systems is informed by theory of constructivism and as such, provides real time interaction with an algorithm's behaviour, that is, it enables a user to change the behaviour of an algorithm's components while it executes. To date, algorithm construction systems provide off line interactions, that is, they require a user to specify prior to the execution of an algorithm's behaviour, which property of its behaviour that they would like to modify and observe. Thus, they enable users to only interact with the behaviour of an algorithm visualisation in real time by changing the speed of its presentation or its view. However, FADA, like algorithm construction systems, enables a user to build his own conceptual understanding of an algorithm's behaviour but, unlike them, enables user to interact with their representations in real time in order to ascertain their correctness. Thus, FADA can be said to be equally informed by the theory of constructionism. Furthermore, FADA, unlike active simulation systems and passive animation systems provides dual representations of an algorithm's behaviour that is, it provides both a visual representation of an algorithm's behaviour and a textual representation of its implementation. Thus, FADA, unlike passive animation systems and active simulation systems, enables users to map the graphical representation of an algorithm's behaviour to that of its underlying implementation.

FADA's Pedagogical and Operational Approach	
Pedagogy	Constructivism, Constructionism, Dual Coding
Operation	Framework, Visualisation API

Table 5-1: FADA's pedagogical and operational characteristics.

In terms of operation, FADA, unlike passive animation systems and active simulation systems, enables users to create their own algorithm implementations. This is achieved through the provision of a framework for common message passing distributed algorithms. This framework is written in a conventional programming language, namely Java and, as such, reflects the manner by which distributed algorithms are implemented in the real world. Unlike algorithm construction systems, FADA facilitates the easy construction of an algorithm visualisation through the provision of a built in visualisation API. This API not only defines the manner by which components of an algorithm's behaviour are rendered, but also, the manner by which a user can interact with them. Through a process of automated annotation, FADA automatically annotates a user's algorithm implementation code with calls to functions of the aforementioned API. Such an action enables users to concentrate solely on the implementation of an algorithm's behaviour and not on that of its visualisation or level of interactivity.

Thus, in order to assess the pedagogical and operational effectiveness of FADA, a number of research questions were posed. With respect to pedagogy, these were:

- To what extent does the algorithm visualisation approach adopted in this thesis enhance the teaching and learning of distributed algorithms?

Concomitant with this question were a number of sub questions.

- To what extent does it facilitate learners to engage in higher order thinking when learning about an algorithm's behaviour?
- To what extent does the software tool under examination facilitate higher order dialogues about an algorithm's behaviour between learners and between learners and instructors?
- To what extent does the embodiment of the dual coding theory within the user interface design of the software tool under examination aid in the algorithmic problem solving process?
- To what extent does the software tool under examination engage learners in an iterative cycle of learning?

With respect to operational effectiveness the following research questions were posed:

- To what extent is FADA easy to use?

99

Associated with this question were a number of sub questions.

- To what extent is FADA easy to learn how to use?
- To what extent is it effective in enabling learners to complete their problem solving tasks?
- To what extent is it both effective and efficient in enabling instructors to create active simulations for use in their own teachings?
- To what extent are both learners and instructors satisfied with the functions and features provided by FADA?

In order to answer such questions, it was necessary to adopt a multi-method approach. This was in order to garner as much data as possible from a variety of view points which could then be analysed and in which one could be more confident compared to using a single method approach. By triangulating the data collected from each of the different methods and user groups deployed, one helps to eliminate the biases that might result from relying exclusively on any one data collection method or source. The following user groups and methods were deployed to assess FADA's effectiveness both on a pedagogical level and on an operational level.

User Groups	Background	Modes of use	Instruments/Methods	Number of participants
Group 1	Undergraduate students with a background knowledge in concurrency, operating systems and networks but not in distributed systems	Interactive presentation and algorithm modification task	Video capture, Direct observation, Questionnaires.	16
Group 2	Postgraduate students with a background	Interactive presentation and algorithm	Video capture, Direct observation, Discussion, Questionnaire.	4

	knowledge in concurrency, operating systems and networks but not in distributed systems	modification task		
Group 3	Postgraduate students in distributed systems	Interactive presentation and algorithm modification task	Video capture, Direct observation, Discussion, Questionnaire.	12
Group 4	Instructors in distributed systems	Algorithm construction task and presentation delivery in class.	Interview, Questionnaire	3

Table 5-2: Breakdown of participant groups within current study and mechanisms deployed to assess FADA's pedagogical and operational effectiveness from each of their perspectives.

It should be noted that prior to the commencement of this study, FADA underwent a number of pilot tests. Each pilot study was designed to replicate the use of FADA within a learning setting. In each study, the author, acting as the instructor, either presented to a sample test audience an algorithm for exploration and discussion or an algorithm for them to modify in some way. The pilot studies were designed to inform and refine the design of the artefact, to gauge initial reaction and feedback and to test and improve the design of questionnaires. All questionnaires were reviewed by a senior lecturer in education for accuracy and appropriateness.

Section 5.2 outlines the manner by which FADA's pedagogical effectiveness was investigated from the perspective of each of four different user groups. First, it outlines the overall methodological approach adopted. Next, it delineates for each user group, the participants' demographics and the manner by which the data was garnered from each group.

101

Section 5.3 describes the manner by which FADA's operational effectiveness was assessed both from the perspective of the learner and the instructor. It also outlines the methodological approach undertaken in each instance, the participants' demographics and the way in which the data was collected.
Section 5.4 concludes with an overview of the chapter.

5.2 Methodological approaches adopted to investigate the pedagogical effectiveness of FADA.

One way of assessing the pedagogical effectiveness of the approach adopted by FADA is to determine to what extent learning has increased as a result of its use. Such an experimental approach operationalises pedagogical effectiveness in terms of the acquisition of target knowledge structures which learners are assumed to glean from learning sessions in which they are exposed to both FADA and alternative media such as text books. In such designs, individual performances on a written post test are taken as evidence for the successful transfer of knowledge structures, which are often classified as either conceptual (what the program does) or procedural (how the algorithm works) [1]. However, the use of such experimental designs begs the question as to what extent the results can be said to internally and externally valid.

Internal validity is concerned with the question, "do the experimental treatments, in fact, make a difference in the specific experiment under scrutiny?". In other words, are the changes observed in the dependent variable (level of target knowledge) due to the effect of the independent variable (the algorithm visualisation system) and not due to some other unintended variable such as history, which are events that happen during the course of the study [107]. Internal validity can be threatened by a number of variables in addition to history. These are maturation, which is biological or psychological changes in the participants during the course of the study, testing, which is the ability for participants to become 'test-wise' due to exposure to a pre-test that is similar to the post test, instrumentation, which refers to changes observed on the dependent variable that are due to the nature of the instrument and not the independent variable (e.g. post-test was easier than the pre-test), and, lastly, experimental mortality, which relates to participants who drop out during the course of the study. (This becomes a threat to internal validity if participants differentially drop out of the experimental and control groups) [107]. External validity concerns itself with the question as to what extent findings in one study be applied to another. If findings in one study are observed in another situation then the results are said to be generalisable or externally valid [107]. In order to achieve 'perfect' internal validity, it necessitates use of an artificial setting, an environment in which no variables operate except those that the researcher introduces. This necessity to create artificial settings in order to explore single variable effects may yield results that have only meaning within that particular setting. 'Humans react to artificially restricted manipulated conditions differently from the way they react to naturally occurring conditions, and if the research is conducted under artificial conditions, then the generalisability of the results (external validity) is severely limited '[108] (p. 361).

Thus, in terms of establishing the true potential pedagogical effectiveness of FADA, there is need to observe its effects in a real world context like, for example, a lecture setting. Hence, there is need of an ethnographic approach. Such an approach assumes that behaviour and, thereby, data are socially situated, context-related, context-dependent and context-rich. To understand a situation, a researcher needs to understand the context in which that behaviour took place because situations affect behaviour and perspectives and vice versa. Ethnographic research is a process of involving methods of inquiry such as interviews, journal notes, participant observation, artefacts, video recordings and so on. The intention of the research is to create as vivid a reconstruction as possible of the group or individual being studied. Such an approach 'is concerned more with description rather than prediction, induction rather than deduction, generation rather than verification of theory, construction rather than enumeration, and subjectivities rather than objective knowledge' [109] (p.39 – 44).

The approach starts with the researcher taking a wide angle lens to gather data, and then, by sifting, sorting, reviewing and reflecting on them, the salient features of the situation emerge. These are then used as the agenda for subsequent focusing [110]. This is achieved by comparing different groups simultaneously and over time, matching the responses given in interviews to observed behaviour, an analysis of deviant and negative cases, calculating frequencies of occurrences and responses, assembling and providing sufficient data that keeps separate raw data from analysis. The validity of the data collected is maintained through the use of multiple devices for recording, using a flexible observation schedule in order to minimise biases, remaining in the situation for a long time in order to over come the Hawthorne effect and using respondent validation and descriptions.

Thus, by definition in order to get an externally valid picture of how the use of FADA within a lecture setting and/or laboratory setting motivates learners, engages their higher order thinking skills, assists instructors, there is need to observe its use by a number of different instructors in a number of different lecture settings over an extended period of time. However, given the nature of the subject domain, the manner by which it is widely taught and the time frame in which this research was to be completed, such an analysis was not possible. Distributed algorithms is not a subject taught in and of itself, but represents a part component of an overall topic known as distributed systems. Across many computer science departments, it is reserved as a module for advanced computer science students and even at that, it is normally only offered to students as a speciality that is, an optional topic and not as a core requirement. Thus, it is not unusual to find one distributed system class per department due to small student numbers. Moreover, many instructors in their teachings prefer not to delve deeply into the topic, preferring instead to concentrate on the development of learners' low level implementation skills, like for example, CORBA and RMI. Others prefer to elucidate students to the presence and behaviour of different distributed algorithms as the need arises during their teachings, making it difficult to pinpoint an exact time for FADA's intervention.

Given this backdrop, it was necessary to rethink the manner by which one proposed to investigate FADA's pedagogical effectiveness. It was decided that such a task would be best served through the use of a case study approach. A case study can be thought of as one type of ethnographic (interpretive) research that involves intensive and detailed study of one individual or of a group as an entity through observation, self reports and other means [111]. It is the study of a 'bounded system' with the focus being either the case or an issue that is illustrated by that case (or cases). 'One of the powerful strengths of a case study is that it can establish cause and effect situated in a real context' [112] (p. 220). 'It provides a unique example of real people in real situations, enabling readers to understand ideas more clearly than simply presenting them with abstract ideas or principle. Case studies can penetrate situations in ways that are not always susceptible to numerical analysis' [110] (p. 200).

'A case study is most valuable when the researcher has little control over events. Associated with a case study are a number of attributes. It is concerned with a rich, vivid description of relevant events and provides a chronological narrative of these events. The study blends a description of these events with analysis thereof focusing on individual actors or groups and seeks to understand their perceptions of events. Analysis of the case seeks to highlight events of specific relevance. The researcher may be integrally involved in the case' [112] (p. 77).

Case study designs may be single case or multiple case designs. 'A single case study is analogous to a single experiment and many of the conditions that justify a single experiment also justify a single case study' [113] (p. 39).

'A single case study design is eminently justifiable under certain conditions, – when the case represents (a) a critical test of an existing theory that is, a case which meets all criteria or conditions for testing a specific theory, (b) a rare or unique circumstance that is, a case that is so rare that warrants further investigation, or (c) representative or typical case that is, a case whose object of study is assumed to behave in ways typical of a class or group, or when the case serves (d) relevatory or (e) longitudinal purposes' [113] (p. 45).

A relevatory case can be defined as a case that represents an opportunity to observe, analyse a phenomenon previously inaccessible to scientific study. A longitudinal case can be defined as a case whose object of study is observed at multiple points in time over an extended period. The theory of interest being how certain conditions change over time and the selected time intervals reflect the stages at which those changes should reveal themselves [113]. However, in choosing a single case study design, caution must be exercised to ensure that the unit of analysis or the case itself is in fact relevant to the issues and questions of interest. In this current study, participants come from broadly similar computer science backgrounds but no one participant could be deemed typical or representative of a group as to entirely represent it. Moreover, the remit of this study was to analyse the pedagogical effectiveness of FADA from both the perspective of the instructor and the learner. Thus, its aim was to analyse the ways in which both parties engage with the software to either assist or grow to a deeper understanding of an algorithm's behaviour. As a consequence of the latter, no one participant could be assumed to be representative of the entire range of interactions possible. Thus, there was need of a multiple case study approach, one which enables the detection of patterns of behaviour which are common to all cases (literal replication) and which are mediated by the software as well as enabling the detection of behaviours which deviate from the common (theoretical replication).

> The need for 'replication is analogous to that used in multiple experiments. Upon uncovering a significant finding from a single experiment, the immediate research goal would be to replicate this finding by conducting a second, third and even fourth experiment. Some of the experiments might attempt to duplicate the exact conditions of the original experiment. Other replications might alter one or two conditions, to see whether the finding would still be duplicated. Only with such replications would the original finding be considered robust and worthy of continued investigation or interest. The logic underlying the use of multiple case studies is the same. Each case must be carefully selected so that it either (a) predicts similar results (literal replication) or (b) predicts contrasting results but for predictable reasons (theoretical replication)' [113] (p. 47).

If such replications are indeed found for several cases, one can have more confidence in the overall result. The development of consistent findings, over multiple cases and even multiple studies can then be considered a very robust finding [113].

In this study a number of cases were selected for analysis and examination on the basis, in the main, of literal rather than theoretical replication. This was with a view to generating a theoretical position with regard to both learner and instructor behaviours. The unit of analysis in each case was holistic and sought to analyse the relationship between the instructor, learner and software and how that relationship impinged upon a learner's understanding of the algorithm's behaviour. To this end, the following cases were included. These were the detailed analysis of FADA's use in a single authentic lecture setting coupled with its use in simulated lecture settings. Moreover, in order to ascertain to what extent learners had acquired an understanding for the concepts presented in each lecture setting, it was necessary to have them complete a task which required them to make explicit that understanding. Such tasks were designed to equate to that given by instructors for learners to complete in laboratory settings. These settings were also included as cases. All selected cases enabled one to focus on FADA's immediate impact on individual learners and to determine to what extent the ability to (1) view an algorithm's behaviour, (2) engage with an algorithm's behaviour in real time, (3) modify or customise an algorithm's implementation assist learners in acquiring an understanding of that algorithm's behaviour.

In all, four participant groups were observed in their interactions with FADA. These consisted of three groups of learners and one group of instructors. The learner groups were designed to differ in terms of their prior knowledge of distributed systems. This was in order to assess to what extent FADA can accommodate and challenge learners of different knowledge levels and experience and also, to give insight into the different ways that each engage with the software to obtain an understanding of an algorithm's behaviour. Each learner group was exposed to FADA in one of two different ways. These were: as an interactive presentation tool within a lecture setting and as a modification tool within a laboratory setting. Both were chosen to shed light on the effect, if any that, viewing an algorithm's behaviour, interacting with it in real time and modifying its implementation has on the learner's understanding of it. The instructor group was chosen to investigate to what extent FADA assisted them in conveying the dynamic and concurrent behaviour of a distributed algorithm.

With respect to issues of reliability and validity of the case study approach, internal validity was maintained through the adoption of 'the analytic tactic of pattern matching' [113] (p. 36) and explanation building. 'Pattern matching can be defined as the making of predictions about the behavioural patterns and comparing these to empirically observed results' [112] (p.81). If the patterns coincide the results can help a case study to strengthen its internal validity [113]. However, in determining the 'closeness of fit' of the data to the predicted pattern the onus is on the researcher to make the value judgement.

'Explanation building goes beyond pattern matching by specifying the causal nature of the links that make up the pattern and then by testing the evidence for those links. 'Explanation building is an iterative process involving first making a theoretical statement and comparing the findings of an initial case study against this statement. This statement may then be revised and compared either to other details of the same case or to facts of a second or subsequent case. In this way, the theoretical position may be refined so as to explain the range of cases. This approach lends itself to multiple case studies and serves to strengthen any conclusions drawn' [113] (p. 120).

External validity was maintained by generalising the findings of one case study to subsequent cases through a process of literal replication. Reliability was preserved through the use of a case study protocol that is, where all procedures within a case were documented so as to facilitate replication and through the maintenance of an archive of the raw data. 'The general way of approaching the reliability problem is to make as many steps as operational as possible and to conduct the research as if someone was always looking over your shoulder' [113] (p.38). Construct validity was addressed through the use of multiple sources of evidence which were deployed 'in a manner encouraging convergent lines of inquiry' [113] (p. 36).

Section 5.2.1 to section 5.2.3 delineates the demographics of participants in each of the three learner groups together with the manner by which each group was exposed to FADA both as an interactive presentation tool and as a modification tool. Equally, it outlines the manner by which data was collected from each group in each of the aforementioned exposure instances. Section 5.2.4 documents the design of questionnaires administered to glean further insight into learners' reactions to and their perceived pedagogical effectiveness of FADA when used as an interactive presentation tool and as a modification tool. Section 5.2.5 delineates the demographics of participants within the instructor group and the manner by which they deployed FADA to assist them in conveying to learners the dynamic behaviour of a distributed algorithm. Lastly, it documents the design of questionnaires administered to garner insight into instructors' perceived pedagogical effectiveness of FADA when used as a tool to assist them in the teaching of distributed algorithms.

5.2.1 Group 1: Learner Demographics

Participants were fourth year computer science undergraduate students taking distributed systems as a specialisation and not as a core requirement. Each participant had a strong background in object oriented programming, as each had been introduced to and used a variety of programming languages from the latter paradigm throughout his four years in university. The class consisted of sixteen students. This class was considered an ideal platform for FADA's deployment as an interactive presentation tool due to the nature of the course material and the teaching style deployed. In this course, students get a firm grounding in, not only, the low level implementation skills required for implementing distributed systems, but also, in the complexities associated with distributed algorithms and their application. Moreover, an interactive teaching style is adopted whereby students are actively encouraged to discover the fundamental principles relating to distributed computing through the consideration of challenging problems which, are posed collectively or in small groups, prior to the presentation of relevant course material. Furthermore, this course introduces students to distributed algorithms over a block period of time and not sporadically. Thus, this enabled the author to assess the potential educational effectiveness of FADA on two fronts. These were: as an interactive presentation tool and as a tool to impart ownership over learning, by enabling learners to customise or modify the behaviour of an algorithm.

5.2.1.1 Group 1: Interactive presentation methodology

The following methodology was followed to determine the pedagogical effectiveness of FADA when used as an interactive presentation tool. The instructor deployed FADA to implement the behaviour of the dining philosophers' algorithm. This is an algorithm which illustrates the problems that occur when many threads of control are competing for limited resources in a distributed system. In order to ensure that each thread gets enough access to limited resources in order to make reasonable progress, it is necessary to ensure fairness. A system is fair if it prevents starvation and deadlock. The analogy of four or more philosophers sitting at a round table in front of a bowl of spaghetti is often used to illustrate the problem. In order to eat, a philosopher must acquire the fork to his immediate right and to his immediate left. The goal of the algorithm is to find a way for the philosophers to share the forks so that they can all eat.

The instructor implemented this algorithm using FADA in a series of five stages. Each stage was designed to introduce participants to a particular concept and to the problem or problems associated with that concept, like for example, the question of how a node should respond to a message which says 'fork taken'. The first three stages were designed to introduce participants to the manner in which communication evolves across all distributed systems through the sending and receiving of messages. The last two stages were designed to introduce participants to the logic of the dining philosophers' algorithm and to problems inherent in its implementation like for example, the problems that occur when two adjacent nodes try to eat at the same time (See figure 5-1) or when all nodes try to eat concurrently.

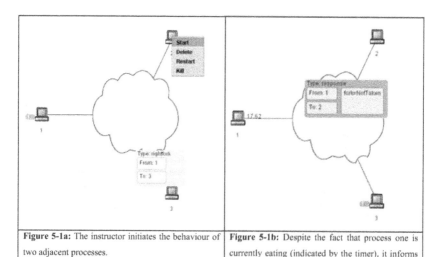

Figure 5-1a: The instructor initiates the behaviour of two adjacent processes.	**Figure 5-1b:** Despite the fact that process one is currently eating (indicated by the timer), it informs process two that it can avail of use of its left fork.

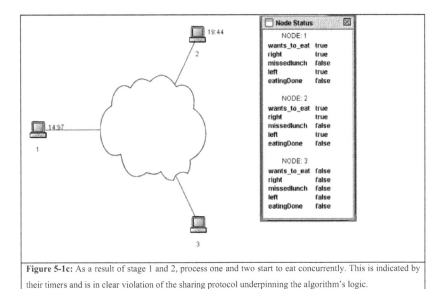

Figure 5-1c: As a result of stage 1 and 2, process one and two start to eat concurrently. This is indicated by their timers and is in clear violation of the sharing protocol underpinning the algorithm's logic.

Figure 5-1: A depiction of the manner by which the instructor deployed FADA to allude learners to the algorithm's failure to account for whether a fork was being used or not that is, its failure to account for atomic operations.

FADA was deployed to actively reinforce each concept and to re-enact the problems inherent with each. This was achieved by the instructor actively switching between the code frame and the simulation frame to visually and interactively illustrate not only, the functionality of the algorithm when simulated but also, the manner by which it was implemented. Through a process of active exploration, participants were encouraged to voice and define solutions to overcome each problem encountered. All lecture proceedings were directly observed by the author and captured on video. This was necessary in order to allow the author to analyse the degree to which the use of FADA and the simulations derived from its use motivated participants' interests, mediated participant-instructor interactions, and prompted participants' higher order thinking. This information was extrapolated not only through the analysis of questions posed by participants during the presentation but also through the analysis of their voiced solutions.

5.2.1.2 Group 1: Modification methodology

In order to assess to what extent participants had acquired an understanding for the concepts presented within the above lecture setting and to assess the pedagogical effectiveness of FADA when used as a modification tool, participants were asked to modify the behaviour of the dining philosophers' algorithm in a laboratory setting to overcome issues of deadlock and starvation (See figure 5-2). These were issues encountered in stage five of the above interactive presentation and for which, solutions were suggested but not implemented.

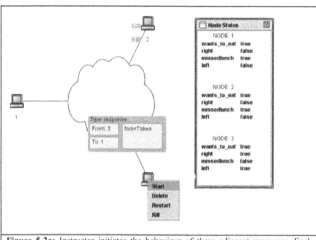

Figure 5-2a: Instructor initiates the behaviour of three adjacent processes. Each sends out a request for the fork to its immediate right and left.

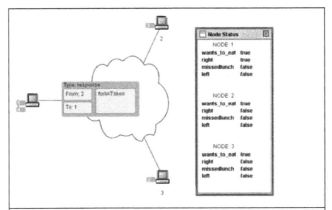

Figure 5-2b: Process two refuses process one's request for use of its left fork as its id is higher than that of process one.

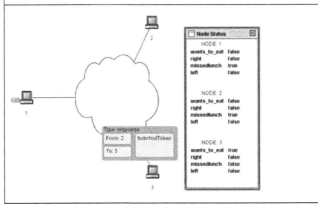

Figure 5-2c: Process two relinquishes possession of its right fork to process three as process three's id is higher than that of process two's.

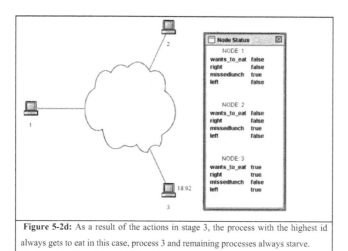

Figure 5-2d: As a result of the actions in stage 3, the process with the highest id always gets to eat in this case, process 3 and remaining processes always starve.

Figure 5-2: A depiction of the manner by which the instructor deployed FADA to allude learners to the issue of starvation associated with the algorithm's process.

Through the analysis of the solutions returned together with data eluded from the video capture, direct observation of the participants by the author and the use of questionnaires, the author was able to decipher the level of participants' understanding, the extent to which FADA had facilitated them in acquiring that understanding either through viewing the algorithm's behaviour, through interacting with it in real time or through modifying its behaviour.

5.2.2 Group 2: Learner Demographics

These were postgraduate students who possessed either an undergraduate qualification or a postgraduate qualification in computer science but, who had no formal knowledge of distributed systems. Each had a strong working knowledge of Java as each had studied it for one or more years prior to their current studies. The group consisted of four participants. This group was considered ideal for FADA's intervention, both as an interactive presentation tool and as a construction tool, due to its size. It was thought that given its size, that one would glean greater insight into the manner by which participants interact with such technology, how it enables them to engage with the subject content, and with their instructor and fellow peers.

5.2.2.1 Group 2: Interactive Presentation Methodology

In order to assess the pedagogical effectiveness of FADA as an interactive presentation tool, the following methodology was deployed. It was designed to mirror closely that deployed by the instructor in group 1. A simulated lecture setting was set up where by the author through collaboration with the participants constructed an active simulation of a distributed banking application. The aim of the latter was to give a real world context to the manner by which transactions are carried out in a distributed system and to introduce participants to the concepts of the lack of global knowledge and partial failure. The application was designed to simulate the transfer of funds between two bank servers within one banking system. As in the methodology deployed with group 1, the application was built in a series of stages. Each stage was implemented to illustrate problems of increasing complexity which can affect the behaviour of the application, like for example, the failure of a transaction (See figure 5-3), the lack of a consistent state and so on. Through a process of active exploration and feedback from participants, the underlying logic of the algorithm was amended to put interventions in place to enable the algorithm to continue functioning despite the presence of one or more failed components. This enabled the author to make explicit participants' understandings of the algorithm's behaviour and enabled her to experiment with the representation in real time to decipher to what degree it was consistent or fault tolerant.

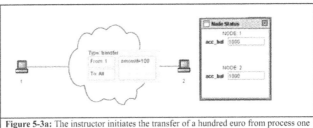

Figure 5-3a: The instructor initiates the transfer of a hundred euro from process one to process two.

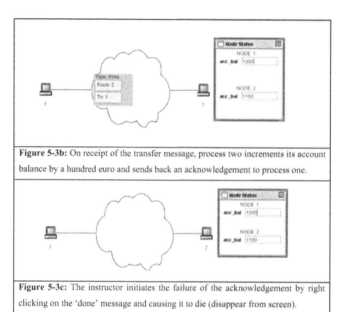

Figure 5-3b: On receipt of the transfer message, process two increments its account balance by a hundred euro and sends back an acknowledgement to process one.

Figure 5-3c: The instructor initiates the failure of the acknowledgement by right clicking on the 'done' message and causing it to die (disappear from screen).

Figure 5-3: A depiction of the manner by which the instructor deployed FADA to investigate whether students would be able to recognise the state inconsistency caused by the loss of the acknowledgement message from process two to process one.

In so doing, it provided the author with the opportunity to highlight the inadequacies in proposed solutions and offered the chance for participants to amend their solutions in light of observed failings. Such interactions served two further purposes to foster active participation by participants and to introduce them to FADA and its framework methods. Through the analysis of video capture, answers derived from appropriate questionnaires, solutions verbalised by participants, the author was again able to analyse to what extent FADA motivated participants, mediated meaningful conversations about the algorithm's behaviour between participants and between participants and instructor and prompted participants' higher order thinking. The latter was extrapolated through the questions posed by participants and through solutions offered by them.

5.2.2.2 Group 2: Modification Methodology

Again, in order to ascertain to what extent participants had acquired an understanding for the concepts presented within the lecture and to assess the pedagogical effectiveness of FADA when used as a modification tool, participants were presented with an active simulation of a distributed address book application. Such an application was initially presented to participants devoid of fault tolerant behaviours. The aim of the exercise was to ascertain the extent of participants' understanding of partial failure, a concept presented to them in the aforementioned lecture setting. The application was based on a client/server topology. The client was implemented to determine whether the server was alive prior to attempting to store or retrieve someone's name and telephone number. Participants were first asked to actively explore the behaviour of the application in real time to decipher what failure scenarios could occur (See Figure 5-4).

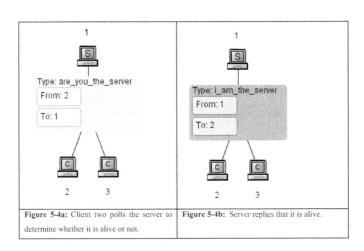

Figure 5-4a: Client two polls the server to determine whether it is alive or not.

Figure 5-4b: Server replies that it is alive.

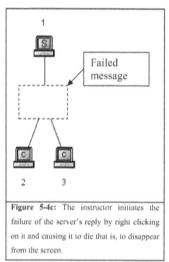

Figure 5-4c: The instructor initiates the failure of the server's reply by right clicking on it and causing it to die that is, to disappear from the screen.

Figure 5-4: A depiction of the manner by which FADA enables learners to investigate issues of partial failure by enabling them to select individual components of the application's process in real time, like for example in the above representation, the server's rely to the client's request, and cause them to fail.

On successful identification of these scenarios, each participant was asked to modify the underlying implementation logic of the application to enable it to handle the loss or failure of one or more of its components. Participants were given freedom to voice questions and to direct the questions to the instructor or to fellow peers. Through the analysis of the video capture and direct observations garnered, the author was able to investigate to what the extent the ability to view and interact with an algorithm's behaviour in real time enables a participant to develop a deep understanding for the failure scenarios that can affect its behaviour. Moreover, it enabled the author to investigate to what extent the ability to modify an algorithm's behaviour together with the ability to interact with those modifications in real time assisted the participant in better understanding the algorithm's process. Equally, it enabled the author to ascertain to what extent FADA, when used as a modification tool, fosters meaningful interactions between participants in order to enable them to arrive at a mutual understanding of the problem at hand.

5.2.3 Group 3: Learner Demographics

In order to assess the pedagogical effectiveness of FADA to accommodate participants of different skill and knowledge levels, it was necessary to locate participants who, not only, had a working knowledge of Java but, who also, had a broad knowledge of distributed systems. Familiarity with the subject domain was required in order to ascertain to what extent FADA enables participants to test or challenge their conceptual understanding of an algorithm's behaviour, whether it leads to changes in their understanding or reinforcement. Equally, familiarity was required to enable participants to act as experts to assess to what extent they believe FADA to be pedagogically effective. To this end, the sample population was taken from a cohort of postgraduate students belonging to a research group specialising in distributed systems. Of this population, twelve students volunteered. Each student had prior knowledge of distributed algorithms as each had either successfully completed an undergraduate module in distributed systems or a post graduate module. Each had between two and four years of experience in distributed systems. All had a working knowledge of Java.

5.2.3.1 Group 3: Interactive Presentation Methodology

As with group 2, participants were subdivided into groups of four. This was done to convenience the participants and to foster settings which enabled one to examine closely the manner by which such individuals engage with FADA. The aim was to determine to what extent FADA mediates their interactions with and conversations about an algorithm's behaviour. Again, each group collaborated with the instructor to build an active simulation of the distributed banking application. The aim of which was manifold; to challenge participants' conceptual understanding of partial failure within the sample system, to mediate meaningful conversation about the algorithm's behaviour between participants and between participants and instructor, to probe their higher order thinking skills in order to enable them to generate and voice solutions to overcome each failure scenario encountered and to introduce them to FADA, its use and framework methods. All interactions were video taped. Questionnaires were administered to glean further insight into participants' reactions to FADA and to what extent they viewed it as pedagogically effective.

5.2.3.2 Group 3: Modification Methodology

Group 3 was presented with the same modification task as group 2. The aim of which was to ascertain, in the first instance, the extent to which the ability to view and engage with an algorithm's behaviour in real time enables a participant to develop a deep conceptual understanding of its behaviour and enables him to identify possible failure scenarios. The task was also designed to enable a participant to modify the algorithm's behaviour to overcome the failure scenarios and to enable him to ascertain through viewing and real time interactivity the degree to which such modifications had achieved their purpose. More over, the task was also designed to ascertain to what extent FADA initiates and mediates meaningful conversations about an algorithm's behaviour between participants.

5.2.4 Questionnaires

In addition to the exploratory case studies, a number of questionnaires were designed to gather data about the participants' perceptions of the pedagogical value of FADA when used as an interactive presentation tool in class and their perceptions of its pedagogical and operational effectiveness when used as a tool to enable them to modify the behaviour of an algorithm. The interactive presentation questionnaire (See Appendix A) was completed at the end of each lecture sitting and the modification questionnaire (See Appendix B) was filled out upon completion of the assigned amendment task. The aim of the interactive presentation questionnaire was to ascertain to what extent participants' believed their understanding of the concepts presented in class had been aided by the use of FADA. It was also designed to ascertain to what extent participants had believed that FADA had motivated them to participate more in class and whether they preferred the teaching approach adopted with FADA to other traditional approaches such as chalk and talk. The modification questionnaire was designed to determine to what extent participants found FADA as an overall application easy to use and to what extent they found its framework easy to use. It also was designed to ascertain from a pedagogical stance whether participants perceived the task of modifying an algorithm's behaviour as assisting them in better understanding its behaviour and whether they perceived the ability to play with, experiment with, the components of an algorithm's behaviour in real time as lending to their understanding of it. All questionnaires were piloted and feedback gained from each pilot used to amend them. In addition to the questionnaires, open-ended discussions were conducted with participants at the end of both the lecture sittings and the task modification sittings. This was in order to garner further and deeper insight into participants' perceptions of FADA's pedagogical and operational effectiveness. In conducting the group discussions, the author's guidance was kept to a minimum to maintain the criterion of non-direction. The respondent's description of the experience/situation was allowed full expression, and the range of responses from participants was maximised. The nature of the group discussions facilitated a wide range of responses with participants being able to challenge and extend each other's ideas [114].

5.2.5 Group 4: Instructor Demographics
In order to ascertain the pedagogical effectiveness of FADA as a tool to assist instructors in conveying the dynamic behaviour of an algorithm or in enabling them to set exercises for their students to complete, it was necessary to locate instructors who would be willing to use FADA in either or both contexts. In all, three instructors were located. All were active computer science lecturers, two of which are currently teaching distributed systems at both undergraduate and postgraduate level and one of which has a background in distributed systems teaching but is not currently teaching the topic. Each hails from one of the following third level institutes. These are Trinity College Dublin, University of Edinburgh and Dublin Institute of Technology. As defined in section 5.2.1.1 and section 5.2.1.2, the instructor (L1) from Trinity College Dublin, used FADA, not only, to build but also to present to students the behaviour of the dining philosophers' algorithm. Equally he used it to set students a task to modify the behaviour of the aforementioned algorithm to overcome problems of deadlock and starvation associated with it. The instructor (L2) from the University of Edinburgh used FADA to set students a task which required them to simulate

the behaviour of one of two algorithms. These were the ring based election algorithm and the bully election algorithm. FADA was deployed with one of two students groups. These were a fourth year computer science undergraduate class and a postgraduate computer science class. The undergraduate class consisted of fifty students and the postgraduate class consisted of thirty five students. The undergraduate class were asked to implement the behaviour of the ring based election algorithm whilst the postgraduate class were asked to implement the behaviours of both the ring based election and the bully algorithm. In each case the instructor had to build using FADA a completed version of each algorithm to act as a template upon correction of students' admissions. The instructor (L3) from the Dublin Institute of Technology used FADA in one of two ways. He used it to build sample simulations for his own use and to enable his research student to build his own representation of the Byzantine's generals' algorithm. In order to investigate to what extent each instructor perceived FADA to be a pedagogically effective tool in assisting him in either conveying to learners the dynamic and concurrent behaviour of a distributed algorithm or in enabling learners to make explicit their own conceptual understanding of an algorithm's process, each was administered a dedicated questionnaire. This was followed up by interviews which were in the case of the instructors from the University of Edinburgh and Dublin Institute of Technology conducted over the telephone. This was simply due to location.

5.3 Operational Effectiveness

This section delineates the methodological approaches adopted to assess the operational effectiveness of FADA from both the perspective of the learner and the instructor. Section 5.3.1 documents the approach adopted to assess operational effectiveness from the viewpoint of the learner. Section 5.3.2 documents the approach adopted to assess operational effectiveness from the perspective of the instructor.

5.3.1 Learner Methodology

FADA's operational effectiveness was assessed using the same three learner groups identified in section 5.2 (See table 5-2). A standard usability metric [115] was deployed to assess FADA's operational effectiveness. This metric entailed assessing FADA's performance with respect to each of the following criteria. These were:

- Learnability, the speed by which novice users can learn to use the system. (Novice users can be defined as individuals who know the task but have little or no knowledge of the system).

- Effectiveness, the percentage of tasks completed, the ratio of successes to failures.

- Efficiency, time to complete task, time to learn, time spent on errors, frequency of use of help documentation.

- User satisfaction, rating scale for usefulness of system, rating scale for satisfaction with functions and features, perception that software supports tasks as needed by users [116, 117].

In order to collect data on each of these measures, a number of strategies were deployed. The video captured from all of the modification sessions outlined in section 5.2 was reanalysed to ascertain FADA's efficiency that is, its efficiency in enabling participants to arrive at solutions to problems posed. It was also analysed together with data gleaned from related questionnaires to ascertain FADA's learnability and level of user satisfaction. The questionnaire consisted of a number of prescribed questions asking participants to rate the level of ease of use of FADA's framework API methods and its developer tools (See Appendix B). FADA's effectiveness was measured by the percentage of tasks that were successfully completed by participants and by the ratio of successes to failures.

5.3.2 Instructor Methodology

In order to investigate to what extent instructors found FADA to be operationally effective in enabling them to create active simulations for use within their own learning settings, it was necessary to administer each a questionnaire which enabled them through a series of closed and open-ended questions to rate the learnability of FADA, its efficiency and effectiveness in enabling them to create active simulations and their overall level of satisfaction with its features (See Appendix C).

5.4 Summary

This chapter has outlined the research methodology which was followed in order to ascertain to what extent the algorithm visualisation approach adopted in this thesis enhances the teaching and learning of distributed algorithms. It has in adopting triangulation tried to ensure the validity of the research. The aim of the chapter was to describe and analyse the techniques and procedures used in the process of data collection so as to enable one at a later date to replicate the process. The methods deployed for data collection included both quantitative and qualitative measures. The former were gleaned from the analysis of returned questionnaires and from the number of correct algorithm implementations received from learners. The latter were gleaned from the use of a case study methodology which included the following data collection methods; video capture, focus group discussions and interviews. The next chapter outlines the manner by which the collected data was analysed and how generalisations were ventured as to the effectiveness of the algorithm simulation approach in assisting learners to acquire a deep understanding of an algorithm's behaviour and in assisting instructors to convey the dynamic and concurrent behaviour of a distributed algorithm.

Chapter 6
Evaluation Findings

6.1 Introduction

This chapter delineates the findings with respect to the multiple case study methodology adopted in this research. In order to assist the reader in interpreting the data derived from each case study, sample movies are provided and enclosed within the accompanying CD. This is to give the reader a true picture of the manner by which they were procured. All findings documented within this chapter are inextricably linked to the manner in which instructors and learners engaged with FADA to enable learners to arrive at an understanding of an algorithm's process. Such interactions were, not only, subtle, but also, manifold and led to a host of concurrent and dynamic changes being reaped on the behaviour of the algorithm being investigated. Such interactions and changes do not lend themselves well to representation by static imagery and text but are more easily captured through the medium of video. Movies or videos, not only, capture the changes reaped upon the algorithm's behaviour through the user's interactions with FADA, but also, the manner by which users engaged with one another to interpret the algorithm's process.

This chapter is subdivided into three main sections. First, it outlines findings arising from three different lecture settings as to FADA's use as a tool to facilitate instructors in conveying to learners the behaviour of an algorithm. Next, it documents findings arising from a number of laboratory settings as to FADA's use as a tool to enable learners to make explicit their own understanding of how an algorithm's behaviour should be changed to overcome set problems encountered with its implementation. For each lecture setting and laboratory setting reviewed, it provides a detailed description and analysis of all proceedings as warranted by the case study methodology and critiques each with respect to each of the four pedagogical research questions outlined in chapter five. Next, it outlines findings arising from the use by three different instructors of FADA and their perceived pedagogical value of it in each instance. Lastly, it delineates findings with respect to FADA's operational effectiveness both from the perspective of the learner and the instructor.

6.2 Findings with respect to FADA's use as an interactive presentation tool

This section is subdivided into a number of subsections. The first section provides a detailed case study analysis of the manner by which FADA assisted instructor (L1) to communicate to learners the behaviour of the dining philosophers' algorithm. The next section also provides a detailed case study analysis of the manner by which the author, acting as an instructor, deployed FADA in one of two different simulated lecture settings to aid her in conveying to learners the behaviour of transactions with in a distributed system. The aim of the analysis as previously stated in chapter five is to allow for literal replication that is, to determine whether similar patterns of behaviour witnessed in the first lecture setting also occurred in the second and third lecture settings and can be deemed a function of FADA's use. This is in order to validate findings arising from the first lecture setting.

6.2.1 Case study 1: Authentic Lecture Setting

In this case study, instructor (L1) used FADA to introduce students to the concept of concurrency and the problems of deadlock and starvation associated with it. This was facilitated through the creation of an active simulation of the dining philosophers' algorithm. The aim of the lecture was to enable the instructor to introduce students to the logic of the algorithm in a gradual manner. This was facilitated by him subdividing the aforementioned logic into a series of stages. These were five in total. Each stage was designed to build upon the former stage and to simulate the behaviour of the algorithm at each stage of implementation. By actively experimenting with each simulation rendered in real time, the instructor was able to engage students in higher order conversations about the algorithm's behaviour and enable them to uncover problems associated with it and identify ways by which to overcome them. Such an approach mirrors that of a constructivist approach to the teaching and learning of distributed algorithms and was deployed to maximise students' involvement within the learning session. This was in order to engender within students higher order thinking so as to enable them to venture reasons as to why set problems were encountered and to voice solutions to overcome them. However solutions relating to the issues of deadlock and starvation were left unrealised. This was in order to enable the instructor to set the latter as an exercise for students to complete in their labs

(See Appendix F for a complete transcript of proceedings taken from the above lecture setting). As a consequence of the solutions returned in response to such an exercise, the instructor was able to gain insight into students' overall understanding of the concept of concurrency

In keeping with the case study methodology undertaken in this research, a detailed 'thick' description of each of the aforementioned stages together with their purpose is given in this section. The first three stages were designed to establish the platform from which the instructor could begin to engage students in meaningful higher order dialogues about the algorithm's behaviour and in particular about deadlock and starvation. They were designed to introduce students to the manner by which one defines the behaviour of an algorithm within FADA and also, to reinforce in students' minds the need to allow for the lack of global knowledge within a distributed system. The remaining two stages were designed to enable the instructor to probe students' higher order understanding of the algorithm's purpose and to ascertain to what extent they would be able to foresee and allow for problems in its implementation such as that caused by two adjacent philosophers attempting to eat at the same time. Section 6.2.1.1 provides a detailed description and analysis of the first three stages of the lecture's proceedings. Section 6.2.1.2 affords a description and analysis of the remaining two stages.

6.2.1.1 Stages 1, 2 and 3.

Stage one was designed to depict and explain the manner by which one defines an algorithm's behaviour whose underlying topology is that of a group within FADA. The aim was to familiarise students with and to enable them to differentiate between those aspects of the algorithm's implementation which are required to realise the group communication mechanism and those aspects which are required to derive the algorithm's logic. This was in order to enable students to ignore the implementation of the former in favour of the latter so as to enable them to concentrate solely on the algorithm's implementation. This was achieved by the instructor highlighting and explaining the relevant lines of code relating to the algorithm's implementation and those relating to the implementation of the communication infrastructure within the code frame.

As a consequence, the first stage of the instructor's presentation depicted a skeletal description of the algorithm's behaviour. It depicted the manner by which a node deciphers the identity of the node to its immediate right and left, the manner by which it initiates the algorithm's behaviour through the sending of requests to its left and right neighbours for the use of their forks and lastly, the manner by which it stores state information locally at the node level. This is information relating to whether or not a node has possession of its left or right fork, whether or not it wants to eat and whether or not it has attempted to eat and failed (See figure 6-1).

```
//Dining Philosophers' Algorithm: Stage 1
import network.*;

public class MyNode extends Node implements GroupNode{

    Vector participants = new Vector();
    int size = 0;

    public MyNode(){
        define("left", new Boolean(false),false);        State information stored
        define("right", new Boolean(false),false);       locally at the node level
        define("wants_to_eat", new Boolean(false),false);
        define("missedlunch", new Boolean(false), false);
    }

    public void receiveMessage(Node sender, Message message){}     No code relating to how
                                                                   a node handles receipt of
    public void run(){                                             a request for its left or
        eat();                 Method to initiate the              right fork has as yet been
    }                          algorithm's process                 implemented
    private void eat(){
        // get the forks...
        setBoolean("wants_to_eat", true);
        Message msg1 = new Message(this.getRight(), "rightfork");
        Message msgr = new Message(this.getLeft(), "leftfork");
        send(msg1);
        send(msgr);
    }


    /* these methods are needed so as
    to enable one to find a node in the chain to send message to
    */

    //determine the previous node up from each node      A method to detect the
    private Node getRight(){                              neighbour to the
        for (int i=0;i<participants.size();i++){          immediate right of a
            //next node is one up from current node       node.
            if (participants.get(i)==this){
                //if node is the last member in group
                //the next node is node 0
                if (i == 0){
                    return participants.get(participants.size() - 1);
                }

                return participants.get(i-1);
            }
        }
        return null;
    }
```

128

```
51    //determine the next node up from each node
52    private Node getLeft(){
53        for (int i=0;i<participants.size();i++){
54            //next node is one up from current node
55            if (participants.get(i)==this){
56                //if node is the last member in group
57                //the next node is node 0
58                if (participants.size()-1==i){
59                    return participants.get(0);
60                }
61                return participants.get(i+1);
62            }
63        }
64        return null;
65    }
```

A method to detect the neighbour to the immediate left of a node.

Figure 6-1: Skeletal description of the algorithm's behaviour.

The aim of the skeletal description was twofold. As stated earlier, it was designed to form the basis from which the instructor could build and introduce students to the logic of the algorithm in a series of stages. Moreover, it was designed to reinforce in students' minds that within a distributed system there is no global knowledge, and that all state information is held locally at the node level and acquired through the sending and receiving of messages. Such a concept was further reinforced in students' minds through the use of active simulation. In the dining philosophers' algorithm in order for a philosopher to be able to eat it must acquire the fork to its immediate right and left. To do so, it needs to send individual requests to each of its immediate neighbours to ascertain whether or not they have possession of the required forks and whether or not they would be willing to relinquish them. By re-enacting this process as a simulation, the instructor reinforced in students' minds the need to allow for a lack of global knowledge within a distributed system. This was achieved by the graphical depiction of a philosopher's actions as dependent upon the state returned by each of its neighbours.

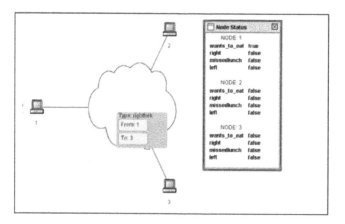

Figure 6-2: A depiction of the simulation used by the instructor to assist him in illustrating to students the concept of a lack of global knowledge within a distributed system. In the above simulation in order for node 1 to be able to eat, it needs to obtain possession of the forks to its immediate left and right. To do so, it first needs to query node 2 and node 3 to determine whether or not they have possession of the required forks and depending upon their replies, node 1 may or may not be able to eat.

The second stage was designed to elaborate upon the message passing behaviour witnessed within stage one. It was designed to portray the manner by which a node handles a request for its right or left fork. This is dependent upon the state of its local variables. This was facilitated through the instructor loading into FADA's code frame a separate algorithm description file, one which contains code relating to the ability of a node to decipher the nature or type of a request that it receives, its ability to respond to that request by creating a new message object and its ability to encapsulate inside that message object a variable stating whether or not it grants permission to the requesting node to obtain use of its fork. Such permission is dependent on whether the receiving node has possession of the required fork. This is information which is stored in its relevant local state variable and is visualised through the 'Node Status' panel in Figure 6-2. Again, the dual representations afforded by FADA provided the platform from which the instructor could reinforce in student's minds the concept of message passing as a means to obtain state information about other members within a distributed system. This was achieved by the instructor actively switching between the code frame and the animation frame, in an attempt to show students both a graphical representation of the message passing behaviour and a textual representation of it. This was in order to enable them to build dual representations of the message passing behaviour.

```
public void receiveMessage(Node sender, Message message) {
    if(message.isType("leftfork"))
    {
        Message response = new Message(sender, "response");
        if(getBoolean("left")) //have it
        {
            response.putString("fork", "Taken");
        }else{ // don't have it

            response.putString("fork", "NotTaken");
        }
        send(response);
    }
    else if(message.isType("rightfork"))
    {
        Message response = new Message(sender, "response");
        if(getBoolean("right")) //have it
        {
            response.putString("fork", "Taken");
        }else{ // don't have it

            response.putString("fork", "NotTaken");
        }
        send(response);
    }
}
```

Figure 6-3: The textual representation of the algorithm's behaviour which the instructor deployed to assist him in conveying to students the manner by which a node detects receipt of a request for its left or right forks.

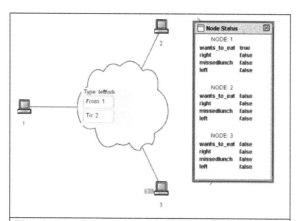

Figure 6.4a: In the above simulation in order for the instructor to be able to reinforce in students' minds the logic of the algorithm's behaviour as documented within Figure 6-3, he needed to graphically represent the reply request protocol underpinning its logic. To do so, he created a simulation consisting of three nodes in which he activated the behaviour of node one. This caused node 1 to send out two individual requests to its nearest neighbours seeking possession of the fork to their immediate left or right. One of those requests is signified in the above depiction by the yellow icon travelling from node 1 to node 2.

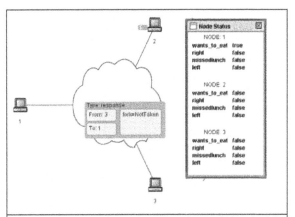

Figure 6.4b: On receipt of the request for the fork to its left, node 3, on the basis of the state of its local 'left' variable replied 'fork not taken' and as a result, granted node 1 permission to obtain possession of the fork.

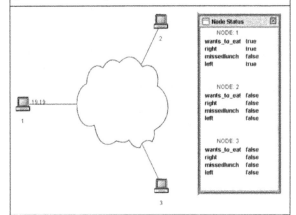

Figure 6.4c: Similarly, node 2 replied in the same manner as node 3 to node 1's request and as a result, gave node 1 leave to take possession of the fork to its immediate left. Now node 1 has possession of both its left and right forks as indicated by the node status pane and can start to eat. This is signified by

the timer depicted beside node 1 in the above simulation.

Figure 6-4: The corresponding graphical representation of the code documented within Figure 6-3 which the instructor used to reinforce in students' minds the logic of message passing behaviour exhibited by the dining philosophers' algorithm.

The third stage was designed to set the dais from which the instructor could begin to gauge students' understanding of the algorithm's behaviour. It was primarily designed to depict the manner by which a node, on receipt of responses to its initial requests for forks, should proceed. Should it on receiving a reply of 'fork not taken' from both its right and left neighbours, reply 'fork taken' and as a consequence, proceed to eat? By default each node was set to reply 'fork not taken' in response to a request for its fork and as a result, cause all requesting nodes to start to eat at the same time. Such behaviour is in violation of the sharing protocol underpinning the algorithm's logic. Between any two nodes, there is only one fork and not two. The aim of the algorithm is to share the fork in a manner which ensures that no one philosopher ever starves.

Thus, in order to ascertain to what extent students were able to recognise this violation, it was necessary for the instructor to revert to the use of simulation. This enabled him to set up a concrete representation of two adjacent nodes eating at the same time and as a result, enabled him to use the derived simulation to probe students' higher order understanding of the algorithm's behaviour. From the replies received in response to his probe, there is evidence to suggest that the use of simulation alerted students to the algorithm's failure to function correctly. This is clearly evidenced by the verbal responses received from students S1, S2 and S3 in Figure 6-6.

134

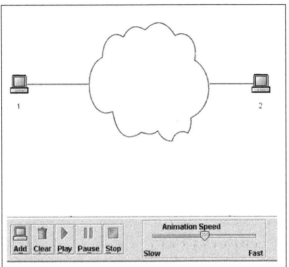

Figure 6.5a: By successively selecting the 'Add' button functionality from the panel running along the bottom of the FADA's interface, the instructor created a simulation consisting of a number of nodes.

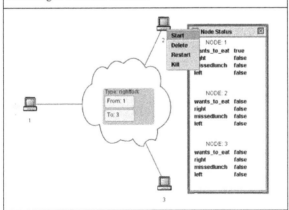

Figure 6.5b: On completion of his set up, he deliberately initiated the behaviour of two adjacent nodes by right clicking

135

on each and selecting the 'start' option from each of their
behavioural panels. As a consequence of his actions, node 1
sent out two separate requests to node 2 and node 3 for use of
the forks to their immediate right or left.

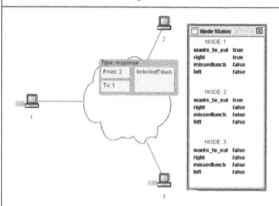

Figure 6.5c: On receipt of a request from node 1, node 2 gave
node 1 permission to use the fork to its immediate left. This is
indicated by the 'fork not taken' message embedded within the
response returned by node 2 to node 1 in the above depiction.

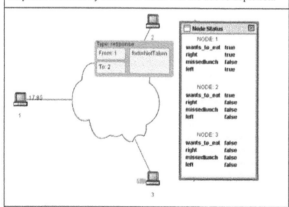

Figure 6.5d: As a consequence of receiving permission from
both node 2 and node 3 to use the fork to the right of node 2

and to use the fork to the left of node 3, node 1 commenced to eat (This is signified by the timer in the above depiction and the true state of both node 1's left and right variables). Yet despite needing both forks in order to continue eating, node 1 incorrectly gave permission to node 2 to use its left fork. This is signified by the message icon travelling from node 1 to node 2. This resulted in node 2 commencing to eat as signified by the next screen shot.

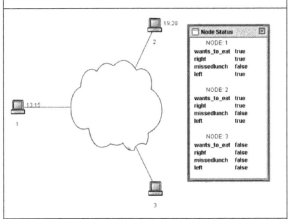

Figure 6.5e: Thus, the current algorithm's implementation enabled both node 1 and 2 to eat concurrently signalling its failure to account for whether a fork was being used or not.

Figure 6-5: A depiction of the simulation created by the instructor to demonstrate the problems incurred when one fails to account for whether a fork is being used or not within the dining philosophers' algorithm.

> *L: Can anyone see anything wrong?*
> *S1: They shouldn't be eating.*
> *L: It shouldn't be possible for them both to be eating.*
> *L: Let me ask you what do you think is wrong?*

S2: *It's not working.*

L: *It's not working ..yip. Let's go a little bit deeper. It's not working because..*

S3: *Because they are doing something that technically they should not be capable of doing. They are both eating despite the fact that to eat you should only have two forks. There are only two between them, so at most, only one should be able to eat and at worse, neither should be able to eat.*

Figure 6-6: A depiction of the dialogue[1] which arose between the students and the instructor as a consequence of the instructor's re-enactment of the algorithm's failure to account for atomic operations within Figure 6-5. From the dialogue, it is clear to see that student (S3) has as a result of the simulation defined with in Figure 6-5 been able to correctly identify the violation in the sharing protocol underpinning the algorithm's behaviour.

But in order to enable students to identify the shortcoming in the algorithm's implementation which led to the aforementioned violation, it was necessary for the instructor to revert to the code frame. This was in order to enable students to map the graphical representation of the algorithm's behaviour as witnessed in figure 6-5 to that of its implementation so as to enable them to pinpoint shortcomings in its implementation. By providing voice over explanations of the code contained within the code frame the instructor scaffolded students in their investigative processes and as a consequence, enabled them to more readily pinpoint the algorithm's shortcoming. This is evidenced by the manner in which student (S3) interrupted the instructor's voice over explanations to assert the exact nature of the algorithm's shortcoming that is, its failure to provide 'provision for whether a fork was being used or not'.

---

[1] To view as a movie, go to the enclosed cd and open the folder *Case1_Authentic/Concurrency* and click on *sharing_violation.mov*.

```
25   public void receiveMessage(Node sender, Message message) {
26
27       if(message.isType("leftfork"))
28       {
29           Message response = new Message(sender, "r
30           if(getBoolean("left")){//have it
31               response.putString("fork", "Taken");
32           }else{ // don't have it
33               response.putString("fork", "NotTaken"
34           }
35           send(response);
36       }else if(message.isType("rightfork")){
37           Message response = new Message(sender, "r
38           if(getBoolean("right")){//have it
39               response.putString("fork", "Taken");
40           }else{ // don't have it
41               response.putString("fork", "NotTaken"
42           }
43           send(response);
44
45       }else if(message.isType("response")){
46           if(sender.equals(this.getRight())){//sender was to my right
47               if(message.getString("fork").compareTo("Taken") ==0){
48                   abandonEating();
49               }else{
50                   if(getBoolean("eating")) setBoolean("right", true);
51               }
52           }
53           else{
54               if(message.getString("fork").compareTo("Taken") ==0){
55                   abandonEating();
56               }else{
57                   if(getBoolean("wants_to_eat")) setBool
58               }
59           }
60           if(getBoolean("left") && getBoolean("right")){
61               // pause to eat, then finish
62               FinishEat e = new FinishEat();
63               schedule(e, 20000);
64           }
65       }
66   }
```

Requesting permission to obtain use of the fork to one's left. If the node is not using it, it grants permission to each and every requesting node to take it. It does not allow for the fact that two adjacent nodes may be requesting use of the same fork at the same time.

On obtaining possession of the fork to its right and left, a node is able to eat.

139

```
67    public void abandonEating(){
68        setBoolean("right", false);
69        setBoolean("left", false);
70        setBoolean("wants_to_eat", false);
71        setBoolean("missedlunch", true);
72    }
73
74    public class FinishEat extends TimerTask{
75        public void run(){
76            //release forks
77            setBoolean("wants_to_eat", false);
78            setBoolean("right", false);
79            setBoolean("left", false);
80            setBoolean("missedlunch", false);
81        }
82    }
83
84    public void run(){
85        eat();
86    }
...
88    private void eat(){
89        // get the forks...
90        setBoolean("wants_to_eat", true);
91        Message msgl = new Message(this.getRight(), "rightfork");
92        Message msgr = new Message(this.getLeft(), "leftfork");
93        send(msgl);
94        send(msgr);
95    }
96
```

On finishing eating, a node releases use of the right and left forks.

A node sending out initial requests for the forks to its left and right

Figure 6-7: The flawed implementation of a node's ability to eat. In the above code, no measures are taken to prevent two adjacent nodes from gaining access to a shared fork at the same time.

L: Ok, lets us look at what each node is doing.

L: Each node is saying, 'Can I have the forks please?'...'Can I have the forks please?' and they are getting back responses saying 'By all means go ahead take the forks.' So they are eating.

L: So that part of the protocol is perfectly fine. That's the right behaviour.

L: If a message comes back saying 'you should eat', you should eat!

L: There would be something wrong, if they didn't eat in that scenario.

L: The place that it seems to be going wrong is that they are being told to eat when they shouldn't be.

140

S3: They are being told the fork is available to them when it is not.

L: The problem is in this algorithm seems to be where two adjacent philosophers both trying to eat seem to not take note of the fact that they are both trying to eat.

S3: So basically there absolutely no provision for whether a fork is being used or not.

L: Exactly.

Figure 6-8: The voice over explanations provided by the instructor of the implementation code contained within Figure 6-7 which assisted students in identifying its shortcoming.

Equally, the simulation enabled the instructor to introduce students to one of the greatest difficulties associated with distributed algorithm design that is, the ability for the algorithm to exhibit correct behaviour in certain scenarios despite being flawed. This was achieved by the instructor actively recreating scenarios of behaviour in which the algorithm appeared to function correctly, like for example, in the scenario where two non adjacent processes try to eat at the same time.

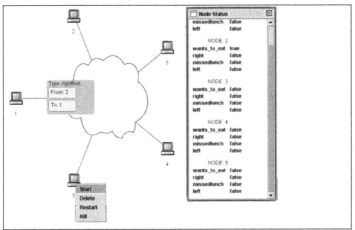

Figure 6-9a: By right clicking on a number of non-adjacent nodes and selecting 'Start' from their behaviour panels their behaviours were initiated. This led to each node requesting access to the fork to its immediate right and left.

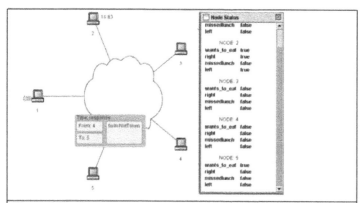

Figure 6-9b: As a consequence of gaining possession of the fork to its immediate right and left, node 2 was able to eat. This is indicated by the timer in the above depiction and by the true state of its left and right variables. These indicate that it has gained possession of the forks to its left and right.

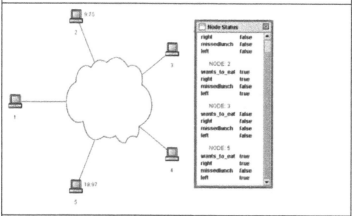

Figure 6-9c: Similarly, as a result of being told that it could have possession of the fork to the immediate left of node 4 and to the immediate right of node 1, node 5 was able to start to eat. Thus, highlighting the capacity for the algorithm to function correctly when non adjacent nodes attempt to eat.

142

Figure 6.9: A depiction of the simulation[1] created by the instructor to assist him in elucidating to students the capacity for the algorithm to function correctly in set circumstances such as when non-adjacent processes attempt to eat.

L: In normal circumstances..........

L: Lets put in lots of philosophers

L: Various philosophers arriving, sitting down trying to eat.

L: There's a philosopher starting to eat...........There's another one starting to eat.

L: There's nothing wrong with those ones eating. There's no conflict there.

L: That's probably the normal case.

L: Behaviour is not working in the sense that it is not actually correct.

L: The computation that it is doing is not correct, but its behaviour seems correct.

Figure 6-10: The use of voice over explanations[1] provided by the instructor to reinforced the correctness of the behaviour exhibited by the simulation in Figure 6-9.

As a by product of the simulations rendered in stage three (See figure 6-5), the instructor was able to elucidate students to the need for atomic operations. These are actions which must be carried out indivisibly for their result to be correct. Atomicity is the key to avoiding undesirable artefacts from concurrency such as that evidenced above, when two philosophers were able to magically turn one fork into two. Such a process was facilitated by the instructor's capacity to ground his explanations for the need for atomic operations in the language of the algorithm's implementation code contained with in the code frame.

L: So the problem occurs then in the creation of the response message.

L: If getBoolean("Left")... we have it fine that would be the good case.

L: However, if one of those philosophers is eating and if the philosopher to the left or right of him tries to eat, he'll be told he can't quite correctly.

L: But if a node is in the process of acquiring the forks and the response messages haven't yet come through to allow him to obtain the forks, my boolean variable won't be set and so I'll happily say 'go ahead, take the fork'. The subtlety in this protocol is that a node has to send out two messages ('LeftFork' and 'RightFork') and get back responses to both those messages and the actual state that the node should expose to the world is really dependent on both the values of those messages. If a message comes in the interim looking for a fork, what the node should really be doing is atomic in some sense, that is, the node should reply 'go ahead have the fork, I haven't got it'.

Section 6.2.1.2 Stages 4 and 5

In stage four, the instructor was able to simulate the behaviour of the algorithm when atomicity was taken into account. This enabled him to set up a scenario whereby deadlock was encountered, that is, a situation in which all philosophers wanted to eat but no forks were available to them as they were all acquired by their neighbours. Consequently, all philosophers were left waiting for their immediate right or left neighbours to relinquish their forks so that they could eat.

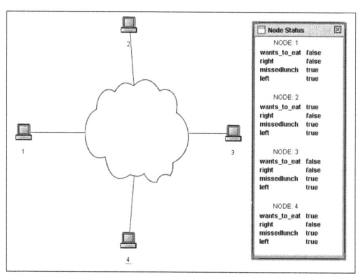

Figure 6-11: A depiction of the manner by which the instructor used simulation to raise students' awareness to the problem of deadlock. Each node has possession of one fork as

indicated by the node status pane. In order to eat they need to gain possession of the fork to their immediate right and left. Each is waiting on the other to release a fork.

L: Is that deadlock?

S4: Yes

L: It's actually not quite deadlock, a kind of deadlock.

S5: They are all waiting.

L: It's livelock. If they all continually come trying to eat at once, they are all going to go away hungry every time.

Figure 6-12: A depiction of the manner by which the instructor used the above simulation[2] in Figure 6-11 to probe students' higher order thinking to ascertain whether or not they would be able to identify the problem of deadlock associated with the current algorithm's implementation.

Again, such a simulation offered the opportunity for the instructor to reinforce in students' mind that despite being flawed, the current algorithm implementation was still able to exhibit some correct behaviour. This was facilitated by the instructor simulating the ability for a single process to be able to eat, for two non adjacent processes to be able to eat at the same time and finally, for the failure of an adjacent process to eat while its immediate right or left neighbour was eating.

As a corollary of the latter experimentations, the instructor[3] was able to engage students in a higher order dialogue as to how they would overcome the issue of dead lock or as in this case, the issue of live lock. Such a process was facilitated by the students' capacity to ground their proposed solutions in the language of the algorithm's implementation code.

L: *Any one got a solution?*

S3:   *Replace the eating message.*

---

[2] To view as a movie, go to the enclosed cd and open the folder '*Case1_Authentic/deadlock*' and click on *deadlock_1.mov*.
[3] To view as a movie, go to the enclosed cd and open the folder '*Case1_Authenti/deadlock*' and click on *deadlock_2.mov*.

L: *Sure.. replace with what? ………Remember we had nothing there before.*

S3:   *No what I am saying is…….We should set the 'eating' variable to true only when we get a 'Not Taken' message back from each of our neighbours.*

From the responses obtained, it is evident that student (S3) had grasped the need for atomicity but had yet to grasp the need for precedence that is, the need for a decision to be made as to which process should obtain the use of a fork first. Should it be the initial requesting process or the subsequent one? In order to assist students in arriving at such an understanding, it was necessary for the instructor to revert to the code frame so as to enable him to convey to students the weakness in the algorithm's implementation that is, its lack of a priority scheme.

L: *So at a high level, just saying 'I want to eat so you can't' is not good enough. Just saying 'by all means, you want it, take it' is not good enough.*

L: *Have to find somewhere in between.*

L: *First of all, if you have the fork, then you shouldn't be able to get it. That's just the state of the thing. 'I have the fork and you don't'.*

L: *But we know that, that by itself, led us to a scenario where we wouldn't have the fork even though we are trying to get that fork.*

L: *So what I've done is I've given the protocol more information…I've said either we have the fork or we're trying to eat and something else.*

L: *I've introduced a little bit of subtlety to it and I've said either 'we have that fork' or 'we are eating' and 'we are going to do some kind of test'.*

L   *This test is going to decide which of us should get the fork.*

L: *That's the point to this.*

L: *Need to have a computation, that can be done by both nodes and that will come out the same. The result will be same and it will give preference to one or the other. The computation will give preference to one or the other irrespective of where that computation is done.*

L: *The test I've put in is that every node has an identifier. If my identifier is larger than your identifier then it is taken.*

146

> *L:*   *what I've implemented is a priority scheme.*
>
> *L:*   *The priority scheme says 'If I already have the fork then there is nothing to debate about...I have the fork, you can't have it, it's taken'.*
>
> *L:*   *Bit if my id is higher than yours and I want to eat then it's taken.*
>
> *L:*   *Correspondingly, if the other node, if it was asked that question, 'who should have the fork?', it would say, 'my id is lower than that node's id so, 'I should give it'.*

As a consequence, the instructor[3] was able to move to stage five and demonstrate the behaviour of the algorithm when priority was taken into account that is, when a scheme was implemented which relinquished the fork to the process with the highest id. However, on simulating the behaviour of the latter, student (S4) was able to immediately decipher the problem associated with such an intervention, that is, the problem of starvation.

> *S4:*   *But by taking into account the node's id, does that not mean that eventually you get..........like node one, who is lower than everyone else would be starved out of the system.*
>
> *L:*   *That's something we would want to look at.*

Hence, the instructor was able to re-enact the problem of starvation through the use of simulation and as a consequence, engage students in a higher order dialogue as to how to overcome it.

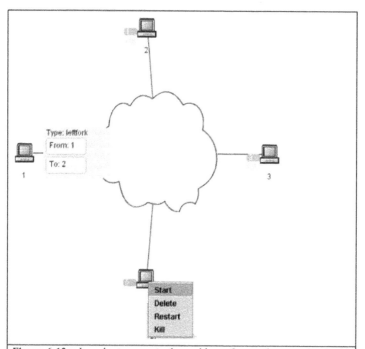

Figure 6-13a: In order to recreate the problem of starvation associated with the algorithm's behaviour, there was need to create a simulation consisting of many nodes in which the behaviour of all nodes was initiated. This was achieved in FADA through successively selecting the 'Add' button functionality in order to add a number of nodes to the animation frame and through a process of right clicking on each node to initiate their behaviours. As a result, all nodes were able to send out requests seeking possession of the forks to their immediate right and left.

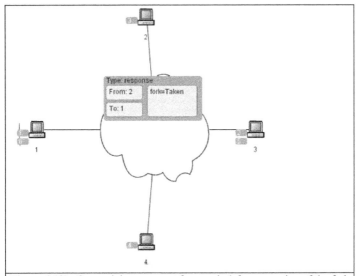

Figure 6-13b: On receiving a request from node 1 for possession of the fork to its left, node 2 replied 'fork taken' and as a result, denied node 1 access to the fork This was because node 2's id was higher than that of node 1's. Thus, node 1 was unable to eat.

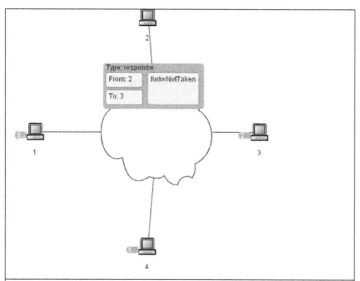

Figure 6-13c: Similarly, on receiving a request from node 3 for possession of the fork to its immediate right, node 2 replied 'fork not taken' and as a result, gave node 3 the fork. Again, this was because node 3's id was higher than that of node 2's.

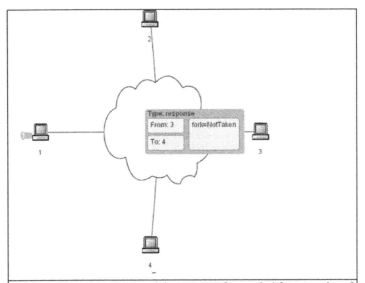

Figure 6-13d: However, on receiving a request from node 4 for possession of the fork to its right, node 3 had to relinquish possession to node 4 as its id was lower than that of node 4's.

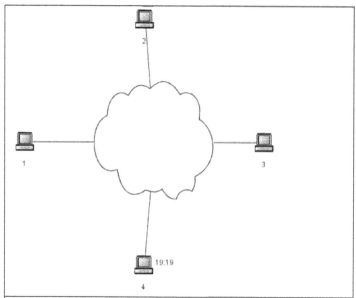

Figure 6-13e: As a consequence, node 4 got to eat and the remaining nodes starved. This was because the priority scheme underpinning the algorithm's behaviour gave unfair preference to the node with the highest id.

Figure 6-13: A graphical depiction of the instructor's use of simulation[4] to allude students to the issue of starvation associated with the algorithm's process and the manner by which he used it to ground higher order discussions as to how to over come it (See Figure 6-14).

L: In fact, what we have now suffers from a simple problem that once we have a chain of nodes, all trying to eat and their messages are being exchanged in an order that kind of binds them together, the top node gets to eat and no one else. That seems inefficient.

L: It is not catastrophic in that system doesn't suffer in potentially nothing can go forward but it does have the starvation problem as mentioned up at the top (by S4).

---

[4] To view as a movie, go to the enclosed cd and open the folder 'Case1_Authentic/Starvation'. From here open *starvation1.mov* and *starvation2.mov*.

L: Every time, a node becomes part of a chain of philosophers sitting down at the table, only one gets to eat and that is, the top one.

L: Any one got a solution? Where should we focus our attention that's the first question?

S4: The id we are using. Need another way of generating the order in which the initial requests were sent out. ...Rather than use the id of the individual making the request ...then highest priority might get to eat rather than highest number.

L: Yeah....The system gives, in the unusual scenario, where everybody comes uniquely together, at the same time, to eat. The system gives automatic priority to the highest identifier.

L: That seems like an unreasonable basis on which to decide priority.

L: Focusing on this calculation, what we need to do is change how we do priority.

L: What should we use? What would be useful?

L: Remember the purpose of the dining philosophers' algorithm is to ensure that no one starves, that's the goal. So if we had some notion of...

S5: Waiting time.

L: Time to starvation that would be useful.

S6: Time from when the initial request was sent out.

Figure 6-14: The dialogue which arose as a consequence of the instructor's re-enactment of the problem of starvation associated with the algorithm's behaviour.

From their responses to his inquiry, it is clear that most students had grasped the need to assign priority to the process that had been waiting the longest to eat. But in making that connection, many students failed to realise that such information was not accounted for within the current implementation of the algorithm's behaviour. Thus, there was need for the instructor[5] to intervene to raise awareness to the fact and to reframe the task so as to provide students with an alternative perspective to enable them to generate another means by which one decides priority.

> *L: Lets park the question of how to generate a valid piece of information.*

---

[5] To view as a movie, go to the folder '*Case1_Authentic/Starvtion*' enclosed on the cd and open *starvation2.mov.*

L: How could I as a philosopher say 'could I have that fork, please?' to each
        node and also, tell them, in a sense, how important this is.

S7:   Put a timer in a message.

L: Lets imagine, I'm about to starve, so I really do need these forks, what could
        I do?

S8:   Use some kind of counter that tracks the need to eat.

L: Yip...I have some kind of counter that expresses.. It could be a boolean 'on'
        or 'off', it could be 'I missed lunch last time' or 'it could be 'It's been three
        days since I last ate'.

S8:   I could increase my priority by switching it on or off.

L: Yeah., so in some ways, it's a piece of information that I could communicate
        that says 'I really need this now'.

As a consequence of such intervention, student (S8) was able to analyse and reflect on the
problem from the new perspective and as a result, offer a potential means by which one
could overcome the problem of starvation through the use of a counter which tracks a
node's need to eat. Such a suggestion enabled the instructor (L1) to close the session by
challenging students to amend the behaviour of the algorithm to overcome the problem of
starvation associated with it. This was set as an exercise for students to complete in their
lab session.

L: Try and implement this.... Try to get rid of the scenario of potential
        starvation caused by basing the ability to eat on the basis of unchanging
        node ids. Modify the code such that the system is fairer to the philosopher.
        When you've done that, you could go further...See if your solution solves the
        problem when a number of philosophers like this...many of whom could eat
        concurrently but for some quirk in the implementation can't. See if that
        solves it and how else you could modify your solution so that for example,
        while node 7 was eating, there's no reason why node 5 couldn't be eating
        and node 3 at the same time'.

6.2.1.3 Discussion

With respect to each of the pedagogical research questions posed in chapter five, there is evidence to suggest from the above analysis that FADA facilitated the instructor in engaging students in higher order conversations about the algorithmic process and in engaging them in higher order thinking about the algorithm's behaviour. This is evidenced by stage three of the implementation process and again, by stage five. Such modes of behaviour were made possible as a direct consequence of the design of FADA's user interface. By providing both a graphical representation and a textual representation of the algorithm's behaviour, FADA enabled students to form referential connections between the two representations and as a result, empowered them to identify shortcomings in the algorithm's logic and to voice solutions to over come each. This is evidenced by stage three of the algorithm implementation process where the graphical representation of two adjacent philosophers eating alerted students to a violation in the sharing protocol underpinning the algorithm's logic. This coupled with a textual representation of its underlying implementation enabled students to identify the shortcoming in the algorithm's behaviour as its failure to account for whether a fork was being used or not. Similarly, in stage five, the graphical representation of the implementation of the priority scheme to overcome the issue of deadlock engaged student's (S4) higher order thinking and enabled him to identify the potential problem of starvation associated with that scheme. As a consequence, this enabled the instructor to engage all students in a higher order dialogue as to how they would overcome the issue. Moreover, the level of real time interactivity afforded by FADA over the algorithm's behaviour assisted in the latter process by enabling the instructor to provide concrete representations of the issue of starvation and also, of the state of each node. Equally, the ability to add additional philosophers to the simulation, to vary its execution speed and to initiate the behaviour of two or more philosophers concurrently enabled the instructor to isolate the problem of starvation and to open it up for separate discussion and experimentation. As a consequence, FADA, indirectly through the actions of the instructor, enabled students to engage in an iterative cycle of learning. The dual representations afforded by FADA exposed students to the algorithm's process in a concrete manner and as such enabled them to reflect upon its behaviour and through a process of active experimentation decipher its correctness. Such cyclic actions enabled students to abstract out and put forward alternate means by which one could overcome problems incurred in the logic of the algorithm and as a consequence, led to further concrete experiences, reflections and active experimentations. Such a process is exemplified by stage three of the algorithm's implementation in which students were first exposed to the problem of two adjacent philosophers eating concurrently and through a process of reflection were able to abstract out and propose an alternate means by which to over come it. This led to further exposure to the issue of deadlock which resulted in further reflections on how to overcome it.

6.2.2 Simulated lecture settings.

Similar to the authentic lecture setting, the author acting as the instructor used FADA to introduce students to the issue of transactions within distributed systems. This was realised through the implementation of a distributed banking application. As in the authentic lecture setting, the author used FADA to build the logic of the distributed banking application in a series of stages. These were three in all. Each stage was designed to introduce students to one or more problems associated with transactions, like for example, partial failure. Such a design served two purposes. These were: to enable the author to simulate the behaviour of the application at each stage of implementation and to engender in students higher order thinking so as to enable them to voice solutions to overcome the shortcomings encountered during each implementation. As a consequence of such a mode of use, similar levels of engagement and high-level dialogue were recorded as that witnessed in the authentic lecture setting, all of which were mediated by FADA and sustained through the author's ability to interact with the simulations in real time. Rather than transcribe and analyse each of the four lectures which occurred, the author chose, for the purposes of this thesis, to analyse two of these as they were representative of the manner by which FADA assisted the author in engaging students' higher order thinking and in engaging them in higher order dialogues about the nature of transactions within distributed systems across all lecture settings (See Appendix G & H for a complete transcript of each of the proceedings). The first to be considered is that which occurred with a subset of students from group 3. These were students who were enrolled as postgraduate students in distributed systems and who had a background in the topic. The second to be considered is that which occurred with students from group 2. These were students, who unlike those in group 3, had no background or prior knowledge of distributed systems but who possessed an undergraduate or postgraduate qualification in computer science. The aim of the analysis was to provide for literal replication, that is, to determine whether similar patterns of higher order thinking and dialogue as those witnessed in the authentic lecture setting also arose in each of the simulated settings and could be deemed a function of FADA's use. This was in order to validate findings from the authentic lecture setting. Equally, the aim of the exercise was not to necessarily formulate and implement the 'best' solutions to problems of partial failure incurred within the distributed banking application but rather to investigate to what extent FADA mediated meaningful conversations about transactions between the instructor and students and between students themselves.

6.2.2.1 Case study 2: Group 3

In this setting, unlike that of the authentic lecture setting, students had prior knowledge of distributed systems. Thus, in order to ascertain their level of understanding of transactions within distributed systems, it was necessary to deploy FADA in a manner which challenged them to make explicit that understanding. This was facilitated through the instructor's use of FADA. She used FADA to build the logic of the banking application from the ground up in response to suggestions put forth by students. This enabled her to concretise their suggestions and through a process of simulation and active experimentation decipher their correctness and completeness. Thus, the instructor deployed FADA in a constructivist manner similar to that witnessed in the authentic lecture setting.

The first stage was designed to challenge students' understanding of the means by which one ensures reliable communication between distinct processes within a distributed system. The aim was to ascertain whether students would be able to realise the need for acknowledgements within the banking application. This is in order to ensure that each transfer message arrives at its intended destination. Such a probe was facilitated through the instructor's use of simulation. The instructor simulated the ability of a process to send a transfer message of a hundred euro to another process. On sending that transfer message, the sending process was deliberately implemented to deduct a hundred euro from its account. From the simulation rendered, only one student was able to spot the application's failure to account for whether or not a transfer message had been received by its intended recipient. Hence, in order to facilitate the remaining students in conceptualising the same failure, it was necessary for the instructor to re-enact the simulation and to deliberately cause the transfer message to fail. Such an action enabled the students to observe at first hand the consequences caused by the loss of the transfer message that was, the loss of a hundred euro from the system.

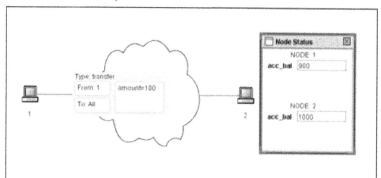

Figure 6-15a: A graphical representation of the simulation deployed by the instructor to re-enact the transfer of a €100 from node 1 to node 2. On sending the transfer message node 1 was implemented to automatically deduct a €100 from its account balance.

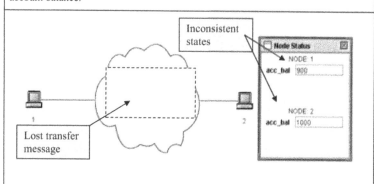

Figure 6-15b: A graphical representation of the manner by which the instructor triggered the failure of the transfer message by right clicking on it whilst in

transfer and causing it to disappear from the screen.

Figure 6-15: An overview of the simulation used by the instructor to assist him in giving students concrete representations of the consequences caused by the loss of the transfer message within the distributed banking application.

> *L: What happens if I lose that message? What happens to the state of my two bank servers?*
>
> *S1: Inconsistent*
>
> *L: How would I overcome that problem?*
>
> *S1: Transactions.*
>
> *L: So in terms of messages, what should I do?*
>
> *S2: You need an acknowledgement basically. You shouldn't subtract unless you receive an acknowledgment.*

Figure 6-16: A depiction of the manner by which the simulation rendered within Figure 6-15 enabled the instructor to engage students in higher order thinking so as to enable them overcome the loss of the €100 from the system.

Subsequently, the author was able to revert to the code frame to modify the behaviour of the application to include acknowledgements. This provided the platform from which the instructor could probe students' higher order thinking further to determine whether they would anticipate the need to allow for the potential loss of the acknowledgment message. Again, such a probe was facilitated through the use of simulation. The instructor visually re-enacted the loss of the acknowledgement message sent from process 2 to process 1 to confirm receipt of its transfer message. Such a graphical representation appeared to openningly challenge students' understanding of transactions and motivate them to dispute the possibility of a solution.

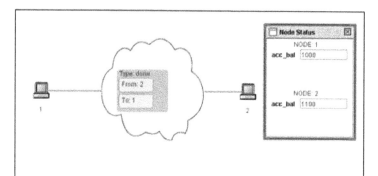

Figure 6-17a: A graphical representation of the amendments made by the instructor to the logic of the above simulation to enable node 2 to acknowledge receipt of node 1's transfer message. This is in order to enable node 1 to reliably deduct a €100 from its account balance only on receipt of an acknowledgement from node 2.

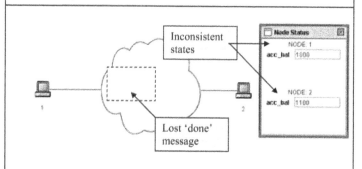

Figure 6-17b: A graphical representation of the manner by which the instructor triggered the failure of the acknowledgment message so as to enable her to probe students' higher order thinking as to how they would over come the presence of an extra €100 within the system.

Figure 6-17: An overview of the simulation deployed by the instructor to assist students in realising a means by which to combat the loss of the acknowledgement

L: *What happens if I lose the acknowledgement? What should I do?*

S2:   *There's no solution for that.*

S1:   *There is a solution.*

Figure 6-18: A depiction of the manner by which the aforementioned simulation in Figure 6-17 challenged students' higher order understanding of how to combat the issue of partial failure within the distributed banking application.

This led to a process of social negotiation which saw students reflect and evaluate each others' alternative perspectives and as a consequence, arrive at a mutual understanding and solution to the problem.

> *S2: In this situation, you cannot solve that as once you lose the communication, it can never happen, hence can never be solved.*

> *S4: What node 1 could do is it could send a message to node saying 'I want to transfer a hundred euro'. Node 2 will do nothing to its account. It will send back a message 'Yeah, I know you are going to send me a hundred euro'. Both accounts will still have a thousand euro. At that stage, node 1 having received the confirmation reduces a hundred euro from its account and sends a further message saying 'Now, add on your hundred'. If node 1 doesn't receive a response after a certain time, it can say 'you never followed up'.*

> *S2: Yeah that's right. That's the timeout procedure. That's the way around the problem.*

> *L: So essentially what node 1 could do is, it could send a transfer message and wait for twenty seconds or so, in order to receive back a reply. If it doesn't receive back a reply in that time, it can resend the transfer message.*

Students proposed the use of timeouts as a means of combating the loss of messages within the banking application but, in so doing, failed to predict the problem associated with the sending of duplicate transfer messages. On detecting the failure of a recipient to acknowledge receipt of its transfer message, a process would time out and resend the transfer message. This would cause the recipient to re-increment his account balance by a further one hundred euro leading to an extra one hundred euro within the system. Thus, in order to assist students in realising the inconsistency caused by the duplication, it was necessary for the instructor to revert to the code frame to modify the application to include the proposed timeout procedure. This enabled her to simulate the new behaviour of the application and as a consequence, enabled her to provide students with a concrete representation of the problem incurred. Students were then subsequently able to decipher a means by which one should acknowledge the receipt of a duplicate message through the use of sequence numbers. By associating with each message a unique identifier, a process was able to determine whether or not it had received that message previously.

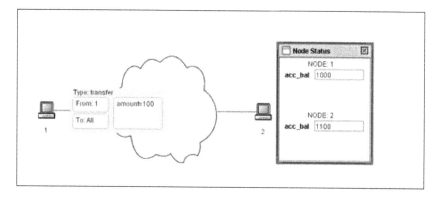

Figure 6-19: An overview of the graphical representation of the timeout procedure deployed by the instructor to assist students in identifying the shortcoming in its behaviour that is, its failure to account for the sending of duplicate transfer messages. In the above depiction, node 1 has timed out, and detected the failure of node 2 to acknowledge receipt of its transfer message. As a consequence, node 1 resends the transfer message to node 2.

> **L:**   *Straight away, I have a timer associated with the (transfer) message. So what should happen when that timer expires, it should resend the transfer message?*
>
> **L:**   *Which it does..*
>
> **S1:** *Gets out of sync again*
>
> **L:**   *So node 2 has added on another one hundred euro, doubled its value. Is there another work around for that?*

> ***L:*** *How can I tell node 2 to ignore the second transfer message?*
>
> ***S1:*** *Sequence numbers.*
>
> ***L:*** *If I associate with each message an id such that node 2 would know that its already received the first   transfer message so it will ignore the second.*

Figure 6-20: An overview of the manner by which the simulation within Figure 6-19 enabled the instructor to engage students in higher order thinking so as to enable them to first identify the algorithm's shortcoming as its failure to allow for the sending of duplicate transfer messages and to enable them to suggest a means by which to overcome it.

6.2.2.2 Case 3: Group 2

Unlike students in group 3, students in group 2 had no formal knowledge of the need for transactions within a distributed system, hence, FADA was used to give them a concrete grounding in that need. This was facilitated through the creation of the distributed banking application. As with group 3, this application was built from the ground up in a series of stages in the presence of students. This was in order to enable them to encounter real world problems associated with the lack of global knowledge within a distributed system and of the problems associated with partial failure. Consequently, students were able to offer solutions to overcome each problem encountered and indirectly through a process of active simulation by the instructor, decipher the correctness of the solutions posed. Subsequently, similar patterns of higher order dialogue were captured as those witnessed between the instructor and students in group 3 and in the authentic lecture setting. Such dialogue arose as a direct consequence of the instructor's use of FADA (See Figure 6-14). As with group 3, the instructor used FADA to implement and simulate the transfer of a hundred euro from one process to another within the system. This was in order to ascertain whether students would be able to identify the potential problem caused by the loss of the transfer message. On transferring a hundred euro, the sending process was implemented to automatically deduct a hundred euro from its account. The [6]simulation rendered by FADA enabled the instructor to re-enact the loss of the transfer message in transit and as a result, enabled her to engage students' higher order thinking to determine whether they would be able to firstly

---

[6] To view as a movie, open the folder '*Case3_group2*' in the enclosed cd and open *lost_ack.mov.*

identify the loss of the hundred euro from the system and secondly, whether they would be able to propose a means by which one could overcome it. From the responses obtained with respect to the instructor's probe, it is evident that student (S2) had garnered a clear understanding of the crux of the problem. He was able to correctly identify that the inconsistent state in each process's bank balance was caused by the failure of the sending process to await receipt of an acknowledgement from the receiving process. But whilst student (S1) was able to propose a means by which one could over come the loss through the use of acknowledgements, he was able to foresee its shortcoming that is, its potential to be lost as well. This is clearly indicated by his use of the 'IF' conditional in his response to the instructor's probe.

> **L:**   Can anyone spot any problems?
>
> **S2:**   Node 1 is still subtracting straight away.
>
> **S1:**   Only want it to subtract when it received back or IF it receives back a 'done' message.

As a consequence, the instructor, as in group 3, was able to amend the algorithm's behaviour to provide a concrete representation of the loss of the acknowledgement message (See Figure 6-17). Again, as a corollary of such actions, she was able to engage students in higher order thinking as to how they would overcome its loss.

> **L:**   What would happen if the 'done' doesn't get through?
>
> **S1:**   You effectively have the same problem on the other side.
>
> **L:**   There's a hundred euro astray. Any ideas as to ...
>
> **S1:**   You need a middle man, some one who can keep track of both of them perhaps.

Interestingly, student (S1) proposed a centralised solution to the problem that is, the use of another process to monitor the behaviour of all other processes and interactions within the system. But in doing so, he failed to foresee the potential problems associated with its loss, that is, he failed to equate the loss of a process to that of a message. Only on elucidation by the instructor was student (S1) able to comprehend the problem.

> L: Right, but what if that middle man fails?
> S1: Then...you would have to cancel the transaction.

In order to enable students to arrive at a solution to the loss of the acknowledgement message, it was necessary for the instructor to intervene to reframe the task in terms of the graphical representation depicted by FADA. Such an invention enabled student (S1) to put forward the use of a timeout procedure as a means of overcoming the loss of the acknowledgement.

> **L:**   What is node 1 doing? It is waiting for a message back.
> **S1:** Yes.
> **L:**   How long should it would for?
> **S1:** Oh, you could set a timer and if it doesn't receive back, well then,...the transfer can't go through or resend the transfer.

Figure 6-21: The manner by which the instructor used the above simulation to help students to arrive at a solution to the loss of the acknowledgement from node 2.

Subsequently, the instructor was able to amend the algorithm's implementation to include the timeout procedure and as a consequence, was able to probe students' higher order thinking as to whether they would be able to identify its shortcomings (See Figure 6-17).

> **L:**   If this message dies, it should resend now. So it resends it...so 2 should automatically send back that done. Things should be...
> **S2:** There's an inconsistency there
> **L:**   There is.
> **S2:** Node 2 is still adding even before node 1, irrespective of whether or not node 1 gets an acknowledgement.

[7]From the simulation rendered (See Figure 6-19), student (S2) was able to correctly decipher the state inconsistency caused by sending of duplicate transfer messages but in so doing, he failed to realise the root cause of the problem. Only on reiteration of the simulation and upon further reflection was he able to ascertain the shortcoming in the solution proposed by student (S1) that is, its failure to account for the sending of two identical transfer messages.

> S2:   It shouldn't be adding because it is the same message.

As a consequence of such a realisation, the instructor was able to move to the last stage of implementation and to demonstrate a means by which one could overcome the receipt of a duplicate message through the use of unique identifiers. By uniquely identifying each message that a receiving process is to receive, the receiving process will know if it has received the same message twice.

> L: So in that instance, we need to tell node 2 that it has already received that
>   message so you need to label those messages. Need to give them some sort
>   of id.

6.2.2.3 Discussion

As with the authentic lecture setting, similar levels of higher order engagement with an algorithm's behaviour were observed in each of the simulated lecture settings analysed. All of which were mediated and sustained through the functionality afforded by FADA. It appeared that the ability to use FADA to isolate and provide concrete representations of set aspects of an algorithm's behaviour enabled the instructor to pose higher order questions about its behaviour and challenged students' prior understanding of it. This motivated students to voice their own solutions and to collaborate to realise a mutual understanding of the problem at hand. This was clearly evident in stage two of the implementation process within case study 2, where the instructor's ability to re-enact the loss of the

---

[7] To view as a movie, open the folder 'Case3_group2' on the enclosed cd and click on *timeout_problem.mov*

acknowledgement message challenged students' understanding of the manner by which one recovers from such a loss.

Such a process was greatly facilitated by the level of real time interactivity afforded by FADA over the algorithm's behaviour. It appeared that the ability to cause one or more of an algorithm's components to fail during execution and the ability to visualise the changes in its state at each stage of implementation enabled the instructor to give students a real world grounding in the need to allow for the lack of global knowledge within a distributed system and for fault tolerance. This was also observed in case study three where the instructor's ability to re-enact the loss of the transfer message enabled her to engage students in higher order thinking as to how they would overcome it.

The creation of concrete representations of the solutions proposed by the students enabled them to reflect upon their soundness and also, collaborate to realise a mutual understanding of each solution's effectiveness. This was evidenced by stage three of the implementation process in case study three where the instructor was able to provide students with a concrete representation of the timeout solution proposed by student (S1) and as a consequence, was able to engage them in the higher order analysis of its correctness. Subsequently, student (S2) was able to reflect upon the solution proposed by student (S1) and upon reiteration of the simulation's behaviour identify its shortcoming as its failure to account for the sending of a duplicate transfer message. As a result of such actions, the students were able to engage in an iterative cycle of learning which enabled them to encounter concrete representations of the application's behaviour at various stages of implementation, which they could reflect upon and indirectly through the actions of the instructor experiment with and amend, leading to further concrete experiences, experimentations and reflections.

In such a setting, FADA differs from other teaching methodologies like for example; 'chalk and talk' in that it affords the instructor the ability to easily capture the dynamic and concurrent behaviour of a distributed algorithm. FADA frees the instructor from having to manually draw each stage of an algorithm's process and enables him to concentrate his time in engaging students in higher order discussions about its behaviour. Such a process is greatly facilitated by the level of real time interactivity afforded by FADA. Unlike static representations of an algorithm's behaviour, FADA enables one to experiment with the

167

behaviour of one or more processes in real time and demonstrate the immediate and concurrent effects of those changes on the overall behaviour of the algorithm and on its state. Equally, FADA enables one to truly test the correctness of the solutions proposed by students by enabling the instructor to amend the behaviour of the algorithm to reflect those changes and to simulate its behaviour in real time. This is something which, as evidenced in case study 3, enables students to arrive at a deep understanding of an algorithm's behaviour.

6.2.2.4 Interactive Presentation Questionnaire

In order to ensure the construct validity of findings arising from the analysis of the various lecture settings, it was necessary to administer a dedicated questionnaire (See Appendix A) to each student at the end of each lecture setting. This was in order to probe students' thoughts on whether they believed that as a result of using FADA that they had a better understanding of the algorithm's behaviour, that it had encouraged them to participate more in class and finally, that they had preferred it to other traditional teaching strategies such as chalk and talk. With respect to understanding, over 85% of students in each subject group believed that their understanding of distributed algorithms had increased as a result of using FADA. Many cited the ability to see and animate the algorithm's behaviour as assisting them in better understanding it.

> *'Because it was graphical, it made it easier to understand than just listening and reading text'.*

> *'Because seeing which philosophers could or could not eat when there were many requests helped me to better understand'.*

Others cited the ability to experiment with the algorithm's behaviour in real time that is, the ability, for example, to cause one or more of its components to fail as assisting them in better understanding it.

'By clearly, quickly and graphically showing the effects that changes have, it made it easier to place such changes within a context'.

'The simple visualisations and failures made them easier to understand and debug'

Finally, others cited the ability to map the graphical representation of an algorithm's behaviour to that of its underlying implementation as enabling them to better understand it and to identify problems associated with its behaviour.

'It allowed you to see the effect of, for example, dropped messages, in a concrete manner, which allowed the solutions to the problem to become more obvious'.

'You imagine what will happen and you get a picture which shows you immediately if you what you imagined your code did actually happens'.

Equally, in each of the subject groups, over 70% of students believed that FADA encouraged them to participate more in class. A similar finding was recorded with respect to whether students preferred FADA to other traditional teaching methodologies like for example, chalk and talk. Over 80% of students in each subject group preferred FADA. This was due to the manner in which it enabled them to render abstract concepts concrete and enabled them to experiment with their behaviours.

'More hands on, more demonstrative, better at communicating the subject'.

'Much easier to understand, less working out to do in your head'

6.3 Findings arising from FADA's use as a modification tool.

In order to ascertain to what extent FADA assisted students in higher order thinking, in engaging in higher order conversations with others, and in identifying and arriving at solutions to the problems posed within the algorithm's implementation, it was necessary to set them a task to complete. c Hence, this section primarily analyses the manner by which

FADA assisted students within group three to arrive at a solution to the problems posed by the issue of partial failure within the distributed address book application. This group was chosen for closer analysis due to their greater levels of experience with software designed for research purposes, their prior knowledge of distributed systems and their greater familiarity with Java. It was thought that by analysing the ways and means by which members of such a subject group interacted with FADA, one would gain greater insight into FADA's effectiveness as a tool in enabling them to identify problems associated with an algorithm's behaviour and in enabling them to define and implement ways by which to overcome those problems. Moreover, one would gain insight into its capacity to challenge students' prior knowledge of distributed systems.

The first to be considered are events which unfolded between a subset of four students from the aforementioned group. This is then followed by the analysis of a subsequent subset, consisting of two students. Again, the aim of the analysis, as stated previously, was to allow for literal replication, that is, to ascertain whether findings arising in the first group were replicated by the second and could be deemed a function of FADA's use.

6.3.1 Case study 4

In this setting, each of the four students was initially presented with an active simulation of the distributed address book application. This is an application which was designed to enable clients to update and retrieve an individual's address from the server. It was initially presented to students devoid of all fault tolerant behaviours. The aim of the exercise was for students to play with the simulation that is, to experiment with its behaviour in real time and on identifying problems associated with its behaviour to amend its implementation to overcome each. One interesting outcome of the latter interactions was the manner by which individuals were motivated and challenged to collaborate to realise a mutual understanding of the best means by which to overcome the issues of partial failure. This is clearly evidenced by the responses given by students with respect to the instructor's initial probe as to how to overcome the issue of server failure. [8]As a consequence of actively playing with the simulation, student (S2) was able to correctly identify the source of the failure as the

---

[8] To view as a movie, open the folder '*Case4_group3*' on the enclosed cd and click on detect_server_failure.mov.

loss of the acknowledgement from the server to the client informing it that it was alive. Subsequently, student (S1) was motivated to put forward a means by which one could overcome the loss by having the server initiate a timer and continually poll the client telling it when it was alive.

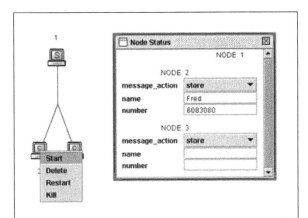

Figure 6_22a: A depiction of the manner by which the student (S2) initiated the behaviour of client2 so as to enable it to store Fred's details at the server. This was achieved by right clicking on client2 and selecting 'Start' from its menu of options.

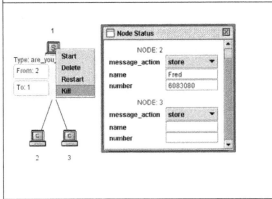

Figure 6_22b: As a consequence of its initiation, client 2

inquires of the server as to whether it is alive or not. Student
(S1) initiates server failure by right clicking on the server and
selecting 'kill' from its menu.

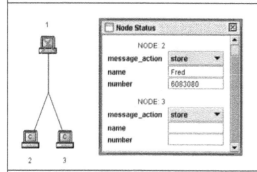

Figure 6_22c: As a consequence of student (S1)'s actions, the
server fails to respond to the client's request. Thus, the client is
unable to send its store message as it does not know whether
the server has failed or its request has failed to reach it.

Figure 6-22: A depiction of the manner by which student (S2) investigated the effects of
server failure on the application's behaviour.

> *L: Given the logic of the algorithm as is what is the first failure scenario that could*
> *affect it?*
>
> *S2: The server fails.*
>
> *L: How would you propose to overcome such a scenario?*
>
> *S2: If I don't receive a response from the server to whom am I going to send the*
> *data?*
>
> *L: So I need to....*
>
> *S1: Server needs to broadcast every twenty seconds that it is, the server.*

This appeared to challenge remaining students to come up with an alternate means by
which one resolves the loss. This led to a period of reflection and experimentation with the
application's behaviour which culminated in student (S2) putting forward the possibility of

two solutions to the problem at hand. These were; the client polling the server prior to sending a store message or the server continually polling its clients telling them when it was alive. However, by stating that the latter solution was easier to implement than the former, student (S2) challenged his peers to implement it.

> *S2: It can be done in two ways actually. The client asking the server whether 'it is the server' or the server broadcasting the 'I am server' all the time. It's easier if the server broadcasts, I would say...*

As a consequence, students failed to realise the efficiency in terms of message passing of the initial solution proposed by student (S1). Only through actively amending the initial given implementation of the application's behaviour to reflect that of the polling client solution were students provided with a concrete representation of the issue of redundancy associated with its behaviour. This was clearly evidenced by student's (S4) attempts to rationalise the logic of the aforementioned approach. By engaging others, student (S4) was able to realise the inefficiencies of always having the client ask the server prior to sending a store message if it was alive. Such a solution introduced latency into the application and meant that the client would always have to wait for an acknowledgement to its initial request prior to sending the store message.

> *S4: I've another problem because I have looked at it the other way. I have the clients polling the server saying 'are you awake'. When the server does when it receives 'are you awake', it says 'yes, I am'. Does now each of my clients have to wait for lets say five or ten seconds and if they don't get a 'yes, I am', do they have to look for another server?*
>
> *S2: It's more complicated that way.*
>
> *S4: It's not about sending the message; it's more about server failure. There's a separate acknowledgment that you send at the beginning of the message 'Are you a server', 'Yes, I am' 'Grand, here's my contact details' but there's another one that the server is constantly doing of like 'Are you awake?'... when you*

don't respond to me, I've got to look for another server or set some boolean variable to say 'definitely, don't send a request to him because he's not awake'.

S2: You have to consider it as a heartbeat thing, you know.

S4: Hmm

S2: The message saying 'I am the server', you have to consider this as a heartbeat approach. If you get it you can send, if you don't you can wait until you get something. It's as simple as that.

S4: Are we overcomplicating it though?

S2: You are overcomplicating it.

S4: Do we need to worry about failure in the server?

S2: Yes, because in the case of failure in the server, it will not send a heartbeat then the clients would wait until another server will be plugged in and it will start sending the heartbeats again. Then, they can continue their work.

S4: But do I need to know whether the server is plugged in or not if I don't want to send it a message or I don't want to update it or I don't want to check it. Does it matter to me?

S2: You should know that the server is there, you should not just send a message because in all cases, you will not get that acknowledgement from the server if it is dead. That's another thing when you send the store message you should get an acknowledgement and if you don't get an acknowledgement you know that the transaction was not done. This was another reason, probably server is down, its not there, unplugged etc.

S4: Is it not…….Is that like not done in the transaction before we send a message? When I send a message, say I am the client and you are the server, what I do is I go 'are you awake', 'Yeah, I am', 'Here's my message'.

S2:Yes, Yes, if we have it this way…If we are going to have the server sending 'I am the server' then going to have to remove the other one that says 'Are you the server?'. If you make the server send that periodically then by default you know that the server is there. You should just store, you don't need to ask 'are you the server? It's as simple as that.

S4: So, I'm just duplicating

S2: Yes, that's a duplication thing.

As a consequence of such social interactions, student (S4) was able to amend the logic of his proposed solution to overcome the issue of redundant message passing by having the client periodically poll the server to ascertain whether it was alive or not and on the basis of the state information held by the client relating to the server's vitality, enable the sending of a store message on a periodic basis. Such a solution eliminated the need for the client to always have to ask prior to sending a store message whether the server was alive or not. However, due to a limitation of the software, the student was unable to realise his solution to the loss of the server that of the addition of a second server as the underlying topology within FADA only currently supports one server.

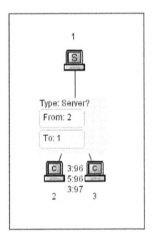

Figure 6-23: A graphical depiction of the manner by student (S4) rendered the behaviour of the distributed address book application to be fault tolerant. In the above representation, the first timer is probing the server every 5 secs to determine whether it is alive. The second timer is enabling client 2 to send a store message every 6 secs. This is dependent on the value of state information held on the client side as to whether the server is alive. The third timer is checking to determine whether the client has received the correct number of acknowledgments from the server's with respect to its store requests.

175

6.3.2 Discussion

With respect to each of the four pedagogical questions outlined in chapter five, there is evidence to suggest, from the above analysis of students' interactions (See Appendix I) with the distributed address book application, that the level of real time interactivity afforded by FADA over its behaviour enabled them to engage in higher order thinking about its process. Student (S2), as a consequence of his ability to cause one or more of the application's components to fail during execution, was able to correctly decipher that the shortcomings in its behaviour were related to its inability to account for the loss of the server and for the loss of server acknowledgements.

Moreover, the ability to easily modify the application's behaviour and simulate its behaviour appeared to motivate and encourage students to engage in higher order discussions about the best means by which to render it fault tolerant. This is clearly evidenced by the manner in which student (S4) deployed FADA to engage peers in higher order discussions about the best means by which a client could determine a server's vitality. Such discussions were facilitated by student (S4)'s capacity to provide graphical representations of his proposed solution coupled with his provision of voice over explanations of the latter. Such actions provided students with a concrete representation of his solution, one which they could reflect upon and isolate shortcomings from.

Moreover, the dual representations afforded by FADA of the application's behaviour enabled students to engage in an iterative cycle of learning. The graphical representations of the application's behaviour enabled students to encounter concrete representations of its process which they could reflect upon, experiment with in real time and abstract from. As a consequence, students were able to identify shortcomings in its behaviour which they could amend through the use of the code frame. Such amendments led to further concrete experiences as each could be executed as a simulation. This is in turn led to further reflections, experimentations and modifications.

6.3.3 Case study 5

Unlike case study four, this case study evolved into a number of distinct stages. These were three in total. Stage one saw both students choose to actively experiment with the distributed address book application on an individual level so as to enable them to each develop his own understanding of its behaviour and of the issues of partial failure affecting its process. Stage two saw students actively collaborate to realise a mutual understanding of the application's behaviour and to decipher ways by which to overcome its shortcomings. Such a process was facilitated not only by the level of real time interactivity afforded by FADA over the application's behaviour, but also, by the creation in tangent of a flow chart. This was created using pen and paper. The flow chart not only tracked students' mutual understanding of the application's process but also, the manner by which they had proposed to deal with issues of partial failure affecting it. Stage three saw students deploy the use of FADA to enable them to verify the logic of the flowchart derived in stage two.

In stage one, as in case study four, the level of real time interactivity afforded by FADA over the application's behaviour enabled student (S1) to develop a high level understanding of it. This is clearly evidenced by the manner in which, he, on completion of his experimentations with the application, was able to articulate his findings. Not only was he able to identify the dual functionality afforded by the application as its ability to store a customer's details and its ability to retrieve them but also, he was able to abstract out the application's overall failure to ensure the reliability of such actions by acknowledging their successful execution. When sending a request to the server to store a customer's details, the server was deliberately implemented by the author not to acknowledge the request, as such, it was implemented to never inform the client that its request had been successfully received.

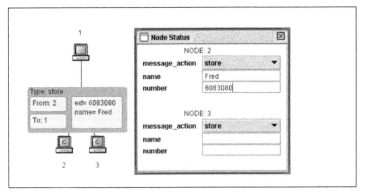

Figure 6-24a: The server receives a request from client 2 to store Fred's details.

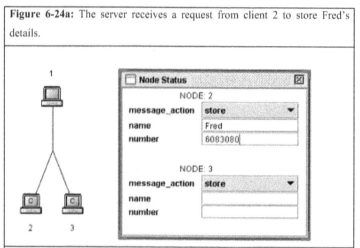

Figure 6-24b: Client 2 is waiting on an acknowledgement from the server to inform it that it has received its request. No acknowledgement is forth coming.

Figure 6-24: A graphical representation of the investigation undertaken by student (S1) to determine whether or not the server would acknowledge receipt of client 2's store request. From the second representation depicted above, one can see that the server has failed to acknowledge client 2's store request and as a consequence, client 2 never knows whether its request has been received by the server and has been successfully completed.

Student (S1) was able, as a consequence of his interactions with the application, to propose a means by which to overcome the aforementioned problem through the use of acknowledgements and a time out procedure. By amending the server to acknowledge receipt of a request sent to it by a client, the client would know that its request had been received. By associating a timer with the transfer of the request, a client would be prevented from waiting indefinitely for a reply and on expiration could resend its request to the server.

> *S1:   The problem here is a client needs to send a request. It should start a timer and leave a certain amount of time for the server to respond. If it doesn't*

respond, it should resend the request. You don't need to ....It's not like we
are....... Actually, I forgot there are two different things here. There's a
store action and a lookup action. So when we are storing something from
the client to the server, we have to make sure it gets stored and
acknowledged. We send the name and the number to the server and wait for
it to acknowledge it. So we have to put a timer on the machine sending it and
if it doesn't time out........Sorry, if the acknowledgement comes back in time
then everything is fine. If the timer runs out, there are two possibilities;
either it didn't get to the server or the reply from the server didn't come
back.

However, whilst the level of real time interactivity afforded by FADA assisted student (S1)
to come to a deep understanding of the application's behaviour, it appeared to challenge
student (S2)'s higher order understanding of message failure with in a distributed system.
This is evidenced by the manner in which he questioned student (S1) about the assumption
or assumptions that he had made about the nature of message failure within the
application's process. In so doing, he raised student's (S1) awareness to FADA's inability
to allow for latency that is, its failure to enable a message to be paused whilst in transit in
order to enable one to investigate the effects that such an action would have on the
application's behaviour.

S2:   *So, what are we assuming about the message? Say, we send a message and*
        we get a confirmation back and then it does arrive.
S1:   *It's delayed, you mean?*
L: *You can kill a message, but you can't delay a message in the simulation.*
S1:   *Don't worry about latency.*
S2:   *So if it doesn't get there we assume that?*
S1:   *If we don't get an acknowledgement back in the time we specify, we assume*
        that its lost or gone.

179

However, in questioning student (S1), similar to findings observed in case study 4, student (S2) was able to refine his immediate understanding of the application's process and refocus his attention on how to resolve the issue of a [9]lost message. This is evidenced by the manner in which he re-engaged with the simulation by actively killing messages and on completion, proposed the use of time out procedures to detect their loss.

S2:   So we can fix that by repeatedly sending a message until we get a reply.

However, whilst student (S1) was able to correctly identify the application's partial failure issues as the loss of the store message and its look up action, it was necessary for the instructor to intervene to raise his awareness and that of student (S2) to the potential loss of the initial request sent by the client to determine whether or not the server was alive. This was necessary as the sending of the two former messages was dependent upon the server being alive (See Figure 6-22).

L: But just before you advance, you have kind of skipped a step. If you run the simulation again and you actually right click on a client and hit 'start', it first detects the presence of.........

S1:   If it's alive or not. I forgot about that. So we have to first check if it's alive or not. If it's not alive then there is no point in sending........So if it's alive, you should start a timer for some predetermined amount of time, keep sending the 'Are you alive?' message until then don't do anything. So once we know that it's alive...can we assume that once it says 'it's alive', it's not going to die in the mean time?

L: Yes

S1:   Once we know that it's alive then we can send a message.

As a consequence of such an intervention, students were able to refocus their attentions and to tackle the issues of partial failure in order of precedence. In order to facilitate them in the latter process, student (S2) proposed the use of a flow chart. This was in order to enable

---

[9] To view the corresponding movie, open folder 'Case5_modification' and open handle_msg_failure.mov.

him to track the logic of the application's control flow and the manner by which they had proposed to overcome each partial failure issue encountered.

In tackling the issue of server failure, student (S1) proposed the use of numbered acknowledgements but on articulation of his proposal to student (S2), and after a period of active experimentation and reflection with the simulation, he reneged upon his solution.

> S1:   *By starting a timer when we send it and if you don't get a numbered acknowledgement, a specific acknowledgement back……..In other words, what your basically doing when you send this message your essentially sending a unique number. Usually, the way this works is you alternate between 0 and 1 so it's like a sliding window protocol. You send a message saying….the first message you send is 'Are you alive?' and we label that id zero and we send that off and start the timer and if we time out we just send it again.*
>
> *……………………………*
>
> S1:   *Let me think……..Do we need to number the alive messages?*

This was because he realised that the process of uniquely identifying each 'alive' message served no other purpose other than to add to an implementation overhead. Instead, he proposed only to associate numbered acknowledgements with the sending of a store message. By associating a unique identifier with each store message, the server could use that identifier to uniquely acknowledge each request sent to it by a client.

> S1:   *No, it's not because it's either alive or not. The alive packets don't have to be numbered. We keep sending the alive packets until we get a reply back. Once, it is alive then send the requests. We'll do one at a time. We'll do store message first. That packet will have to have an id associated with it. Next step, start the timer and essentially wait. So the decision here is a time out….question mark… yes or no. If yes, go here… If timeout…*
>
> S2:   *Send another message*
>
> S1:   *Send the exact same message thing again.*

181

However, in proposing the use of numbered acknowledgements, student (S2) looked perplexed and questioned their need.

> S2:   *Do we need to number the replies?*

Only through a process of higher order engagement with student (S1) was one able to decipher the root of student (S2)'s internal cognitive conflict. Student (S2) had amended the flow chart to acknowledge the receipt of a store message by sending back its contents and in so doing, had correctly spotted the overhead in terms of redundancy of using both methods, that is, of using both numbered acknowledgements and the contents of a message to confirm receipt of that message. By discussing this with student (S1), they were able to reach a consensus and decide on the use of one method but not both. They decided for reasons of practicality to use the content of a message as a means of confirming receipt of a message. This was because the flowchart had already been updated with the latter solution.

> S2:   *What do I need the id for?*
>
> S1:   *Because, I'm sending two names at the same time Bill and Fred.*
>
> S2:   *If I'm going to acknowledge them by going through this (points to flowchart drawing)*
>
> S1:   *But I don't know in what order the server will reply.*
>
> S2:   *The acknowledgment will consist of…….If the server sends a message back what's it going to be? Will it contain the same name and number that I just sent?*
>
> S1:   *That's one way of doing it.*
>
>   *… … … … … … … … … …*
>
> S1:   *It's irrelevant which system you choose. It doesn't make a difference. Just as long as we get back some information to acknowledge that you stored the correct information.*
>
> S2:   *So which system are we choosing?*
>
> S1:   *We may as well send back the name and number and ignore the id.*

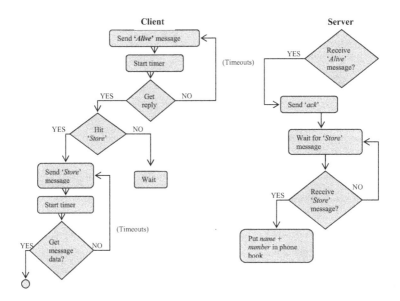

Figure 6-25: An overview of the flowchart logic created by student (S1) and student (S2).

However, in updating the flowchart, student (S1) realised the fruitlessness in maintaining such an artefact particularly with respect to capturing the behaviour of distinct processes within a distributed system. The flowchart failed to enable them to adequately capture the concept of concurrency within the application's behaviour that is, it failed to enable them to effectively capture the creation and sending of multiple requests by a client or clients within the application. This is clearly evidenced by student (S1)'s reactions to student (S2)'s attempts to modify the logic of the chart to depict the sending of multiple requests and also, by the comments made by the instructor as to the quality of his edits.

> S1:   We need to fix the stage in here. This checks the content we are storing. We
>   need to redraw it as it's a bit of a mess. Oh, Jesus, we are going to have to

183

> *start a timer for each message that it sends. A flow chart isn't the best way*
> *to support this.*
>
> ....
>
> *L: It's like abstract art.*

Yet, the task of trying to articulate his dissatisfaction with the flowchart to student (S2) appeared to allude student (S1) to the overhead in the design of the application's initial process that of always having to poll the server prior to sending a request.

> *S1:   Do you know what I am saying here. This works fine for sending one*
> *message but imagine we are sending........This flowchart doesn't handle*
> *essentially concurrency because you could send a message......I don't*
> *know.......Every time, you are sending message, you are sending an 'alive'*
> *message first?*

[10]This provided the instructor with an opportunity to engage students in a higher order dialogue as to an alternate means by which to detect the loss of the server.

> *L: Ok, well now, lets put it this way. That is the way the application is built at*
> *present but it's not set in stone. You may come up with alternative ways by*
> *which I can determine whether the server is alive. Is there another way that*
> *I can determine ....*

Such a dialogue appeared to challenge students' prior understanding of message passing within a distributed system and alert them to the need to account for redundancy in their solutions. Yet despite uncovering a more efficient means by which to detect the presence of the server, neither student opted to implement it, rather each chose to use FADA to test the viability of their initial solution documented within the flowchart. This may have been

---

[10] To view as a movie, open folder '*Case5_group3*' on the enclosed cd and click on
flowchart_shortcoming.mov

because of the easy manner by which FADA enabled one to amend the behaviour of the application, challenged them to realise a graphical and active representation of their flowchart's logic.

> S1:   *You can determine it's alive by receiving back an acknowledgement. I mean that's another way of determining it's alive.*
>
> L: *But is there a way that I can get round having to always ask 'Are you alive?'. How can I presume it's alive? What can the server do to help me as a client?*
>
> S1:   *The server can resend......Is that a three point acknowledgement thing? I don't remember how this works. Because, it's failure....*
>
> L: *Ok, all I'm saying is that it's a bit redundant having the client always ask the server 'Are you alive?', 'Are you alive?'*
>
> S1:   *I'm not sure it is. I'm trying to remember the way it works in reality.*
>
> L: *Could not the server continually poll the client?*
>
> S1:   *OK, alright. The problem is that I'm trying to think of the way an actual reply request mechanism works. So you are saying, we can also have a polling server which broadcasts essentially a heart beat to the clients. If that's the case then we don't have to worry about the alive messages as we are getting a heart beat.*

In order to do so, it was necessary for them, in the first instance, to map the logic of the flowchart to that of the application's implementation. This was in order to enable them to clarify and identify any shortcomings in their higher order understanding of the application's process and also, to enable them to quickly locate areas within its implementation which needed to be amended in order to render them fault tolerant. [11]As a consequence of student (S2)'s verbal mapping of the logic of the flowchart to that of the application's implementation, student (S2) was able to spot the inadequacies within the former that is, its failure, in the first instance, to account for the sending of a look up action.

---

[11] To view as a movie, open folder '*Case5_group3*' on the enclosed cd and click on *modify_flowchart_logic.mov*

On receiving a reply back from the server, the application was automatically implemented to either send a store message or a look up action. However, student (S2) failed to capture the dual functionality afforded by the application within the flowchart. Only on elucidation by student (S1) was student (S2) able to amend his own understanding of the application's behaviour and that of the flowchart's.   Thus, the graphical representation afforded by the flowchart coupled with the textual representation afforded by FADA of the application's implementation enabled students to attain a deeper understanding of the application's process.

S1:   *If we receive back that which says 'I am the server'*

S2:   *Then we go here and send a message.*

S1:   *Does that say 'Hit store'?*

S2:   *If you hit store then you say yes to that. If you don't this is going to wait.*

S1:   *No. It's either one or the other.*

S2:   *It's either one or what?*

S1:   *or else find number*

......

S2:   *We are missing a piece then.*

S1:   *What are we missing?*

S2:   *If you hit store then this, you don't hit store then we...find is it? Find number? ....Send find message*

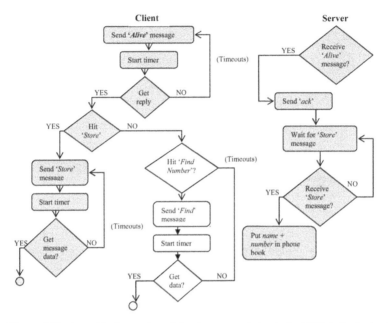

Figure 6-26: A graphical overview of the changes made by student (S2) to the logic of the client's side to capture its ability to query the server for a customer's contact details. All changes are depicted in white in the above representation.

Only on modifying the application's implementation were students able to decipher the robustness and correctness of their proposed solutions to the issues of partial failure affecting the application's process. This is clearly evidenced by the manner in which student (S2) amended the behaviour of the server side to acknowledge receipt of a store message by sending back a copy of it. However, in attempting to do so, student (S1) intervened to alert student (S2) to what he considered to be a shortcoming in its implementation that is, its failure to allow them to compare the two messages to decipher whether they were the same.

S1: *I can see problems trying to compare the two message objects because*

S2: *Of this (pointing to the original message instance)?*

S1: *No, when this is called again it will be a different object. It will be a new message. We can't just compare the objects. Do you see what I am saying? This gets called every time a thing comes into the machine; a message comes into the machine. We are going to have to compare these two.*

S2: *What?*

S1: *It's a new method being run. When the methods are run again, it will a new message object...so we won't be able to compare the two so that won't work. We should just do it the real simple way. The problem here is that we've said lets just send the same object back that not going to work essentially...So what we should do is send back a..........If we get anything back it implies that it has been received because we are not sending two in a row.*

But in so doing, student (S1) failed to realise that the failure to compare the messages was not due to the fact that the messages were separate message objects but due to the fact that student (S2) was attempting to send back a copy of a message which had the same destination address as that of its sender. Such an implementation would mean that upon execution the message rather than being sent to its intended destination (the client), would be sent to the server itself. This would result in the client continually timing out waiting on an acknowledgement from the server to its store message. As a consequence of student (S1)'s intervention and student (S2)'s failure to defend or simulate his amendments, a decision was made to only enable a client to send at most one request at any one given time. This resulted in them creating a blank acknowledgement message which the server would send to confirm receipt of a client's request.

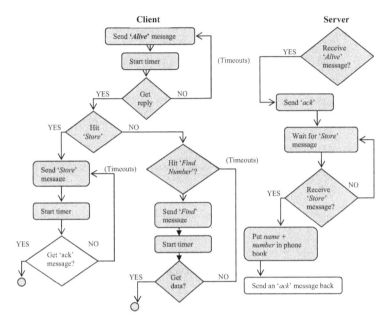

Figure 6-27: A graphical overview of the amendments made by the students to the flowchart to depict the capacity of the server to acknowledge receipt of a 'store' with a simple 'ack' message. All amendments are depicted in white in the above representation.

In so doing, the students reduced the level of flexibility and level of sophistication afforded by the application by only enabling a client to send at most one request at any given time. If clients were to send more than one request at any given time, given the latter implementation they would not as a consequence know which of their requests had been received by the server and in what order. However, such an implementation challenged students (S1) higher order understanding of the manner in which a reliable reply request protocol works within a distributed system. This caused him to engage in a process of reflection which saw him re-evaluate his decision to abandon student (S2)'s initial proposal and confirm its plausibility. Yet despite this, he chose not to revert to the solution. This may have been because he had reconciled himself to the assumption that a client would only ever send one request at any given time and based upon that assumption, there was no need to compare the acknowledgment returned by the server to that of the original message as the mere presence of the acknowledgment confirmed its receipt.

> *S1:   We could have done it by sending back the exact same thing using a global temporary object that's what we should have done.*

However, interestingly, on executing the behaviour of their agreed upon solution, students encountered the exact same problem that they would have encountered had they simulated the initial solution that is, the acknowledgement rather than being sent to the requesting client was returned to the server. This was because students had unwittingly passed a copy of the original store message to the client rather than the new message object they had created.

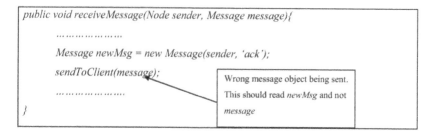

```
public void receiveMessage(Node sender, Message message){

    ... ... ... ... ... ...

    Message newMsg = new Message(sender, 'ack');

    sendToClient(message);                 Wrong message object being sent.
                                           This should read newMsg and not
    ... ... ... ... ... ....                message
}
```

Figure 6-28: A depiction of the students' failure to pass the correct message object to the *sendToClient* method so as to enable the server to acknowledge receipt of a client's request with a simple blank message called 'ack'. In the above implementation, students have in fact passed to the *sendToClient* method a copy of the original store request () sent to the server by the client. This message has associated with it the server's address and will result in the server continually sending to himself a copy of the client's store request.

However, despite being able to correct their mistakes through editing the implementation of the latter within the code frame, neither student was able to back track and map the logic of the aforementioned corrections to that of student (S2)'s initial solution. This may have been because neither student had a concrete cognitive representation of the initial solution in action as it had never been simulated. Perhaps if they had, then the graphical representations afforded by such a simulation may have assisted them in realising the added value of student (S2)'s initial solution and its level of sophistication. Such a conjecture is plausible as the ability to simulate the application's behaviour at various stages of implementation appeared to assist students in identifying further shortcomings in their higher order understanding of its process. This is clearly evidenced by the manner in which they had implemented the behaviour of the timeout procedures deployed to detect the loss of the server and that of the client's store messages. On simulating the latter, students were confronted by a number of endlessly repeating timers.

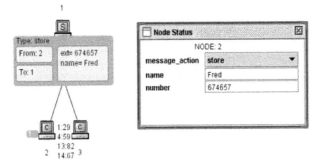

Figure 6-29: A graphical representation of the consequences incurred by the students' failure to realise the need within the application's process to cancel the timeout procedures on logical completion of their functions.

This appeared, in the first instance, to baffle them, but, subsequently, forced them to engage in a process of reflection which saw them recognise the need to cancel each upon completion of its function.

S2:   *Why isn't this dying?*

.....

S1:   *What actually went wrong that time?*

S2:   *You're suppose to cancel the timers.*

However, in order to enable them to determine when and where to cancel each timer, it was necessary for them to revert to the code frame. This was in order to enable them to iterate through the logic of the application's implementation to identify appropriate locations in which to cancel a timer. However, whilst student (S1) was able to correctly decipher the high level need to cancel a timer once it had finished executing, he failed to realise that within the current implementation all timers were executing within one or more loop structures. However, these loop structures were hidden from view. They were encapsulated inside the logic of a particular method of the framework's API which when invoked executes the behaviour of a timer repeatedly at set intervals. Such a decision was taken to encapsulate the latter functionality so as to ease the burden in terms of implementation time of realising the timer behaviour. Thus, in order for students to be able to cancel a timer, it was necessary for them to locate the logical point within the application's behaviour when that timer's functionality was no longer required. This is when the client has received an acknowledgement from the server to say that it has successfully received its request. In order for students to be able to realise this, it was necessary for the instructor to intervene. As a consequence of her intervention, students were able to reframe their higher level understanding of the purpose of each timer and its function. As a result, they were able to implement their behaviour appropriately.

S1:   *Ok, open up the client code.*

S2:   *When we call a timer like so when do we need to cancel it?*

S1:   *So what happens is... when the timer times out, it will send it again so we*
        haven't taken into account when actually get it back. W should kill straight
        after schedule shouldn't we?

L: *No*

S2:   *Hang on (checking flowchart)*

L: *You are creating a timer on the store message for what reason?*

S1:   *So that we can distinguish between that and the 'alive' messages.*

L: *No, what's the purpose of the timer on the store message?*

S2:   *So that we…*

S1:   *Waiting for an echo.*

L: *So….essentially, you send off a store message, you need to determine whether the server has stored that message or not.*

S1:   *Yeah so?*

L: *So surely if the server acknowledges the store then I should cancel the timer.*

6.3.4   Discussion

As in case study four, the ability to actively engage with the application's behaviour in real time by causing one or more of its components to fail and or by changing its state enabled students to develop a high level understanding of its process and of the issues of partial failure affecting it. This is evidenced by the manner in which the ability to initiate a client's request, to associate with that request a customer's details and to, subsequently, cause that request to fail during transit, enabled student (S1) to correctly identify the application's overall shortcoming as its failure to offset the loss of a request through the use of a timeout procedure coupled with that of acknowledgements. Moreover, there is evidence to suggest that the ability to engage with an application's behaviour in real time challenged students' prior understanding of distributed system concepts and motivated them to engage the services of others so as to enable them to arrive at a deeper understanding of them. This is evidenced by the manner in which the ability to re-enact the loss of a message prompted student (S2) to engage student (S1) in a higher order discussion as to its meaning. Did it, in the context of the application mean that the message was delayed or that the message was lost?   As a consequence of such interactions, student (S2) was able to reframe his understanding of a failed message and subsequently, like student (S1) decipher a means by which to over come it.

Moreover, there is evidence to suggest that the ability to modify the application's behaviour and to simulate its process, further enabled students to identify shortcomings in their understanding of it. This is evidenced by the manner in which the task of modifying the application's behaviour to reflect that of the flowchart alerted students to inadequacies within the latter that is, its failure to terminate the behaviour of timers on logical completion of their tasks. On amending and simulating the behaviour of the application to reflect that of the flowchart students were confronted with a number of endlessly repeating timers. Such a confrontation alerted them to the need, not only, to cancel the timers but to also cancel them from the client side as this is from where they had originated. The ability to switch to the code frame scaffolded students in the aforementioned task by enabling them to quickly locate the region within the implementation code that needed to be changed.

Equally, the ability to enable students to immediately upon modification of the application's behaviour to simulate its process, allowed students to verify the logic of their amendments and to decipher whether they had functioned as first thought. This is clearly evidenced by the manner in which students simulated the behaviour of the server after modifying its implementation to send an acknowledgement to a client to confirm receipt of its request. In so doing, students were graphically alerted to the logical error in their implementation that is, its failure to send the acknowledgment message to the client. As a consequence, they were able to map the logical error to the relevant section of code within the server's implementation. By reverting to the implementation held within the code frame, students were able to amend its behaviour to correct the error and to re-execute it to verify its correctness.

As a consequence, students were able to engage in an iterative cycle of learning. The ability to simulate the behaviour of the application enabled them to encounter concrete representations of its behaviour, which they could reflect upon and abstract from. The ability to amend the behaviour of the application led to further concrete experiences which subsequently led to further reflections and amendments. However, it should be noted that in order for students to successfully identify all of the application's partial failure issues and to realise ways by which to overcome them, it was necessary for the instructor to intervene at different intervals. This was in order to reframe problems so as to assist students in realising solutions. This was clearly evidenced by the manner in which the instructor intervened to scaffold and facilitate students to realise a solution to the problem of endlessly repeating timers.

6.3.5 Modification Questionnaire

Again, in order to ensure the construct validity of findings arising from the analysis of each of the laboratory settings, it was necessary to administer a questionnaire (See Appendix B) at the end of each session. This was in order to ascertain to what extent students perceived the capacity to modify the behaviour of the application as helping them to better understand it, to what extent they found the ability to interact with the behaviour of application in real time helped them to better understand it and to what extent they believed that the use of visualisations helped them to better understand the application's process. With respect to modification, all students within [12]group 2 and 3 and 95% of students in [13]group 1 believed that it enabled them to acquire a better understanding of the application's behaviour. With regards to real time interaction, again all students in groups 1, 2 and 3 believed that the ability to interact with, play with the components of the application's behaviour in real time helped them to better understand it. 79% of students in group 1 believed that visualisations helped them to better understand the application. 100% of students within [14]group 3 believed that visualisation in general assists them in understanding how an algorithm functions. A similar finding was recorded in group one with 100% of students believing that visualisation assists them in understanding the behaviour of an algorithm.

6.4: Findings with respect to instructors' perceptions of FADA's pedagogical value.

Given the capacities in which each of the three instructors used FADA, outlined in chapter five, each was asked to reflect upon and define what he perceived as its pedagogical value in that instance.

The instructor (L2) used FADA to set students a task which required them to simulate the behaviour of one of two algorithms. These were the ring based election algorithm and the bully election algorithm. The undergraduate class was asked to implement the behaviour of the ring based election algorithm whilst the postgraduate class was asked to implement both, the ring based election algorithm and the bully algorithm. In each case, each implementation had to allow for the need to detect failure that is, to detect the loss of a

---

[12] Total participant number between group two and three was sixteen
[13] Total participant number within group 1 was sixteen.
[14] Total participant number in group 3 was four.

message and/or node and depending on whether the status of a failed node was that of a monitor, to permit the election of a new monitor. Each student group was offered a basic tutorial on the use of FADA. This focused on the use of its interface features like for example, its wizard. However, details relating to the manner in which one deployed the relevant methods of the framework API to derive the logic of an algorithm were left largely un-investigated. This was in order to ascertain to what extent students would be able to garner an understanding of the aforementioned methods from their independent study of their behaviours as documented within the relevant help files encapsulated inside FADA.

In the above capacity, the instructor believed that FADA had a 'twofold' pedagogical effect. It enabled students, in the first instance, not only to visualise their own conceptual understanding of an algorithm's behaviour, but also, enabled them to visualise and observe its concurrent and dynamic operations. The latter is something which is not easily captured using text or diagrammatical means. In the second instance, it provided an environment which scaffolded and enabled students to concentrate solely on the implementation of the algorithm's logic without having to worry about the implementation of low level details like for example, that of infrastructure.

> 'It's a two-fold pedagogical value. First of all, I think visualisation of distributed algorithms is a good thing because it enables the student to see what's going on, in particular, as some algorithms have nodes operating in parallel. This is an inherent limitation to all text or diagrammatical representations as it is more or less bound to a sequential form. The second value is that students are enabled to actually implement an algorithm without too much worry about details of the infrastructure. They can in fact focus on the algorithm and how it works and won't get distracted by system specific or low level details. FADA lets them focus nicely on the high level aspects of the algorithms'.

Moreover, he believed, in line with the theory of constructionism, that by requiring students to build their own understanding of an algorithm's behaviour, students gain, as a consequence of the greater effort required, a better understanding of its process.

'I found that students who implemented the Bully algorithm using FADA seems to spend much more time thinking about what's going on in that algorithm than before. Previously, I believed some students might have learnt off by heart steps of the algorithm without actually understanding its concepts.'

In [15]each student group, one hundred percent of students completed the task. The average mark awarded for the undergraduate group was seventy nine percent and that of the postgraduate group was seventy percent. The postgraduate group were found to be more challenged by the exercise. This was due to the heterogeneous nature of their academic backgrounds. Many of these students had come from non-computer science backgrounds and thus, were learning how to programme for the first time. Hence, they found the task more difficult to complete than the undergraduate students. The undergraduate students had three years prior experience of programming within the object oriented paradigm.

'The MSc students with their more heterogeneous background (some having done undergraduate degrees in entirely different subject areas) were more challenged with this coursework. However, I believe this had nothing to do with the material or FADA, but can be attributed to the fact that some students didn't know Java at the start of the semester and were struggling to learn Java whilst already progressing through the course.'

With respect to the instructor (L1), as previously defined in chapter five, he deployed FADA in one of two different ways. These were as an interactive presentation device in class and as a tool to enable students to modify the behaviour of the dining philosophers' algorithm to overcome problems of deadlock and starvation associated with its implementation. As an interactive presentation tool, he believed that FADA had a two fold pedagogical effect in that instance. It provided dual representations of the algorithm's behaviour, which he could deploy to scaffold students in mapping the source of a graphical error in the algorithm's behaviour to that of a particular section in its implementation.

---

[15] Total participant number in the undergraduate group was fifty and in the postgraduate group was thirty five.

Moreover, it enabled him to actively modify the behaviour of the algorithm in real time and to demonstrate visually the changes reaped upon it by that modification. Such perceptions echoed those of students within the learning setting (See section 6.2.2.4).

> 'It is useful to be able to point to the code, modify it and demonstrate the change'

However, unlike instructor (L2), instructor (L1) would have preferred the use of an API that reflected the implementation of low level details relating to the algorithm's behaviour like for example, those relating to infrastructure. This was in order to give students a real world grounding in and understanding of the implementation overheads involved in such a process. In terms of its pedagogical value as a modification tool, the instructor believed that its value lay in its ability to enable him through a process of simulation to quickly ascertain students' conceptual understanding of the algorithm's dynamic and concurrent process. As a consequence, this in turn enabled him to reflect upon his own teaching practices when presenting such material so as to enable him to better assist students in acquiring a base understanding of its behaviour.

> 'It enabled me to quickly see whether a student had successfully completed the work. It also quickly showed any problems students may have had and alerted me to the need to better cover them in class'.

Moreover, like instructor (L2), he believed that the overall pedagogical value of enabling students to modify the behaviour on algorithm lay in its ability to enable them to acquire a deep understanding of the algorithm's process. This was facilitated through the students' ability to modify, simulate and actively experiment with the algorithm's behaviour in real time.

> 'Being able to play with the algorithm in real time was nice........it helped them to know if their solution was correct and enabled them to correct it if it wasn't'

198

Like instructor (L1) and instructor (L2), the instructor (L3) used FADA in one of two different ways. These were as a tool to enable him to build sample simulations for his own use and as a tool to enable his own research student to build his own representation of an algorithm's behaviour. From his reflections on his own use of FADA, he believed that its pedagogical value lay in its ability to enable him to dynamically capture and convey to others visually the changes reaped by an algorithm's behaviour on the state and behaviour of each process within a distributed system. This is behaviour which is not easily captured by traditional teaching methodologies like for example, chalk and talk or power point presentation slides.

> 'Teaching a topic like networks, which is inherently dynamic by its nature, just cannot be done well using chalk and talk or even power point, whereas a dynamic representation of a dynamic process provides learners with the opportunities to develop a deeper and more authentic understanding of the processes involved.'

Moreover, he believed, similar to instructor (L1), that the provision of dual representations of an algorithm's behaviour enabled him to assist and scaffold others in mapping problems incurred in the graphical representation of an algorithm's behaviour to that of its implementation.

> 'The idea of a multi-modal way of teaching networks is wonderful since it will appeal to a greater range of learners with different learning preferences, and it can also help scaffold the learning experience for the student by providing both an algorithmic and visual representation of a process'.

Equally, he believed that by enabling students to create their own representations of an algorithm's behaviour, to simulate the latter and experiment with them in real time that FADA enabled them to acquire a deeper understanding of its process. This he believed was greatly facilitated by FADA's added capacity to enable them on identifying shortcomings within the algorithm's behaviour to amend its implementation and to re-simulate it so as to enable them to further experiment with the algorithm's behaviour in real time and modify it.

6.5: Operational Effectiveness

This section is subdivided into two main subsections. First, it outlines findings with respect to what extent learners within each of the three student groups outlined in section 5.2 found FADA to be easy to learn how to use, effective in enabling them to complete their tasks and efficient in enabling them to modify the behaviour of an algorithm in a timely manner. Secondly, it documents findings from the view point of the instructors defined in section 5.2 as to what extent they found FADA easy to learn how to use, effective in enabling them to create sample active simulations for use in their own teachings and efficient in enabling them to create the simulations in a timely manner. Moreover, it documents findings as to what extent instructors were satisfied with the overall features and functionality provided by FADA.

6.5.1 The operational effectiveness of FADA from the viewpoint of the learners within group 1, 2 and 3.

With respect to how easy FADA was to learn how to use, all student groups, bar group 1, were given a two hour window in which to amend the behaviour of their respective algorithms to overcome set problems of partial failure affecting its process like for example, the loss of a message. Prior to each of the simulated lecture settings, no student had encountered FADA and thus, was not familiar with it as a piece of software or with its function. From the analysis of the video captured, all students successfully completed their initial task of identifying all possible failure scenarios that could affect the behaviour of the algorithms and subsequently, were able to put forward solutions to overcome each within the two hour time period given to them. In order for them to arrive at those solutions, it was necessary for them to familiarise themselves first with the interactive features of each simulation and, second, to experiment with them to investigate what effects the loss of, for example, a message, would have on the algorithm's behaviour.

In the case of group 2 and 3, all students correctly identified the partial failure issues relating to the distributed address book application as its failure to account for the loss of the server, the loss of a client's store message and equally, the loss of a client's look up request. All students within the aforementioned groups successfully implemented solutions to overcome the loss of the server and the store message but no student implemented a solution to overcome the loss of the look up request. This was because there was not enough time within the two hour slot to do so, but all, were able to verbally recognise that the implementation of the solution was the same as that for the store message. In order for students to be able to realise their solutions, it was necessary for them to consult the inbuilt help documentation to ascertain what methods of the FADA's framework API they should deploy in each instance.

With respect to group 1, they were given a one week period in which to complete their task of amending the behaviour of the dining philosophers' algorithm to overcome issues of deadlock and starvation. Of the sixteen students within the group, 75% successfully completed the task that is, implemented solutions to overcome the issues of deadlock and starvation associated with the dining philosophers' algorithm's process.

With respect to FADA's effectiveness in enabling each student group to complete their tasks, students were asked, via a questionnaire (See Appendix B), to rate the ease of use of each of the methods belonging to the framework's API, which they had deployed to enable them to render the behaviour of the algorithm as fault tolerant. A five point likert scale was deployed to enable them to rate the ease of use of each method on a scale ranging from very easy to very hard. Over 70% of students within group 2 and 3 found methods relating to each of the following easy to use. These were; create a node, create a message, retrieve content from a message, put content in a message and send a message. Similarly, 70% of students in group 1 found the task of creating a message, creating a node, and sending a message easy to implement. With respect to the ability to be able to create a timeout procedure within FADA, 16% of students in group 3 found this task hard to implement, whilst 23% of students in group 1 equally found it hard to implement. This may have been due to the fact that in order to create a time out procedure within FADA, a three step process is required, which involves creating the timer object, scheduling the timer instance for execution and defining what action it should take on elapsing. All other framework methods within FADA require only one step of customisation in order for their behaviours to be realised (See Appendix E for a break down of all findings derived from the administration of the usability questionnaire).

6.5.2 The operational effectiveness of FADA from the viewpoint of the instructors.

From the analysis of each of the instructor's responses to questions posed within the questionnaire defined in Appendix C, the following findings were garnered. All three instructors found FADA easy to learn how to use. All used it to create sample active simulations for use within their own learning settings.   All found the support documentation enclosed within FADA to be clear, concise and complete. Each took on average one to three hours to create a simulation of an algorithm's behaviour using FADA. All found FADA's framework methods to be in the main easy to use. However, both instructor (L1) and instructor (L2) expressed a need for the execution of the time out procedures to be synchronised with that of the animation speed. By not having them synchronised, it was possible for the behaviour of a timeout procedure to be invoked prior to the safe arrival of a message which was intended to negate its function.

> L2:   *'Problems with timers relate to the use of 'real-time' timers instead of 'simulation-time' timers. Sending messages (and their visualisation) can take some noticeable time, especially if messages are sent individually and the networks become some what larger. For the bully algorithm, I wanted to implement a time out mechanism to determine whether a response is sent in time or a node might have crashed. With larger networks, however, I found that my timers timed out as slow sending of messages caused network congestion. Using 'simulation time', this would have had less impact as time would conceivably pass 'slower' while all messages are being sent. My solution is here is actually a quick and dirty hack. I have just set the timers to empirically determine the values that work well for small and medium sized networks.'*

6.6 Summary

The aim of this research was to investigate to what extent the algorithm visualisation approach adopted in this thesis enhances the teaching and learning of distributed algorithms. In order to answer this question, it was necessary to encompass the viewpoint of the learner and the instructor and also, to assess the effectiveness of the approach from a pedagogical stance and an operational one. To do so, a multiple case study methodology was adopted. This enabled the author to assess the pedagogical and operational effectiveness of FADA within real contexts and hence, provided a real world insight into its use and potential.

With respect to pedagogical effectiveness, one of four research questions were posed. These were designed to explore to what extent FADA enabled learners to engage in higher order thinking about an algorithm's behaviour, facilitated them to engage in higher order discussions about an algorithm's process, supported them in solving algorithmic problems and lastly, enabled them to engage in an iterative cycle of learning. Findings showed that when used as an interactive presentation tool within a lecture setting the level of real time interactivity afforded by FADA over an algorithm's behaviour enabled learners to engage in higher order thinking about its process. Moreover, the capacity to isolate and simulate set aspects of an algorithm's behaviour and actively experiment with them in real time enabled instructors to challenge learners' understanding of its process and as a consequence, enabled them to engage learners in discussion. The dual representations provided by FADA of an algorithm's process enabled instructors to scaffold learners in mapping the depiction of graphical errors in an algorithm's behaviour to that of its implementation. Furthermore, the ability to amend the behaviour of an algorithm, to simulate the changes made and to actively experiment with them enabled instructors to engage learners in an iterative cycle of learning so as to enable them to arrive at a deeper understanding of the algorithm's process.

When used as a tool to set tasks for learners to complete, findings showed that the level of real time interactivity afforded by FADA over an algorithm's behaviour enabled learners to experiment with their understanding of its process and enabled them to identify shortcomings in the latter. Moreover, the ability to easily amend and simulate the behaviour of an algorithm, challenged learners' understanding of its process and motivated them to seek the assistance of others to arrive at a deeper understanding of it. The dual representations afforded by FADA of an algorithm's behaviour enabled learners to map the logic of the graphical representation to that of its implementation and as a consequence, enabled them, to quickly identify shortcomings in its implementation.

In terms of operational effectiveness, FADA was found from the viewpoint of the learner and the instructor to be easy to learn how to use and effective in enabling them to complete their tasks in an efficient manner. All learners, despite having not encountered the software previously, were able to negotiate its functionality to enable them to correctly identify shortcomings in an algorithm's process and amend its implementation to overcome them. All instructors were able to create sample active simulations for their own use. Moreover, they were able to create them on average within a three hour time frame. On the whole, learners and instructors were satisfied with the functions and features provided by FADA, with one notable exception, the need to synchronise the implementation of the time out procedures with that of the simulation speed. By triangulating all of the data collected from the various data collection tools deployed within this study, the validity of the above findings was consolidated.

Chapter 7
Conclusions

7.1 Introduction

To date a spectrum of algorithm visualisation systems (AVs) exist to assist in the teaching and learning of distributed algorithms but despite their proliferation, these systems have failed to catch on in mainstream computer science education. This is because many of them suffer from one or more of the following problems. These are: a lack of a deep model of engagement with an algorithm's process while it executes, time and effort required to return an algorithm visualisation and a lack of empirical evidence as to their pedagogical effectiveness. This thesis has described how an algorithm visualisation system, known as FADA, addresses these challenges through the development of a model of engagement that enables a learner when interacting with the behaviour of an algorithm to engage his higher order thinking skills of analysis, synthesis and evaluation, through the development of a framework which facilitates the quick and easy creation of highly interactive algorithm simulations and through the provision of results from a number of case studies as to the effectiveness of active simulation systems in motivating and engaging learners to experiment with their understanding of an algorithm's behaviour in a deep manner. First, this thesis described how FADA's design was informed by design principles derived from the analysis and critique of currently available AVs and by the author's own experiences of building a highly interactive simulation of the token ring algorithm. Lastly, it describes a number of case studies conducted with FADA to explore its pedagogical and operational effectiveness, both from the perspective of the learner and the instructor. The following sections summarise the main research findings, the limitations of the research and directions for future research.

7.2 Summary of research findings

During the course of this study, two research questions were posed. These were:

1   To what extent does the algorithm visualisation approach adopted in this thesis enhance the teaching and learning of distributed algorithms?

2   To what extent is FADA easy to use?

The former was designed to assess FADA's pedagogical effectiveness, whilst the latter was designed to assess FADA's operational effectiveness. In order to facilitate answering, each was subdivided into a number of subsidiary questions. These were in terms of pedagogical effectiveness:

- To what extent does FADA facilitate learners to engage in higher order thinking when learning about an algorithm's behaviour?

- To what extent does FADA facilitate higher order dialogues about an algorithm's behaviour between learners and between learners and the instructor?

- To what extent does the embodiment of the dual coding theory within the user interface design of FADA aid in the algorithm problem solving process?

- To what extent does FADA engage learners in an iterative cycle of learning?

Subsidiary questions relating to FADA's operational effectiveness were:

- To what extent is FADA easy to learn how to use?

- To what extent is it effective in enabling learners to complete their problem solving tasks?

- To what extent is it both effective and efficient in enabling instructors to create active simulations for use in their own teachings?

- To what extent are both learners and instructors satisfied with the functions and features provided by FADA?

The following two sections present the main conclusions drawn from each of these questions.

7.2.1 Pedagogical effectiveness

With regard to what extent FADA facilitated learners in engaging in higher order thinking about an algorithm's behaviour, learners were found, as a consequence of the level of real time interactivity afforded by FADA over an algorithm's behaviour, to be able to identify the shortcomings in its process and as a result, were able to put forward ways by which to overcome them. This is clearly evidenced within each of the lecture settings and within each of the laboratory settings. Indirectly through the actions of the instructor within the authentic lecture setting, learners were able to identify the issue of deadlock and through a process of mapping its graphical visualisation to that of its implementation were able to identify the algorithm's shortcoming as its failure to account for atomic operations. Similarly, within the laboratory settings, learners were able to identify the shortcomings within each of the applications' behaviours and as a consequence, were able to put forward ways by which to overcome them.

As a consequence of their ability to implement their own proposed solutions to set problems encountered within the applications' behaviours, learners were able to engage the assistance of others to ascertain their level of correctness. This is evidenced by the manner in which student (S4) within case study four engaged the assistance of student (S2) to assist him in overcoming the burden of latency associated with his solution of always having the client, prior to sending a store message, check to determine whether the server was alive.

The dual representations afforded by FADA assisted learners in realising their solutions by enabling them to map the errors in the graphical representation of an algorithm's behaviour to that of its underlying implementation. This is evidenced in case study three were the visual depiction of each bank server's local bank balance alerted student (S1) to the failure of the sending bank server to await receipt of an acknowledgement to its transfer message prior to deducting a hundred euro from its account.

Given the nature of FADA's user interface design, it lended itself well to engaging learners in an iterative cycle of learning. Learners could by experimenting with an algorithm's behaviour in real time identify shortcomings in its process, reflect upon them, abstract and implement ways by which to overcome them. By implementing their solutions to the latter failings, learners were confronted with further concrete representations of the algorithm's behaviour which they could play with. This led to further experimentations, reflections and concrete experiences. This is clearly evidenced in stage three of case study one where learners were first exposed to the graphical representation of two philosophers eating concurrently and through a process of reflection were able to abstract out and propose an alternate means by which to overcome it. Such a process led to further exposure to the issue of deadlock which resulted in more reflections and amendments

207

However, in accepting the claim that FADA facilitated learners in engaging in (a) higher order thinking about an algorithm's behaviour, (b) higher order discussions about an algorithm's process, (c) an iterative cycle of learning and (d) scaffolding them to realise solutions to algorithmic problems through the use of the dual representations afforded by it, one must acknowledge the role of the instructor in realising each of these outcomes.   In each case study, it was necessary for the instructor to intervene at varying intervals in order to reframe the problem at hand so as to enable learners to either proceed with the task in hand or to come to a higher order understanding of it. This is clearly evidenced in case study one where it was necessary for the instructor to intervene so as to enable learners to realise a solution to the issue of starvation. By altering learners' conceptual perception of the use of time as the only means by which one could convey the concept of starvation, learners were able to put forward an alternate means by which to convey the latter concept, that is, through the use of a counter which tracks the number of times a philosopher has attempted to eat and failed. Similarly, in case study five, it was necessary for the instructor to intervene to assist learners in realising a solution to the apparent problem of endlessly repeating timers. By reframing learners' understanding of the need for the aforementioned timers, they were able to determine the cause of their continual execution as relating to their failure to cancel the timers operations on logical completion of their function. Thus, from all of the above findings, one can conclude that the role of FADA in enabling learners to come to a higher order understanding of an algorithm's behaviour is a mediating one. FADA provides the platform from which both learners and instructors can work to establish a mutual understanding of an algorithm's behaviour. It in fact becomes what Papert termed as 'an object to think with' [123] (p. 11). It enables learners either through their own actions or indirectly through those of the instructor to externalise their conceptual understanding of an algorithm's process and enables them through a process of direct manipulation of its behaviour during execution to identify shortcomings in that understanding and to implement ways by which to overcome them. Moreover, it enables them to seek the assistance of others to help them overcome gaps in their own understanding of an algorithm's behaviour. By providing learners with the capacity to observe the behaviour of an algorithm visually, to experiment with its process in real time and to amend its implementation, FADA enables learners to come to a deep understanding of an algorithm's behaviour. This is something simply not possible with pen and paper. Textual and diagrammatical representations do not lend themselves well to the illustration of algorithmic behaviours which are dynamic and concurrent. Moreover, they do not enable one to truly test the correctness of their logic as they do not afford a means by which one can render their behaviours active and open to experimentation. This is evidenced in case study five where only upon amending the behaviour of the distributed address book to reflect the logic of the flowchart was student (S1) and student (S2) able to uncover the shortcomings in their flowchart's logic and ultimately in their understanding of the application's behaviour.

7.2.2 Operational effectiveness

With respect to what extent FADA was found to be effective in enabling the creation of active simulations in a timely and efficient manner, findings from the use of FADA by one of three different instructors showed that it enabled them to create a simulation in, on average, a three hour time frame. Such a finding is significant if one were to compare it to that recorded by the author in creating the token ring simulation and that recorded by users in Stasko and Hundhausens' study of the Samba system [118]. The former needed fifty plus hours to create her simulation whilst the latter required thirty three point two hours on average to create a visualisation. However, before taking these findings on board, one must acknowledge that in order to build an active simulation of an algorithm's behaviour in FADA, a firm understanding of Java and the object oriented paradigm is required. Yet, despite such an overhead, this did not seem to deter users and in particular, novice learners. This is clearly evidenced by the hundred percent completion rates recorded by learners within the Edinburgh sample and especially within the postgraduate sample. These were learners, who were learning Java for the first time and who, unlike those within each of the case study settings, had to independently use FADA to build an implementation of the algorithm's behaviour from the ground up and were reliant on FADA's inbuilt help files as the sole source of assistance. Thus, it appeared, as witnessed within each of the case study settings, that the level of scaffolding afforded by FADA through the use of its inbuilt help files, its wizard, its sample simulations and internal console window offset and eased the burden of implementation for users. Moreover, it appeared that the ability to graphically visualise the behaviour of an algorithm at different intervals during its creation assisted users in quickly identifying the shortcomings in their implementation logic. This is clearly evidenced in case study five, where the graphical representation of amendments made by student (S1) and student (S2) to the logic of the distributed address book application in line with that defined by their flowchart alluded them to their failure to cancel the behaviour of their time out procedures on logical completion of their operations. Thus, one can conclude that the provision of the framework together with a development environment that scaffolds the algorithm implementation process greatly reduces the time and level of complexity associated with creating an active simulation of an algorithm's behaviour.

7.3 Limitations of work

Despite the interesting findings recorded by this research, there are limitations to the significance of the work. However, in considering these limitations, one must bear in mind the difficulties incurred in creating active simulations and in gaining access to lecture settings across different educational institutes as documented within chapter five.

- A major focus of this research was the manner by which one of two different instructors (one being the author) deployed FADA within a lecture setting to assist them in conveying to learners the behaviour of a distributed algorithm. To generalise the results and, in particular those relating to FADA's pedagogical effectiveness in each instance, there is need to observe a number of different instructors deploying FADA using a number of different teaching strategies in a number of different lecture settings. In the current study, both instructors deployed FADA using a constructivist teaching approach. There is need to investigate whether similar findings would be recorded if FADA was deployed in a less engaging manner akin to that of 'chalk and talk'.

- The duration of each lecture setting was short. Each lasted on average between one and two hours. In order to get a truer picture of the manner by which FADA assisted instructors in conveying the behaviour of an algorithm, there is need to observe their use of FADA over a longer period of time and also, the manner by which they deploy it to teach a number of different algorithms.

- Equally, the duration of the modification tasks was short. Each learner within group two and three spent on average two hours completing their tasks. In order to derive a closer examination of the ways by which FADA facilitated them in engaging in higher order thinking about an algorithm's process, in engaging in higher order discussions about an algorithm's behaviour, in scaffolding them to realise solutions to the algorithmic problems posed and in engaging in an iterative cycle of learning, there is need to extend the period of observation over a number of months. Moreover, there is need, not only, to train the video camera on the group of learners as a whole, but also, on each learner's interface, this is in order to capture the true manner by which FADA mediated their conversations and the extent to which its features facilitated them in attaining an understanding of an algorithm's behaviour. By training the camera on each learner's interface, one captures his inner thoughts and processes through out the task as his interactions with the features of the interface can be regarded as a physical manifestation of them. In this study, due to financial constraints, the author had at her disposal a single video camera, thus, on the moment decisions had to be made as to where to train its lens, either on an individual learner's machine or on the group as a whole. Such decisions were made by the author as she saw fit. Consequently, she was not able to capture graphically all interesting events that occurred between individual students and FADA in each setting.

7.4 Future Work

- Currently, FADA is designed to assist in the teaching and learning of message passing distributed algorithms. Such a topic represents a part component of an overall topic known as distributed systems. From the analysis of feedback obtained from the instructors, there is need to extend FADA's capability to assist in the teaching of middleware systems like for example, CORBA.

- In order to validate further observations made in this study, to extend upon conclusions drawn and to provide for a degree of generalisability, there is need to observe a number of different instructors deploying FADA using a number of different teaching techniques in a number of different lecture settings.

- As with all software, there is room to improve upon its interface design and level of functionality afforded. Again, from the analysis of feedback derived from instructors there is need to amend FADA to synchronise the execution of the time out procedures with that of the animation speed. Moreover, the failure scenarios should be expanded upon to enable one to snip the underlying network to ascertain what effect the enforced separation of processes would have on their behaviours. Equally, there is need to enable a process to belong to more than one group at a time. Lastly, the code frame should be amended to enable one to have the implementation code relating to the behaviours of one or more nodes open at the same time. This is particularly important if one is working on the implementation or modification of an algorithm that utilises a client/server topology. In order to achieve this, a tabbed pane interface should be considered.

7.5 Conclusions

In summary, the main contributions of this research are:

- The development of an algorithm visualisation system that engages learners in higher order thinking about an algorithm's behaviour.
- The development of a novel framework to facilitate the easy and quick creation of an active algorithm simulation.
- Results from exploratory case studies as to the effectiveness of active simulation systems in engaging and motivating learners to experiment with their understanding of an algorithm's process in a deep manner.

Appendix A

This questionnaire is to be filled out by students whose lecturers' have used FADA as an interactive presentation tool within class. The aim of the questionnaire is to investigate the effectiveness of FADA when used as a teaching aid.

1. How did the lecturer used FADA in class?		
2. Did the use of FADA by the lecturer help you to better understand the concepts presented in class?	*Yes*	*No*
If you answered *Yes* **(to question 2) then can you explain in what ways FADA helped you to better understand?**		
If you answered *No* **(to question 2) then can you explain why FADA did not help you to understand the concepts presented in class?**		
3. Did the use of FADA by the lecturer encourage you to participate more in class?	*Yes*	*No*
If you answered *Yes* **(to question 3) then in what ways did you participate in class**		
4. Did the use of FADA by the lecturer in class increase your interest in the subject matter?	*Yes*	*No*
If you answered *Yes* **(to question 4) then how did FADA increase your interest in the subject matter?**		
5. Describe, if there are any ways in which the lecturer could use FADA to better aid your learning?		
6. Is this the first time you have encountered the subject matter presented in class?	*Yes*	*No*

If you answered *No* (to question 6) then can you tell me where you encountered the subject matter before?

7. How does today's presentation of the material via the use of FADA compare in terms of learning to your prior experience?

Appendix B

This questionnaire is designed to ascertain how easy FADA is as an application to use, whether it is an effective learning tool. To answer this questionnaire, please place a tick (e.g. X) in the box which most closely matches your findings in relation to FADA.

1. How easy was each of the following algorithm behaviours to implement in FADA?

Algorithm Behaviour	Very Easy	Easy	Moderate	Hard	Very Hard
Create a node					
Create a message					
Put content in a message					
Retrieve content from a message					
Send a message					
Decipher between different messages					
Create a variable					
Create a timeout					
Alter node image					

2. Modifying the behaviour of an algorithm helped me better understand it?

Strongly agree	Agree	Neither agree or disagree	Disagree	Strongly disagree

3. Simulations rendered by FADA were easy to understand?

Strongly agree	Agree	Neither agree or disagree	Disagree	Strongly disagree

4. Interacting with/ playing with the components of an algorithm simulation helped me to better understand its behaviour?

Strongly agree	Agree	Neither agree or disagree	Disagree	Strongly disagree

5. Instructions, provided by FADA by way of its inbuilt help system, to implement the behaviour of an algorithm, were easy to understand?

Strongly agree	Agree	Neither agree or disagree	Disagree	Strongly disagree

6. How easy was FADA to use? Please describe any difficulties you may have experienced?

6. Visualisation is an important part of helping me understand how an algorithm functions?

Strongly agree	Agree	Neither agree or disagree	Disagree	Strongly disagree

7. Has your understanding of distributed algorithms increased as a result of using FADA? If *Yes,* then in what ways?

8. Have you used FADA outside of class or exercises that require its use? If *Yes,* then for what purposes did you use it?

Appendix C

This questionnaire is aimed at lecturers or those persons who teach distributed algorithms. It is designed to investigate how easy FADA is as an application to use, the length of time required to build a simulation using it and whether it is an effective teaching tool. To answer the questions posed in this questionnaire, please select the option in each question that most closely matches your findings in relation to FADA. To do this, circle the appropriate answer.

1. How easy was it to use FADA to build your own simulation of an algorithm's behaviour?

Very easy	Easy	Moderate	Hard	Very hard

2. Instructions to build a description of an algorithm as a simulation are clear

Strongly agree	Agree	Neither agree or disagree	Disagree	Strongly disagree

3. Instructions to build a description of an algorithm as a simulation are complete

Strongly agree	Agree	Neither agree or disagree	Disagree	Strongly disagree

4. Instructions to build a description of an algorithm as a simulation are concise

Strongly agree	Agree	Neither agree or disagree	Disagree	Strongly disagree

Appendix C

5. How easy was each of the following algorithm behaviours to implement in FADA?

Algorithm Behaviour	Very Easy	Easy	Moderate	Hard	Very Hard
Create a node					
Create a message					
Put content in a message					
Retrieve content from a message					
Send a message					
Decipher between different messages					
Create a variable					
Create a timeout					
Alter node image					

6. How long on average did it take you to implement an algorithm simulation?

7. Would you use this application in your future teachings?	Yes	No

If *No* then why not?

8. Please list the approaches you would consider using with FADA in teaching or otherwise?

9. Is there any features you would like to see implemented in FADA? Why?

Appendix D

Below is a description of findings arising from the administration of the questionnaire defined in Appendix B to each of the three learner groups defined in section 5.2 on completion of their algorithm modification task.

1. How easy was each of the following algorithm behaviours to implement in FADA?
1a. Create a node type

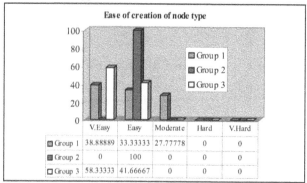

	V.Easy	Easy	Moderate	Hard	V.Hard
Group 1	38.88889	33.33333	27.77778	0	0
Group 2	0	100	0	0	0
Group 3	58.33333	41.66667	0	0	0

1b. Create a message

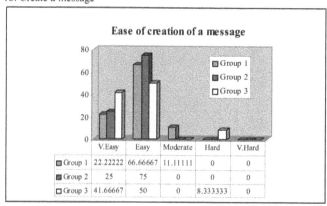

	V.Easy	Easy	Moderate	Hard	V.Hard
Group 1	22.22222	66.66667	11.11111	0	0
Group 2	25	75	0	0	0
Group 3	41.66667	50	0	8.333333	0

1c. Put content in a message

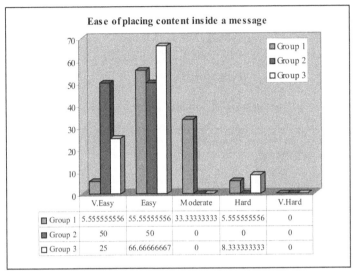

1d. Retrieve content from a message

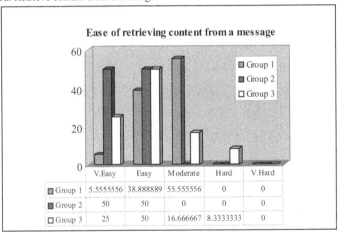

1e. Send a message

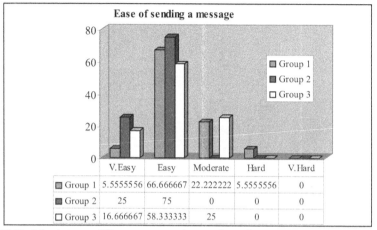

1f. Decipher between different messages that a node receives

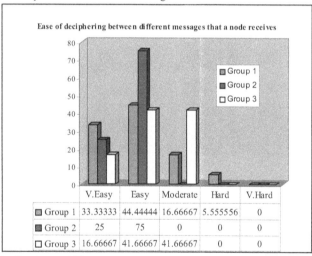

1g. Create a variable

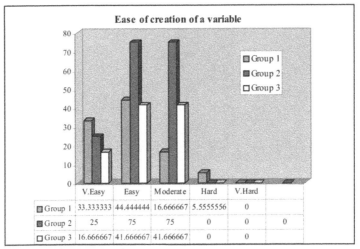

1h. Create a time out procedure.

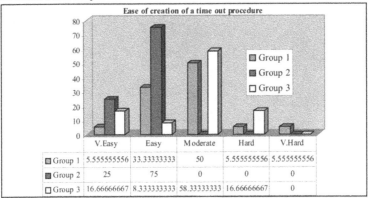

2. Modifying the behaviour of an algorithm helped me better understand it?

223

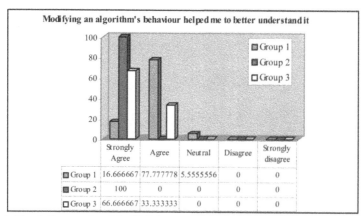

Modifying an algorithm's behaviour helped me to better understand it

	Strongly Agree	Agree	Neutral	Disagree	Strongly disagree
Group 1	16.666667	77.777778	5.5555556	0	0
Group 2	100	0	0	0	0
Group 3	66.666667	33.333333	0	0	0

3. Simulations rendered by FADA were easy to understand?

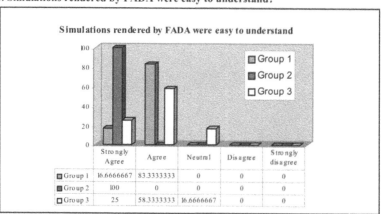

Simulations rendered by FADA were easy to understand

	Strongly Agree	Agree	Neutral	Disagree	Strongly disagree
Group 1	16.6666667	83.3333333	0	0	0
Group 2	100	0	0	0	0
Group 3	25	58.3333333	16.6666667	0	0

4. Interacting with/ playing with the components of an algorithm simulation helped me to better understand the algorithm's behaviour?

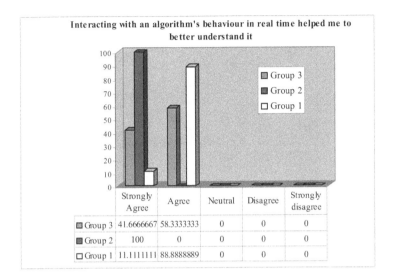

	Strongly Agree	Agree	Neutral	Disagree	Strongly disagree
Group 3	41.6666667	58.3333333	0	0	0
Group 2	100	0	0	0	0
Group 1	11.1111111	88.8888889	0	0	0

5. Instructions, provided by FADA by way of its built in help system, to implement the behaviour of an algorithm were easy to understand?

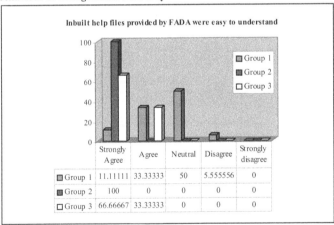

	Strongly Agree	Agree	Neutral	Disagree	Strongly disagree
Group 1	11.11111	33.33333	50	5.555556	0
Group 2	100	0	0	0	0
Group 3	66.66667	33.33333	0	0	0

6. Visualisation is an important part of helping me understand how an algorithm functions?

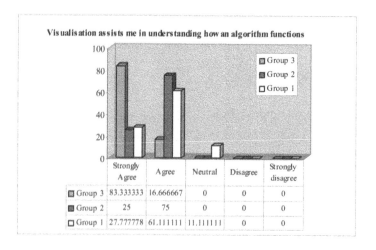

Visualisation assists me in understanding how an algorithm functions

	Strongly Agree	Agree	Neutral	Disagree	Strongly disagree
Group 3	83.333333	16.666667	0	0	0
Group 2	25	75	0	0	0
Group 1	27.777778	61.111111	11.111111	0	0

Appendix E

Below is a description of findings arising from the administration of the questionnaire defined in Appendix C to each of the three instructors defined in section 5.2 on completion of building each of their algorithm simulations.

1. How easy was it to use FADA to build your own simulation of an algorithm's behaviour?

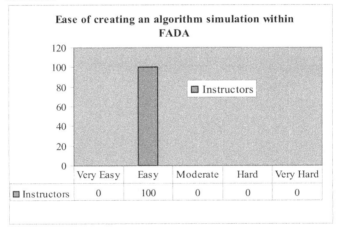

	Very Easy	Easy	Moderate	Hard	Very Hard
Instructors	0	100	0	0	0

2. Instructions to build a description of an algorithm as a simulation are clear

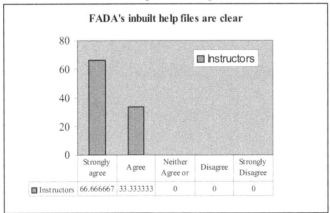

	Strongly agree	Agree	Neither Agree or	Disagree	Strongly Disagree
Instructors	66.666667	33.333333	0	0	0

227

Appendix E

3. Instructions to build a description of an algorithm as a simulation are complete

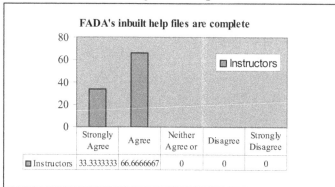

4. Instructions to build a description of an algorithm as a simulation are concise

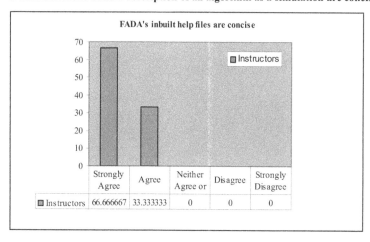

5. How easy was each of the following algorithm behaviours to implement in FADA?

5a. Create a node type

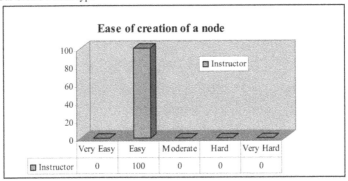

5b. Create a message

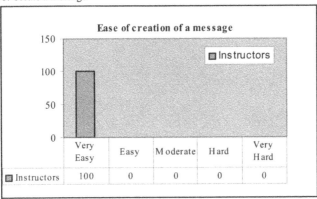

5c. Put content in a message

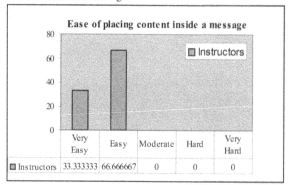

	Very Easy	Easy	Moderate	Hard	Very Hard
▣ Instructors	33.333333	66.666667	0	0	0

5d. Retrieve content from a message

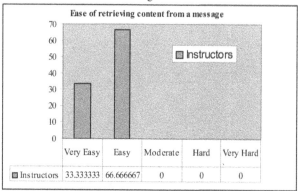

	Very Easy	Easy	Moderate	Hard	Very Hard
▣ Instructors	33.333333	66.666667	0	0	0

5e. Send a message

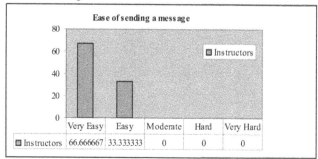

	Very Easy	Easy	Moderate	Hard	Very Hard
▣ Instructors	66.666667	33.333333	0	0	0

5f. Decipher between different messages a node receives

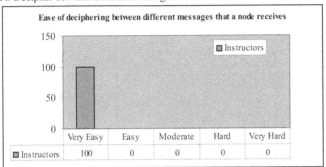

5g. Create a variable

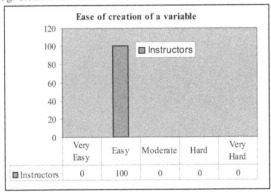

5h. Create a timeout procedure

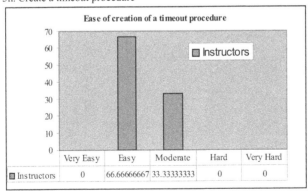

5i. Change a node's image

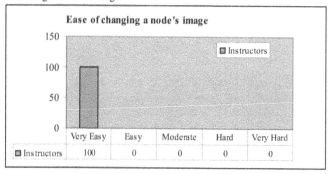

Appendix F

Case Study 1: Transcript

A description of the dialogue which arose between instructor (L1) and learners as a consequence of FADA's use within the authentic lecture setting. In this setting, the instructor used FADA to assist him in conveying to learners the behaviour of the dining philosophers' algorithm.

Stage 3

L: What I am going to do now is to start....two
     So the scenario here is that two philosophers have arrived and they are both trying to eat. They are getting responses saying 'Not Taken'.
     Now, you've got two philosophers eating. Can any one see anything wrong?

S1: They shouldn't be eating.

L: It shouldn't be possible for them both to be eating.
     Let me ask you what do you think is wrong?

S1: It's not working.

L: It's not working...yip. Lets go a bit deeper. It's not working because...

S2: Because they are doing something that technically they should not be capable of doing. They are both eating despite the fact that to eat, you   should only have two forks. There are only two forks between them.
     So at most, only one should be able to eat and, at worse, neither should be able to eat.

L: Ok, lets us look at what each node is doing. Each node is saying 'can I have the forks please', 'can I have the forks please'.
     And they are getting back responses saying 'by all means go ahead take the forks'. So they are eating. So that part of the protocol is perfectly fine. That's the right behaviour. If a message comes back saying 'you should eat', you should eat! There would be something wrong, if they didn't eat in that scenario. The place where it seems to be going wrong is that they are being told to eat when they shouldn't be.

S2: They are being told the fork is available to them when it is not.

Stage 4

L: In normal circumstances..... Lets put in lots of philosophers.
     Various philosophers arriving, sitting down trying to eat
     There's a philosopher starting to eat. There's another one starting to eat. There's nothing wrong with those ones eating. There's no conflict there. That's probably the normal case.

S3: Those last two shouldn't have been able to eat.

L: In that scenario, the system is working. Behaviour is not working in the sense that it is not actually correct. The computation that it is doing is not correct, but its behaviour seems correct.

S3: Sorry, 6 and 8 shouldn't be able to eat

L: Who shouldn't have been able to eat?

S3: Because, they'd be sharing a common fork, wouldn't they?

L: I can't remember which ones I started, but my point was...
     If I've made a mistake I apologise....My point was to select philosophers which are

entitled to eat concurrently. And, it is possible to select philosophers who are able to eat concurrently. We are assuming there is a fork between each of those.

That system can appear to be correct under normal or reasonably normal circumstances. It just seems to fail when we have adjacent philosophers trying to eat. Both seem to have magically turned one fork into two. The problem in this algorithm seems to be, where two adjacent philosophers both trying to eat, seem to not take note of the fact they are both trying to eat.

S2:   So basically, there is absolutely no provision for whether a fork is being used or not.
L: Exactly.....
L: So the problem occurs in the message that is being sent back that is, in the response code... in the creation of the response message. If getBoolean('left')..We have it fine that would be the good case. Can simulate that in a moment. However, if one of those philosophers is eating and if the philosopher beside him to the left or right of him... tries to eat he'll be told he can't, quite correctly. But if a node is in the process of acquiring forks and the response messages haven't yet come through to allow him to obtain the forks, my boolean variable won't be set and so I'll happily say 'go ahead, take the fork'. The subtlety in this protocol is that a node has to send out two messages ('leftfork' and 'rightfork') and get back responses to both those messages and the actual state that the node should expose to the world is really dependent on both the values of those messages. If a message comes in the interim looking for a fork, what the node should really be doing is atomic in some sense, that is, the node should reply 'go ahead, have the fork, I haven't got it'. Now, I could try and build in some kind of fancy message delay. I know, I'm waiting to get responses to my initial messages so I'll wait and I won't respond to the interim message until I get the initial responses back. I could do all kinds of sophisticated things like that but rather then go for that of solution, I'm going to try and solve it rather simply.
L: Rather than testing whether or not I have the fork to my left or right, I'm going to use this 'eating' boolean that I've mentioned earlier. I'm going to set it to true, when I decide I want to eat, and set it to false when I finish eating. Why can't I use getBoolean("eating") as the test rather than 'do I have the right or left fork?'. So it's effectively almost pre-allocating...I'm going to definitely grab the two forks. So if someone to my left or right comes looking for them, I won't let them have them. Clear this. Keep it simple with just four. Test the simple case. When doing this kind of thing, it's always useful to build up a series of tests...and to test the straight forward cases first. So does the basic behaviour still work, seems to. Likewise, if I decided to add that one in there. You would expect that that would be allowed to eat. I should also test the state which I should have tested before the previous one. This should not succeed. Fork is taken...The timer hasn't started there...everything is fine. However, I'm going to slow down the animation
speed. You can play with these things... Play with who starts what and when... I'm picking a case that I know is a bit funny.
I've got everybody deciding they want to eat at the same time.
What do you think will happen before it comes back?
S1:   They are all going to send a message 'fork taken'

L: So what's going to happen? Every one is dependent on every one else to get to eat. They are all going to say they are eating so no one eats.
       Is that deadlock?
S2:   Yes
L: It's actually not quite deadlock, a kind of deadlock.
S3:   They are all waiting.
L: It's live lock. If they all continually come back trying to eat at once,
       They are all going to go away hungry every time.
       If we were able to click on these nodes and see their state, you'd see that 'missed lunch' was now there. So that's not really a solution.
       Although in normal circumstances.....I'm going to slow the animation down...What do you think, will anyone be allowed to eat? No one eats, yeah? Let me add in one or two more nodes. I'm going to start a lot of them and I'm going to put some spaces around the place as well. Speed it up. You do get some nodes getting to eat. So again, if you had some complicated system based upon this protocol and you tested it, you would see some correct behaviours being exhibited. But, we actually know that there is failure in there, there's the live lock situation in there.
       It seems to be when a bunch of connected nodes are trying to eat; they are all going to block each other.
L: Lets just focus on the problem. The problem is that this test is too coarse grained. Just because I want to eat, doesn't mean that I should
       be able to block everyone around me who wants to eat. That leads to a potential for deadlock. Any one got a solution?
S2:   Replace the eating message
L: Sure... replace with what? Remember we had nothing there before.
S2:   No, what I am saying is....We should set 'eating' variable
       to true only when we get a 'Not Taken' message back from each of our neighbours.

Stage 5
L: So at a high level, just saying 'I want to eat so you can't' is not good enough. Just saying 'by all means you want it, take it' is not good enough.   Have to find somewhere in between. First of all, if you have the fork, then you shouldn't be able to get it.   That's just the state of the thing. 'I have the fork and you don't.   But we know that, that by itself, led us to a scenario where we wouldn't have the fork even though we are trying to get that fork. So what I have done is I've given the protocol more information... I've said either we have the fork or we're trying to eat and something else. Just saying either 'we have the fork' or 'we're trying to eat' is the same thing as saying 'we are trying to eat'.
       Introduce a little bit of subtlety to it and I've said either 'we have that fork' or 'we are eating' and 'we are going to some kind of test'. This test is going to decide which of us should get the fork. That's the point to this. Need to have a computation, that can be done by both nodes and that will come out the same. The result will be same and it will give preference to one or the other. The computation will give preference to one or the other irrespective of where that computation is done. The test I've put in is that every node has an identifier. If my identifier is larger than your identifier then it is taken. What I've done is implemented a priority scheme. The priority scheme

235

says 'If I already have the fork then there is nothing to debate about'. I have the fork, you can't have it, it's taken. But if my id is higher than yours and I want to eat then it's taken. Correspondingly, if the other node was asked that question, 'who should have the fork?' It would say, 'my id is lower than that node's Id so, I should give it'.

S3:   But by taking into account the node's id, does that not mean that eventually you get....like node 1, who is lower than everyone else would be starved out of the system.

L: That's something we would want to look at. But before we go to that, I just want to run it. Lets see... Standard behaviour still works. While that's taken, should be able to see that node 2 won't get it. It's taken...We have it. Everything seems to be fine.

Now what we'll do...We'll start off...I'm going to slow down the animation so I can do it. We'll start off a bunch of them concurrently which seemed to be the problem last time. Everybody was trying to eat, the only test was whether or not they were eating and that seemed to cause everybody to block each other. Fork is taken. 3 says 'its taken'. Being told that it's 'not taken' though because its id is higher than node 2.

So node 3 has got to eat. So previously, what happened was when we had three nodes like that none of them got to eat because they all backed off.

Now, have a scenario where one of them has got to eat. Still not quite working. Node one should have eaten but it's not bad. It's an improvement. What I want to do now is to have everybody eating. Now, we'll speed up the animation. Everybody is asking for their left and their right. A message comes back based on the new test which is either 'I have it' or 'I don't but you're not getting it because, my id is greater than yours'. That looked right...Partially right, at least somebody is going ahead. We've got rid of that live lock scenario.

At least, somebody has started... but far, far too many nodes being prevented from eating. In fact, what we have now suffers from a simple problem that once we have a chain of nodes, all trying to eat and their messages are being exchanged in an order that kind

of binds them together, the top node gets to eat and no one else. That seems inefficient. It is not catastrophic in that system doesn't suffer in that potentially nothing can go forward but it does have the starvation problem as mentioned up at the top. It is quite easy in that scenario for any one of those nodes to be starved. As every time, they become part of the chain of philosophers sitting down at the table, only one gets to eat and that is, the top one.

L: How can we solve that? Anybody? What could we do? Where should we focus our attention that's the first question.

S3:   The id we are using. Need another way of generating the order in which the initial requests were sent out. Rather than the id of the individual who is making the request. Then highest priority might get to eat rather than highest number.

L: Yeah.. The system gives, in the unusual scenario, where everybody comes uniquely together, at the same time, to eat. The system gives automatic priority to the highest identifier.

236

That seems like an unreasonable basis on which to decide priority.

Focusing on this calculation, what we need to do is change how we do priority. How are we doing it at the moment? We are just getting the identifier of each sender. I want to show you a slight variation on this because that's really cheating. That's taking information that we probably don't have in a real distributed system. I've changed it slightly to getting the id of my right or left, depending on whether I want the fork to my right or left. I'm not depending now on that sender. I'm depending now on my protocol which understands the structure of the communication system. But it's still the same problem. I'm using an identifier. We should use something else, what should we use?

What would be useful? Remember, the purpose of the dining philosophers' algorithm is to ensure that nobody starves, that's the goal. So if we have some notion of....

S3:   Waiting time

L: Time to starvation that would be useful. How could we introduce that into the protocol?

S3:   Time from when the initial request was sent out.

L: Lets park the question of how to generate a valid piece of information. How could I as a philosopher say 'could I have that fork, please?' to each node and also, tell them, in a sense, how important this is?

S4:   Put a timer in a message.

L: Lets imagine, I'm about to starve, so I really do need these forks, what could I do?

S5:   Use some kind of counter that tracks the need to eat.

L: Yip...I have some kind of counter that expresses..

It could be a boolean 'on' or 'off'. It could be 'I missed lunch last time' or it could be 'it's been three days since I last ate'.

S5:   I could increase my priority by switching it on or off.

L: Yeah, so in some ways, it's a piece of information that I could communicate that says 'I really need this now'. What I could do is add it to the message in the same way that, we have a message there that signifies 'fork taken'. I could add urgency to the original message. So way down here. At the very bottom, where we actually sent off the right and left fork messages. I could augment them with some information that says how really urgent this is to me. And then, rather than doing the calculation based on how important I am in the system, my id is. The calculation could be done based on that piece of information. Will the calculation come out the same on both sides? The philosopher to my left and myself. If I have a notion of how hungry I am, and they have a notion of how hungry they are, and, if the algorithm is based on testing those two values against each other, and giving it to the most hungry philosopher, it should.

As long as the same values cross over. So that's a possible solution. Try and implement this. Try to get rid of the scenario of potential starvation caused by basing the ability to eat on the basis of unchanging node ids. Modify the code such that the system is fairer to the philosopher. When you've done that, you could go further.. See if your solution solves the problem when a number of philosophers like this... many of whom could eat concurrently but for some quirk in the

237

implementation can't. See if that solves it and how else, you could modify your solution so that for example, while node 7 was eating, there's no reason why node 5 couldn't be eating and node 3 at the same time.

Appendix G

Case Study 2: Transcript

A description of the dialogue which arose between the author, acting as the instructor, and participants from group 3, within the simulated lecture setting. In this setting, the instructor used FADA to assist him in conveying to learners the concept of transactions within a distributed system.

L: What should happen when node 2 receives that message?

S1:   Add it to his balance

L: What should node 1 do?

S2:   Subtract it, after getting a confirmation

L: When node 1 sends off that message it should deduct 100 euro from
        its account.

L: But, you are probably a step ahead of me but we'll see.   Lets see what happens
        Straight away node 1 deducts 100 euro and when node 2 receives the transfer
        message it adds on a 100 euros. As'ad don't say anything just yet. What happens if
        I lose that message? What happens to the state of my two bank servers?

S1:   Inconsistent

L: How would I overcome that problem?

S1:   Transactions

L: So in terms of messages what should I do?

S2:   You need an acknowledgement basically.
        You shouldn't subtract unless you receive the acknowledgement.

L: Node 1 shouldn't subtract until it receives like a 'done' message back from
        2.

S3:   How does node 2 know that node 1 got the 'done' message?

L: Very good

S2:   That's the two phase commit protocol.

L: Node 1 shouldn't deduct the 100 euro until it receives the ack message. So
        I need to figure out whether I have received such a message.
        I need to decipher the name of the message that I have just received. To do that, I
        use the *isType* method and only when it gets that message should it do this.

L: Lets see what happens. I'm just going to let it run first as I know that this will work.
        Node 1 will deduct as soon as it gets that ack message. So Colin, your question was
        what happens if I lose that ack message? So again, I'm in an inconsistent state. So
        what should I do?

S2:   There's no solution for that.

S1:   Transaction manager

S3:   There is a solution

L: There is one work around.

S2:   In this situation, you cannot solve that as once you lose the communication, it can
        never happen, hence can never be solved.

L: What could node 1 do?

239

S4:   What node 1 could do is it could send a message to node 2 saying ' I want to transfer 100 euro'. Node 2 will do nothing to its account. It will send back a message saying 'yeah, I know you are going to send me a 100 euro'. Both accounts will still have a 1000 euro. At that stage, node 1 having received the confirmation reduces 100 from its account and sends a further message saying 'now, add on your 100'. If node 1 doesn't receive a response after a certain time, it can say 'you never followed up'.

S2:   Yeah. That's right. That's the time out procedure. That's the way around the problem.

L: So essentially what node 1 could do is it could send a transfer message and wait for 20 secs or so in order to receive back a reply. If doesn't receive back a reply in that time, it can resend the transfer message.

S3:   What were you doing in the timer run method again?

L: I've associated the timer with the transfer message so when the timer expires I want to resend out the same message again

S3:   So you want to do *newMsg.putInt()* don't you?

L: Yeah...Do I not have that....

S3:   No...

L: Oh yeah. Thank you.

L: Straight away, I have a timer associated with the message. So what should happen when that timer expires, it should resend out the transfer message, which, it does. Question, if I start this again and that message gets lost, can anyone tell me what happens?

S3:   Gets out of sync again

L: Yes, so node 2 has added on another 100 euro. Doubled its value is there another work for that? How can I tell node 2 to ignore the second transfer message?

S1:   Sequence numbers

L: If I associate with each message an id such that node 2 would know already that it has already received the first transfer message so it will ignore the second. That should allow for some consistency in the two bank servers.

Appendix H

<u>Case Study 3: Transcript</u>
A description of the dialogue which arose between the author, acting as the instructor, and participants from group 2, within the simulated lecture setting. In this setting, the instructor used FADA to assist him in conveying to learners the concept of transactions within a distributed system.

L: Can anyone spot any problems? (*Viewing simulation*)
S2:   Node 1 is still subtracting straight away
L: Only want it to subtract when it receives back..
S1:   Or if it receives back a 'done' message
        Amends the behaviour of the application such that node 1 only subtracts on receipt of an acknowledgment to its transfer message.
L: I want to subtract the amount from my balance. What would happen if the 'done' message doesn't get through?
        Simulates lost of acknowledgement
S1:   You effectively have the same problem on the other side
S2:   Your balance has gone up by two hundred
S2:   Oh.. That's because you've received two transfer messages
L: There's a hundred euro astray. Any ideas as to....
S1:   You need a middle man, someone who can keep track of both of them perhaps
L: Right...But what if that middle man fails?
S1:   Then.. You have to cancel the transaction
S2:   There's no point in sending another message
L: Not as it presently stands but there's a way to
        ....Node 1 is sitting waiting for a message back
        (*Pointing to animation frame*)
S1:   Hmmm
L: How long should it wait for?
S1   Oh, you could set a time out and if he doesn't receive it back.
S1:   Well then... the transfer can't go through or resend the transfer
        Implements the timeout procedure put forward by student S1
L: If this message dies, it should resend now.
L: So it resends it...so 2 should automatically send back that 'done'.
        Things should be....
S2:   There's an inconsistency there.
L: Yes, There is. We need to figure out exactly where that is.
        There's a hundred euro extra or missing.
S2:   Number two is still adding even before number one,
        irrespective of whether or not one gets an acknowledgement.
S1:   hmmm
L: Right, we'll run it again
        Re-executes the simulation
L: So two adds straight away when it gets a transfer message so when it gets another transfer message, its going to add another hundred euro
S2:   It shouldn't be adding...because it's the same message.

241

Appendix H

L: So in that instance, we need to tell node 2 that it has already received that message so you need to label those messages. Need to give them some sort of id.

Appendix I

Case Study 4: Transcript

A description of the dialogue which arose between learners from group 3 when deploying FADA to modify the behaviour of the distributed address book application to render it fault tolerant.

S3   It's an address book for clients and they store the data on the server. The algorithm is to update the server with the clients' changes

S2   Was it not doing this before

S4   Yes, but there was no acknowledgements so there was no way of knowing whether the server had updated itself

S4   Presumably it's a collaborative address book and we can all retrieve data?

L   Yes (demonstrates the retrieve functionality)

L   Given the logic of the algorithm as is what is the first failure scenario that could affect it?

S2   The server fails

L   How would you propose to over come such a scenario?

S2   If I don't receive a response from the server then to whom am I going to send the data

L   So I need to …….

S1   Server needs to broadcast every twenty seconds that it is the server

S2   It can be done in two ways actually. The client asking the server whether 'it is the server' or the server broadcasting the 'I am server' all the time. It's easier if the server broadcasts, I would say……..I don't know

S4   Only because of this implementation, that is because all messages go directly to the server

S2   That's the fail silent approach. If you don't receive from the server this kind of message 'I am server' all the time then you know its failed…… it's a fail silent

S3   So the server is going to periodically send a message

Later…..

S4   Is the message that the server is constantly sending out not just one of 'I am awake'?

S1   Well, its 'I am a server'. It's a reference to me as a server

S2   Its both. Its saying 'I am awake' and 'I am the server'

S4   Is the 'I am server' message not the acknowledgement? You've got two options from the client's perspective…..The client needs to know 'you're a server' but, it also needs to know that……… so your combining the two, the polling message is also the acknowledgement that the client can send the store message now

S1   The server is announcing its presence by saying it's available to take messages. The client doesn't have to poll it just has to listen

S2   We have to change the client because at the minute when the client receives 'I am server' message, it automatically sends a store message. So we need to change it so that it only sends a message when we want it to send it.

S1   Need to remove code from the receiveMessage method and place inside an alternative method.

243

Appendix I

Later...

S4: I've another problem because I have looked at it the other way. I have the clients polling the server saying 'Are you awake?' What the server does when it receives 'Are you awake?' it says 'Yes, I am'

Does now each of my clients have to wait for lets say five or ten seconds and if they don't get a 'Yes, I am', do they have to look for another server?

S2: It's more complicated that way.

S4: It's not about sending the message. It's more about server failure. There's a separate acknowledgement that you send at the beginning of the message 'Are you the server?', 'Yes, I am', 'Grand, here's my contact details' but there's another one that the server is constantly doing of like 'Are you awake?'...when you don't respond to me, I've got to look for another server or set some boolean variable to say 'Definitely, don't send a request to him because he's not awake'.

S2: You have to consider it as a heartbeat thing, you know.

S4: Hmmm.

S2: The message saying 'I am the server', you have to consider this as a heartbeat approach. If you get it you can send, if you don't you can wait until you get something. It's as simple as that.

S4: Are we overcomplicating it though?

S2: You are overcomplicating it.

S4: Do we need to worry about failure in the server?

S2: Yes, because in the case of failure in the server, it will not send a heartbeat. Then the clients would wait until another server is plugged in. It will start sending the heartbeats again. Then, they can continue their work.

S4: But do I need to know whether the server is plugged in or not if I don't want to send it a message or I don't want to update it or I don't want to check it. Does it matter to me?

S2: You should know that the server is there, you should not just send a message because in all cases, you will not get that acknowledgement from the server if it is dead. That's another thing when you send the store message you should get an acknowledgement. And if you don't get an acknowledgement you know that the transaction was not done. This was another reason, probably the server is down, it's not there unplugged etc.

Appendix J

Case Study 5: Transcript
A description of the manner by which participants from group 3, engaged with FADA to render the behaviour of the distributed address book application fault tolerant.

S1   A client needs to send a request. It should start a timer and leave a certain amount of time for the server to reply. If it doesn't, it should resend the request......... [Pauses]........ I forgot there are two different things here...a store action and a look up action. So when we are storing something from the client to the server, we have to make sure the information gets stored and acknowledged. We have to put a timer on the client sending the message. If the acknowledgement comes back in time everything is fine. If the timer runs out... there are two possibilities either it didn't get to the server or the reply from the server didn't get through. Are you with me?

S2   Yes

S1   With a situation like that if the message doesn't get to the server, the server hasn't been updated. If it does get to the server but the message gets lost on the way back, the server has that information but we don't realise it has that information so we have to number the acknowledgements

S2   Well...can we add a timer onto a message?

S1   No, the message themselves can't contain timers, the nodes themselves can start clocks

S2   Are we assuming messages will die?

S1   No, we are trying to build fault tolerance into the system

S2   So what are we assuming about the messages then?

S2   Say, we send a message to the server and we don't get back a confirmation of that message and then it does arrive

S1   You means its delayed

L   You can kill a message, you can't delay one as such

S1   So don't worry about latency

S2   So if you don't get a response in the period of the timer have to assume message is lost and not delayed
Plays with simulation............realised they forgot to take into consideration the alive message

S1   So if server is not alive, no point in me sending the store message. So if it's not alive then you should again start a timer for some predetermined amount of time. You should keep sending the 'are you alive' message and until them don't do anything. Can we assume that once it says it's alive, it's not going to die in the mean time?

L   Yes

S1   So once we know its alive we can start sending messages to store.
Takes out pen and paper

S1	Failure modes are just the messages being lost. Once the server is up we can assume it not going to die. Two ways in which messages can get lost, on the way to the server and on the way back. *Draws on paper*
S2	But we can still kill a server. *Demonstrates with simulation*
S1	No we are not going to kill the server; we are not trying to simulate server failures. Only mode of failure we are looking at is message failures
S2	How do you kill a message? *Plays with animation to reinforce his understanding of it.*
L	Right click on the message object
S2	So if a message doesn't get through at the moment, nothing happens. Clients can't store
S1	That's right, that's what should happen
S2	Need to fix that........so we can fix that by repeating sending a message until we get a reply
S1	By starting a timer when we send it, and if we don't get a numbered acknowledgement, a specific acknowledgement back. ... In other words what you're basically doing is you're sending a message, an unique id. Usually the way the id works it alternates between 0 and 1. So you send me a message saying 'are you alive' we label that 0, we send that off and start the timer. If we timeout, we just send it again........let me think.............
S1	Do we need to number the 'alive' message
L	Is it really necessary?
S1	No, its not. Because it's irrelevant to you either the server's alive or it's not. So we are waiting for it to come back and say 'I'm alive'. Keep resending the alive packets til we get a reply
S2	**Initiates the drawing of the flowchart**
S1	Need to deal with failure of each separately. lets do the store message first
S1	Send store message *S2 draws on flow chart*
S2	Is it storing a name and number?
S1	Doesn't matter they are only parameters?
S1	The message will have to have an id associated with it
S2	Ok *Draws on flowchart*
S1	Next start timer and essentially wait *(S2 draws on chart)*
S1	If timeout... so...draw timeout? Yes, no *(S2 draws decision symbol on flowchart)*.... If timeout equals no then we still have to wait for........hold on........
S2	We should receive an acknowledgement here like if it timeouts and we don't receive the acknowledgement then it doesn't matter.
S1	Its irrelevant, doesn't matter. Clients can only, A client doesn't know if the packet was lost on the way or on the way back from the server and it can't ever know. The client has to look after his own fault tolerance and the server has to look after his
S2	So send another
S1	Send the exact same message again *(Draws on flowchart)*

S2	If timer doesn't time out
S1	If it doesn't that we received so we got it back. Does it?..........yes, yes
S2	Yes
S2	It's successful that's it
S2	That's to store........looking up will be pretty the same just different parameters
	Both recheck the logic of the flowchart and agree that the amendments to the client side are finished, now decide to do the server side
S2	Do we need to check the server once its up, its up
S1	*(Reflecting.)* There's something not right here *(Pointing to flow chart)*
S1	Client side isn't complete, we haven't checked the acknowledgement. If client gets the acknowledgement check the id. If it doesn't get an acknowledgement, resend the 'alive' message.
S1	I'm confused.........
S2	Why do we need an id on the store message?
S1	Because we might send two store messages at the same time
S1	Imagine, I'm the client and you are the server. Lets do a role play, I send you this (paper), you get it and send me an ack.
S2	Which is what?
S1	You send me back an ack with a number such as 0. If you send me back an ack 0 or say string' fred' I know what you are talking about
S2	Ok, you send a message, you receive an acknowledgement, then you going to send another message
S2	Does it matter which message gets acknowledged?
S1	Yes, because if I want to store two messages say 'fred' and 'bill'. Fred will be 0 and bill will be 1. These are their ids
S2	But each time you make a new message, you create a new id. If I send this message again will it have the same id?
S1	I won't send again unless I timeout
S2	But if you do timeout, you send the message with the same id. Right?
S1	Yes, sorry…yeah, yeah
Later……	
S1	Need timers for each message you send. Flowchart isn't the best way to structure this?
L	What would be the best way?
S1	*(Reflects)*
S2	Do we need to show for multiple messages?
S1	Do you know what I am saying here, flow charts work fine if we are sending one message, it doesn't handle concurrency because………Is it the case that every time you are sending a message, you have to send an 'alive' message first
L	That is the way the algorithm is implemented at present but it is not set in stone. You may come up with an alternative means by which to determine that the server is alive. If there another way I can determine this?
S1	We can determine this by receiving the ack
L	But is there a way I can get round having to always ask the server before I can send a store message whether it's alive? How can I presume it's alive?

247

S1   ....

L   What can the server do to help me as a client?

S1   Could the server...... Is that a three point acknowledgement thing? I don't remember how this works?

L   OK, it's a bit redundant the client having to ask 'are you alive' 'are you alive'

S1   I'm not sure it is? I'm trying to remember what way it works in reality

L   Could not the server continually poll the clients

S1   Alright yeah, I'm trying to think of it in the way a request reply mechanism works. So you are saying we could also have a server broadcasting essentially a heart beat to the clients. If that is the case, we don't need to worry about the 'alive' message. Is that what you mean?

L   Yes, I'm just trying to give you alternatives

S1   I just thought we were constrained by the current implementation.

L: Your not

Modifying the behaviour of the application to reflect the logic of the flowchart

Reading flow chart logic

S2:   Send a message 'alive', start timer. If you get a reply... You do or you don't... If message 'I am server' that means I got a reply back, I can store. If you haven't got a reply, keep sending til you get a reply.

S1:   OK

Reading application implementation within the code frame

S2:   If message action equals 'store'. This is get message where's the sending of the message now.

S1:   No, this is the receiving of the message so we have to receive the............

S2:   What about....we've got the reply back....

S1:   Where's the same run method? Down here, it's this part. This is where we say 'are you the server', right?

Reading the flow chart

S2:   Ok, you're over here.

S1:   If we receive back that which says 'I am the server'

S2:   Then we go here then we send a message. So if.......

L: All that basically means is?

S2:   We right click on it

L: So it stores it.

S2:   And if we don't then ....eh?

S1:   Does that say 'hit store'?

S2:   If you hit store then you say yes to that. If you don't do this, its going to wait.

S1:   No, it's either one or the other.

S2:   It's either one or what?

S1:   Else find number

Reading implementation code within the code frame

S2:   Yeah but look, this goes if you type in 'Fred' then you do this, if you don't type in that....

L: No. All this line here is doing is reading the value of message action. So if message action is store you can do this but if its find number

S1:   Try and get the name. We don't have to worry about that as it's pre-coded.. So once we've sent it.........So in both case once you've sent it then you need to start timers again

S2:   We are missing a piece then

S1:   What are we missing?

S2:   If you hit store then this, if you don't hit store then we find is it? Find number....send find message

S1:   Remember this is receive message and the only time.........wait a second......If you receive a message back and it's a store message. This is going to be the acknowledgement coming back because we are receiving a message back.

S2:   No

L: No, No you're wrong

S1:   Am I wrong?

L: All its basically asking is the value of message action 'store'

S1:   Ok

        Reading client side code within the code frame

L: So it's basically doing there is its received back a message saying 'I am server' then all I'm doing is checking to see if message action is set to 'store' or 'find number'. If its set to store then I can create a new message and send to store. If its findNumber then I can create a message to find

S1:   Oh, ok. Got you. Receive message is a two stage process first of all it receives....yeah, yeah.   So once we send a message then we have to start a timer

S2:   Ok.

        Lecturer comments on the condition of the flow chart

L: It's like abstract art

S1:   Send store.....so the message comes back. It pulls the data from the form and then it sends the message. Actually the name here ...receiveMessage is almost.........Handle message would be a better name for that method. First of all we've got if message type is 'I am server' then do this then send whatever you want to send else if message is type acknowledgement then

S2:   Yeah ok

S1:   We'll get to that

        Pointing to code frame

S2:   Hit store, yes, send to store, start timer here

S1:   So lets start the timer. Cut and paste. Only need to run it once, don't we? Because if we don't get it back in say 20 sec or whatever it is

S2:   we send it again. We need a different message here, that's sending that message so we need a different message.

S1:   Ok, Sorry say that again.

S2:   That's sending the server message so that's what that is going to send, we need separate timers

        Implements the code

249

S1: One timer for the alive part and one timer for the acknowledgement. Ok that's grand. Do we need three timers…that could be just a message fail……….

S2: We need to do different things each one is sending different things. This one is going to send a store message, so we need to send this message again (pointing to the message)

L: So you are resending the store is it?

S2: Yes

S1: Are we going to fall into a recursive trap? So you are going to try resend once

S2: No, we are using this instead (Schedule method)

S1: So in other words, keep sending it every 10 secs

S2: No we'll send it……..we'll give it 20 secs

Finishes implementation, traces logic by rechecking against the logic of the flowchart

S2: Send message, yes, Start timer, yes, If it doesn't come back, times out, send it again

S1: Every 10 secs keep on…..in other words going to be stuck in that forever

L: So where have you resent the store message?

S1: Haven't done that yet we are getting to that now

L: Can't do it like that

S1: Where's new message declared? No it's inside an if. Make it global. Will that work? Is that because…….

L: You need to recreate the store message in order to resend it back out.
So you really need to copy

S1: Get the information back. That's probably the easiest way to do it as the information is still sitting here (*Pointing to animation frame*). What you are saying, take it from the form again. We'll do it like that but that's not a realistic way of doing it like that. Normally you'd store it in a different variable when the timer gets called, pull it from the form again

S2: Why don't we……….. But we have it here already just send it like this (*Pointing to code*)

S1: Cut this stuff out again

S2: But we don't need to as we have got the message

L: You can't pass a parameter in and out of a class name

S2: That's true. How do you pass it?

L: Need to pass it through a constructor

S2: OK

S1: I'm going to need to ask an implementation question. I'm curious about the implementation. What are the limitations of this? Can you write any program here at the moment and it will simulate it? What are its limitations? I presume the simulator can't get any program and draw it.

L: It will simulate any program that's written using my API. I can create persistent variables in normal java code and run it along with it but they won't be simulated or you won't see them… but to get the logic of your code.

S1: Well, we just grab it from the form.

L: It's just the easiest way.

S1:   But if we do that though, it means we can't ....we couldn't send multiple requests at the same time which means... We now would get rid of the ability to do that because if its relying on that way to get the data back again, the data would be gone by the time............ Say you sent in Fred and write it off, send it off and then send Mary and send it off ...and when we get back the fred thing the data is lost because you've wiped it from the form. That's why you'd use other variable. So it's not a realistic situation. So if you are going to pull it from the form again then that means we'll never be able to send more than two messages at the same time because the data is essentially lost if that's what's being essentially stored. Is that what you want us to do? I'd never write it like that because it would never work in the real world. I don't know what you are trying to get at.

L: But if you think of the purpose of the exercise........

S1:   It is an unrealistic way of simulating something. I've just told you why. I couldn't send more than two bits of information, two numbers, at the same time using that system of retrieving the data and sending it. It would be lost immediately.
        Lets just do it the simple way, the really bad way. (To S2) Do you understand what I am saying?

S2:   I think we should do like this?

S1:   Lets have a look

L: See if yours actually works.

S1:   That's what I'm almost curious about. Lets see if we can break this thing.
        Checks the logic of the code within the code frame

S2:   Ok, start a timer, if it doesn't come back; send a message again that's all taken care here. The message we are passing through a constructor.

S1:   So basically send a copy to the constructor. So that timer has a copy of that message that was sent. So that timer object is associated with that actual message. Ok right

S2:   So now if it comes through, need to get an acknowledgement. Acknowledgement is the server side.

S1:   Should just echo back the same message, exact same message.

S2:   'I am server' that's done, 'store' 'Puts it in address book' (reading code)

S1:   Define is for variables. Why are we doing this? Why are we defining a string variable?

L: What define will actually do is it will visualise

S1:   Oh right

L: It will visualise name and number (points to animation frame)

S1:   It's a simulation piece of code. We can ignore this.

S2:   Put it in the book there then we need to

S1:   We need to acknowledge it.

S2:   Send the exact same message back

S1:   Send a message send to client.........does it know which client to send it to?

L: Question......What message are you sending back?

S1:   As an acknowledgement, sending back the exact same message because the timer at the other end will know it, it will look at and compare them to the data.

L: So what is message?

S1:   Message is whatever the message object is. It should be the exact same object.

251

L: It's a simulation tool so it has to be able to draw that object. In a real programming environment, you can pass objects all the time but I need to draw this object.

S1:   Visually it should be the exact same thing being sent back, it just literally an echo. So just echo it back

S2:   Send that, hit store message, yes, receive store message, Yes, put in phone book, yes, send message data back, yes

S1:   So this is for store, should we do find number or should we bother

L: See if it works

S1:   Yes, Lets I'm curious (*compiles it and executes it*)
        In simulation, S2 starts client 2. Client 2 sends a request to the server. The acknowledgement from the server is sent to the server itself and not to client 2.
        Syntax errors are flagged (global variables)
        Simulation display an infinite number of timers (Solution haven't cancelled any timers)

L: None of the timer threads have been cancelled. You can cancel timers by calling the cancel method.

S2:   Why isn't this dying? Delete. Its not dead

L: Because none of the timer threads have been cancelled.

S1:   What actually went wrong that time?

S2:   You're suppose to cancel our timers

S1:   So ok, open the client code.

S2:   When we call a timer like so when do we need to cancel it?

S1:   So what happens is.....When the timer times out, it will send it again so we haven't taken into account when actually get it back. We should kill it straight after schedule shouldn't we?

L: No,

S2:   Hang on. (*Checks the flowchart*)

L: You are creating a timer on the store message for what reason?

S1:   So we can distinguish between that and the alive message

L: No what's the purpose of the timer on the store message

S2:   So that we........

S1:   waiting for the echo

L: So... essentially you send off a store message you need to determine whether the server has stored that message or not

S1:   Yeah, so

L: So surely if the server acknowledges the store then I should cancel the timer.

S1:   You have to compare them as well. Oh gum. We have to check if it's the same object essentially but we haven't done that.

S2:   OK look..... Here...If we get a store message back that means it's been received here

S1:   So check if it's the same message object

L: what you are doing on the client side is creating the store message so...

S2:   Oh yeah

L: what you need to check is the acknowledgement for the store message

S2:   yeah, yeah (*Implements it*)

252

S1: I can see problems trying to compare the two message objects because

S2: of this

S1: No when this is called again. It will be a different object. It will be a new message. We can't just compare the objects. Do you see what I am saying? This gets called every time a thing comes into the machine; a message comes into the machine. We are going to have to compare these two.

S2: What?

S1: It's a new method being run. When the methods are run again, it will be a new message object

S2: Yeah that's true

S1: So we won't be able to compare the two so that won't work. We should just do it the real simple way. The problem here is that we've said lets just send the same object back that's not going to work essentially I don't think the simulator can't handle it either.......... So what we should do is send back a

L: But all the acknowledgement is, is a message

S2: So we don't need to compare, do we? We send this message right and we don't do any thing until we get an acknowledgement

S1: OK fair enough

S2: Then we are going to say that replies that

S1: If we get anything back it implies that's its been received.

S2: All we need to do is wait for anything an acknowledgement

Interpreting the code within the code frame

S1: If message type equals this type 'ack' then cancel timer (implements timer)

L: Where is the acknowledgement coming from?

S2: Send message back here

L: Yes, Tim you're thinking?

S1: We could have done it by sending back the exact same thing using a global temporary object that's what we should have done. Its irrelevant which way you do it, all the same thing

S2: I'll just check that I have cancelled both timers (rechecks logic)

Amends code

S1: Lets run it and see if it works.

Corrects errors

L: Why is it going up and down? (The ack from server to client 2)

Never associated an address with the message object

S1: It doesn't know where to send it to. Do you have to specify an address?

L: Need to go to the server side to figure out the address for the server

S1: Need to specify an address; I presume its part of the message.

L: Yes

Multiple timers showing

L: Only if it gets to the client will it be cancelled.

S1: That was nice, the way it simulated that... because it really didn't know where to go

L: The address is associated with the message object. So you specify the address when you create the message object

S1: we didn't do that yet.

L: See here, you are just passing in the last message that was sent. sendToClient (message). That message object is going to have the address of the server so it is always going to send it to itself.

L: Did you want to send the acknowledgement back

S1:   I thought the send to client will automatically know where the client was

S2:   Yes it does............. but we haven't specified the sender

S1:   Oh, pardon me.

Executes normally

S1:   Now we can start testing whether our fault tolerance works because we've actually tested nothing so far. So we are going to cancel a message on the way there first.

L: If you want to change the speed, that will make it faster but not the timer. I never associated the timer with

S1:   Actual real time.

L: Which is a pity

Infinite timers

S1:   Change all timers to three seconds

S2:   Run through it (code logic) and make sure. Where does it start?

S1:   This is the server side

S2:   Need client

L: First timer is for 'i'm alive', second is for 'store'

Slow right down so you can kill the first message

S1:   I don't think it will get back in time

L: The interval is too small. Initially runs for three seconds and waits for one sec before executing

S2:   Start the timer, wait for a second start it again

L: that won't give the server a chance to get the reply back in time

In order for the message to travel back it needs longer.

S1:   Animation and real time aren't sync. Set it bigger to 6 secs.

S2:   It's not working

S1:   Speed up the animation. Right click on it, kill the ack. It is working

Where's that starting from? There's no timer to say do something again. It's stuck in a loop somewhere

S2:   It certainly is.

S1:   It keeps storing. Once we get the acknowledgement back do we cancel it? Why is it trying to send it again?

S2:   Can you print something out?

L: Yes, to the console window within the application

S1:   Throw in a load of '*System.out.println*' lines, put "At stage 1", "At stage 2", "At stage 3"

Problem with echoing back same object decide to change to grab from form

Opens console window

S2 reads from the console window and spots the resend

S2:   See that........ storeFail1 again

S1:   Yeah it ran it twice in a row there. …..First of all it's clearly not working as these are two different packets and they shouldn't be the same packet. See the way there are two different colours.

S2:   What?

S1   There are two packets being sent, the same thing is being sent immediately so. First of all there are no timers here so there must be something wrong
        Did you see little timers started there?

L: The initial store timer did start and then it was cancelled.

S2:   Can we try this a different way. If we don't do it like this

S1   What do you think is the problem?

S2:   I think this is the problem

S1:   That what's the problem was, we shouldn't have passed in that object to the constructor. We don't really need it

S2:   We can get the information from the form

S1:   There was two packets being sent and they shouldn't be the same ones
        So.. there was two colours, a blue and a purple. I saw sometimes two packets being sent even though we never sent two packets. There is something funny going on there.

L: like as if it was duplicating

S1:   Yeah, because we didn't cancel anything it started going wrong so something funny was going wrong at the very start before we tried to test any fail safe stuff. If you don't do anything it should run once and stop. So we are not going to kill anything.
        Error, problem with the constructor, still passing the message object to it

S2:   I believe my friends that did work

S1:   Now if you kill what happens?

S2:   It will work

S1:   We are going to kill one on the way first.

S2:   Kill the alive on the way out.

L: Now try to kill a store message. Very good, so that's it, is it?

S1:   No, we want to kill messages on the way back now
        Kill that.
        Do we ask it to store?

L: It does as soon as it receives the acknowledgement

S1:   When we run it just doing whatever the action is

L: Now we want to kill the reply from the server to say that it stores. In other words the fourth packet.

S1:   I'm curious just send it from both.   It's storing the same thing so I think it is……
        It's doing something very odd here.
        Checks the console window.

S1:   Something is calling this and it shouldn't be. There's a thread in the simulation calling this again and again. The question is why wasn't that killed?
        I think I know what is wrong. There are two clients, right? This client is sending 'Tim' and 'one', this client is sending nothing. So what way are we acknowledging it? We're just sending an acknowledgement. Is it comparing the data, so it shouldn't make a difference. It's just an acknowledgement. We also don't know which timer

is generating that. Run the simulation again and put data in both clients. Put data 'Tim, one' and 'Bill, two' in the two clients. If this works there is some odd problem with the simulator

Rechecks logic of server

S1: What if it receives multiple requests at the same time? Is it multi threaded? Does it queue them?

S2: Because there is only one server.............

S1: So we don't have to keep checking it to see if it is server. What do you think is the problem? So you said it sent 'I am server' twice to the first client
We didn't send two 'are you server', did we?
What I am thinking because the simulation and timers are running at different speeds, I think when we start both clients at the same time, the processor, itself is doing .. its achieving two things. Nothing is synchronised here that's the problem.

S2: But even if nothing is synchronised it should still work because

S1: No that might explain why it sent another 'are you the server' thing. I didn't see... I know you saw two 'I am the server' coming back but did you see two 'are you the server' going forward?

Reruns the simulation

Normal case not working

S1: Did you change anything in the code?

S2: I don't think I started the second client

L: No you didn't

S1: 'Are you server' message twice

L: Did the timer run out before the client received back 'I am the server' message?

S1: It must have. You go to change the timers. Put them to 20, no 10.

L: The interval is going to be?

S2: 15 seconds

Starts one

L: The timer was cancelled.

S2: That works.

Enters in data

Adds data and starts second client

Start both together

Starts one and waits 'til its first message is acknowledged before starting the second ˙ client.

Starts both clients together.

Problem was the timers, not giving messages enough time to return.

Tests the fault tolerance.

Starts client one and then client two and randomly kills messages.

Kill the acknowledgment to the store for client 2 and then quickly sends another store.

BIBLIOGRAPHY

[1]   C. Hundhausen, "Towards effective algorithm visualisation artefacts: Designing for participation and communication in an undergraduate algorithms course", Department of computer science and information science, University of Oregon, PhD, 1999, p. 1-150

[2]   J. Stasko and A. Lawrence, "Empirically Assessing Algorithm Animations as Learning Aids," In *the MIT Press*. Cambridge, MA: The MIT Press, 1998.

[3]   B. Koldehofe, "Distributed Algorithms and Educational Simulation/Visualisation in Collaborative Environments", Department of Computer Science and Engineering, Chalmers University of Technology, PhD, 2005, p. 1 - 173

[4]   E. Ackermann, "Chapter 2: Perspective Taking & Object Construction Two Keys to Learning," In *Constructionism in Practice: Designing, Thinking and Learning in the Digital World*, K. Resnick, Ed., 1996, p. 25-35.

[5]   M. D. Byrne, R. Catrambone, and J. T. Stasko, "Evaluating Animations as Student Aids in Learning Computer Algorithms," *Computers and Education*, vol. 33, pp. 253-278, 1999.

[6]   A. W. Lawrence, A. Badre, and J. Stasko, "Empirically evaluating the use of animation to teach algorithms," Presented at Proceedings of the 1994 IEEE Symposium on Visual Languages, St. Louis, MO, 1994. pp. 48 - 54

[7]   J. Stasko, A. Badre, and C. Lewis, "Do Algorithm Animations Assist Learning? An Empirical Study and Analysis," Presented at Proceedings of the INTERCHI '93 Conference on Human Factors in Computing Systems, Amsterdam, Netherlands, 1993. pp. 61-66

[8]   C. D. Hundhausen and S. A. Douglas, "Using visualisations to learn algorithms: Should students construct their own, or view an expert's?" Presented at IEEE Symposium on Visual Languages, Los Alamitos, CA, 2000. pp. 21-28

[9]   C. Hundhausen, S. Douglas, and J. Stasko, "A meta study of algorithm visualisation effectiveness," *Journal of Visual languages and computing*, vol. 13, pp. 259-290, 2002.

[10]   J. S. Gurka and W. Citrin, "Testing the effectiveness of algorithm animation," Presented at IEEE Symposium on Visual Languages, Los Alamitos, 1996. pp. 182 - 189

[11]   C. Kehoe and J. T. Stasko, "Using Animations to Learn about Algorithms: An Ethnographic Case Study," Georgia Institute of Technology, Atlanta, Technical Report GIT-GVU-96-20, September 1996.

[12]   J. Stasko, "Using Student-Built Algorithm Animations as Learning Aids," Presented at Proceedings of the SIGCSE Session, ACM Meetings, San Jose, CA, 1997. pp. 25-29

[13]   S. R. Hansen, N. H. Narayanan, and D. Schrimpsher, "Helping learners visualise and comprehend algorithms," *Interactive Multimedia Electronic Journal of Computer Enhanced Learning*, vol. 2, pp. 10-16, 2000.

[14]   J. Roschelle, "Designing for cognitive communication: Epistemic Fidelity or mediating collaborative inquiry," In *Computers, Communication and Mental Models*, D. K. Kovacs, Ed. London: Taylor & Francis, 1996, p. 13-25.

[15]   A. Paivio, "The empirical case for dual coding," In *Imagery, Memory and Cognition: Essays in Honor of Allan Paivio*, J. C. Yuille, Ed. Hillsdale, NJ: Lawrence Erlbaum Associates, 1983.

[16]   R. E. Mayer and R. B. Anderson, "Animations need narrations: an experimental test of a dual code hypothesis," *Journal of Educational Psychology*, vol. 83, pp. 484-490, 1991.

[17]   A. Paivio, "Dual Coding Theory: Retrospect and Current Status," *Canadian Journal of Psychology*, vol. 45, pp. 255-287, 1991.

[18]   L. Najjar, "Dual Coding as a Possible Explanation for the Effects of Multimedia on Learning," Georgia Institute of Technology, Altanta GIT-GVU-95-29, 1995.

[19]   R. Dunn and K. Dunn, *Teaching Students through their individual learning styles: A practical Approach*: Prentice Hall, Reston Publishing, 1978, p. 1-421.

[20]   R. Riding and S. Rayner, *Cognitive Styles and Learning Strategies*: David Fulton Publishers, 1997, p. 1-217.

[21]   B. Shearer, *The MIDAS handbook of multiple intelligences in the classroom.* Columbus, Ohio: Greyden Press, 1996, p. 1-217.

[22]   H. Gardner, *Frames of Mind: The Theory of Multiple Intelligences.* New York: Basic Books, 1983, p. 1-440.

[23]   D. Kelly, *On the Dynamic Multiple Intelligence informed Personalisation of the Learning Environment*, Department of Computer Science, Trinity College Dublin. PhD, 2005, p. 1-240.

[24]   A. Paivio, *Mental Representations: A Dual Coding Approach.* Oxford: Clarendon Press, 1986.

[25]   S. M. Alessi and S. R. Trollip, "Learning Principles and Approaches," In *Multimedia for Learning: Methods and Development*, S. R. Trollip, Ed. London: Allyn and Bacon, 2001, p. 16- 47.

[26]   D. Jonassen and T. Mayes, "A Manifesto for a Constructivist Approach to Technology in Higher Education," In *Designing Constructivist Learning Environments*, J. Lowyck, Ed. Heidelberg: Springer-Verlag, 1993, p. 232-247.

[27]   C. D. Hundhausen, S. A. Douglas, and J. T. Stasko, "A Meta-Study of Algorithm Visualisation Effectiveness," *Journal of Visual Languages and Computing*, vol. 13, pp. 259-290, 2002.

[28]   D. J. Jarc, M. B. Feldman, and R. S. Heller, "Accessing the benefits of interactive prediction using web based algorithm animation courseware," Presented at Proceedings of the SIGCSE 2000, Austin, Texas, 2000. pp. 377-381

[29]   D. J. Jarc, "Assessing the benefits of interactivity and the influence of learning styles on the effectiveness of algorithm animation using web based data structures courseware", Department of Electrical Engineering and Computer Science, George Washington University, PhD, 1999, p. 1 - 232

[30]   J. Paiget, *The Science of Education and the Psychology of the Child.* New York: Grossmon, 1970, p. 1-300.

[31]   D. F. Sewell, *New Tools for New Minds: A Cognitive Perspective on the Use of Computers in the Classroom.* London: Harvester Wheatsheaf, 1990.

[32]   T. Mayes and C. Fowler, "Learning technology and usability: a framework for understanding courseware," *Interacting with Computers*, vol. 11, pp. 485-497, 1999.

[33]   S. Papert, *MindStorms: Children, Computers and Powerful Ideas*, Second Edition ed. New York: Harvester Wheatsheaf, 1993, p. 1-230.

[34]   S. Papert, "An Introduction to the 5th Anniversary Collection," In *Constructionist Learning*, I. Harrell, Ed. Cambridge, MA: MIT Media Laboratory, 1990.

[35]   S. Grissom, M. F. McNally, and T. Naps, "Algorithm Visualisation in CS Education: Comparing Levels of Student Engagement," 2003. pp. 87 - 94

[36]   C. Hundhausen, "The Search for an Empirical and Theoretical Foundation for Algorithm Visualisation," Unpublished Technical Report, Department of Computer & Information Science, University of Oregon, Eugene, Oregon 1993.

[37]   R. Baecker, "Two systems which produce animated representations of the execution of computer programs," Presented at SIGCSE Bulletin, 1975. pp. 158-167

[38]   J. Stasko, "TANGO: a framework and system for algorithm animation," *IEEE Computer*, vol. 23, pp. 27-39, 1990.

[39]   C. Hundhausen and S. Douglas, "A language and System for Constructing and Presenting Low Fidelity Algorithm Visualisations," In *Software Visualisation: State of the Art Survey, LNCS 2269*, S. Diehl, Ed. New York: Springer Verlag, 2002, p. 227-240.

[40]   E. A. KirkPatrick, "An Experimental Study of Memory," *Psychological Review*, vol. 1, pp. 602-609, 1894.

[41]   R. N. Shephard, "Recognition memory for words, sentences and pictures," *Journal of Verbal Learning and Verbal Behaviour*, vol. 5, pp. 201-204, 1967.

[42]   R. S. Nickerson, "Short term memory for complex meaningful visual configurations: a demonstration of capacity," *Canadian Journal of Psychology*, vol. 19, pp. 155-160, 1965.

[43]   L. Standing, "Learning 10,000 pictures," *Journal of Experimental Psychology*, vol. 25, pp. 207-222, 1973.

[44]   A. Paivio and K. Csapo, "Picture superiority in free recall: imagery or dual coding?" In *Images in mind: The Evolution of a Theory*, A. Paivio, Ed. London: Harvester Wheatsheaf, 1991, p. 210- 225.

[45]   D. L. Nelson, U. S. Reed, and R. J. Walling, "Picture Superiority Effect," *Journal of Experimental Psychology: Human Learning and Memory*, vol. 3, pp. 485-497, 1977.

[46]   J. R. Anderson, "Arguments concerning representations for mental imagery," *Psychological Review*, vol. 85, pp. 249-277, 1978.

[47]   J. H. Larkin and H. A. Simon, "Why a diagram is (sometimes) worth ten thousand words?" *Cognitive Science*, vol. 11, pp. 65-99, 1987.

[48]   J. Morton, "Interaction of information in word recognition," *Psychological Review*, vol. 76, pp. 165-178, 1969.

[49]   S. Madigan, "Picture Memory," In *Imagery, Memory and Cognition: Essays in honor of Allan Paivio*, J. C. Yuille, Ed. Hillsdale, NJ: Lawrence Erlbaum Assciates, 1983, p. 205 -215.

[50]   S. Kobayashi, "Theoretical issues concerning the superiority of pictures over words and sentences in memory," *Perceptual and Motor Skills*, vol. 63, pp. 783-792, 1986.

[51]   J. R. Anderson, *The architecture of cognition*. Cambridge, MA: Harvard University Press, 1983.

[52]   M. Bauer and P. N. Johnson-Laird, "How diagrams can improve reasoning," *Psychological Science*, vol. 4, pp. 327-378, 1993.

[53]   J. Roschelle, "Designing for cognitive communication: Epistemic fidelity or mediating collaborative inquiry?," *The Arachnet Electronic Journal on Virtual Culture*, vol. 2, 1994.

[54]   K. Rasmussen, "Hypermedia and learning styles:can performance be influenced," *Journal of Multimedia and Hypermedia*, vol. 7, 1998.

[55]   C. Cooper, *Individual Differences*. London: Routledge, 2002.

[56]   S. Messick, "Bridging cognition and personality in education: The role of style in performance and development," *European Journal of Personality*, vol. 10, pp. 353 - 376, 1996.

[57]   R. J. Sternberg and E. L. Grigorenko, *A capsule of history of theory and research on styles*. Mahwah, NJ: LEA, 2001.

[58]   S. M. Alessi and S. R. Trollip, "Simulations," In *Multimedia for Learning (Methods and Development)*, Bacon, Ed. Boston, 2001, p. 213 -269.

[59]   N. Ford and S. Y. Chen, "Individual differences, hypermedia navigation and learning: an empirical study," *Educational Multimedia and Hypermedia*, vol. 9, pp. 281-312, 2000.

[60]   E. V. Glaserfield, "Constructivism in education," In *International encyclopedia of education*. Oxford: Pergamon Press, 1989, p. 162- 163.

[61]   M. H. Brown, *Algorithm Animation*. Cambridge, MA: The MIT Press, 1988.

[62]   M. Brown and R. Sedgewick, "Techniques for algorithm animation," *IEEE Software*, vol. 2, pp. 28-39, 1985.

[63]   J. Stasko, "The path-transition paradigm: A practical methodology for adding animation to program interfaces," *Journal of Visual Languages and Computing*, vol. 1, pp. 213-236, 1990.

[64]   J. Stasko, "Smooth, continuous animation for portraying algorithms and processes," In *Software visualisation: programming as a multimedia experience*, B. Price, Ed. Cambridge, MA: The MIT Press, 1998, p. 103-118.

[65]   M. Brown and J. Hershberger, "Color and sound in algorithm animation," *Computer*, vol. 25, pp. 52-63, 1992.

[66]   J. Stasko and J. Wehrli, "Three dimensional computation visualisation," Presented at IEEE Symposium on Visual Languages, Bergen, Norway, 1993. pp. 100-107

[67]   M. Brown and M. Najork, "Algorithm animation using 3D interactive graphics," Presented at ACM Symposium on user interface software and technology, Atlanta, GA, 1993. pp. 93-100

[68]   P. Gloor, "Animated Algorithms," In *Software visualisation: programming as a multimedia experience*, B. Price, Ed. Cambridge, MA: The MIT Press, 1998, p. 409 - 416.

[69]   T. L. Naps, J. R. Eagan, and L. Norton, "JHAVE - An environment to actively engage students in web-based algorithm visualisations," Presented at Proceedings of the 31st SIGCSE Technical Symposium on Computer Science Education, Austin Texas, 2000. pp. 109-113

[70]   D. E. W. Tileston, *10 best teaching practices, how brain research, learning styles and standards define teaching competencies*. New York: Sage Publication Inc (USA): Corwin Press, 2000.

[71]   B. S. Bloom, M. D. Engelhart, E. J. Hurst, W. H. Hill, and D. R. Krathwohl, *Taxonomy of Educational Objectives: The Classification of Educational Goals: Handbook I Cognitive Domain*. London: Longman Group Ltd., 1972, p. 1-201

[72]   T. Naps, R. Fleischer, M. McNally, G. Robling, C. Hundhausen, S. Rodger, V. Aimstrum, A. Korhonen, J. A. Velazquez-Iturbide, W. Dann, and L. Malmi, "Exploring the Role of Visualisation and Engagement in Computer Science Education," Presented at ACM SIGCSE Bulletin, 2003. pp. 131 - 152

[73]   A. W. Lawrence, "Empirical studies of the value of algorithm animation in algorithm understanding", Department of Computer science, Georgia Institute of Technology, Unpublished Ph.D. dissertation,1993.

[74]   A. Sears and R. Wolfe, "'Visual analysis: adding breadth to a computer graphics course'," Presented at SIGCSE Technical Symposium, Nashville, TN, 1995. pp. 195-198.

[75]   S. Hansen, N. H. Narayanan, and M. Hegarty, "Designing Educationally Effective Algorithm Visualizations," *Journal of Visual Languages and Computing*, vol. 13, pp. 291-317, 2002.

[76]   M. H. Brown, "Exploring algorithms using Balsa-II," *IEEE Computer*, vol. 21, pp. 14-36, 1988.

[77]   J. Stasko and E. Kraemer, "A methodology for building application-specific visualisations of parallel programs," *Journal of Parallel and Distributed Computing*, vol. 18, pp. 258-264, 1993.

[78]   M. Ben-Ari, N. Myller, E. Sutinen, and J. Tarhio, "Perspectives on program animation with Jeliot," In *Software Visualisation: International Seminar*, S. Diehl, Ed. Dagstuhl, Germany: Springer, 2001, p. 31-35.

[79]   A. Korhonen, "Visual Algorithm Simulation", Department of Computer Science and Engineering, Helsinki University of Technology, PhD,2003, p. 1-135

[80]   W. Pierson and S. H. Rodger, "Web-based Animation of Data Structures Using Jawaa," Presented at Proceedings of the 29th SIGCSE Technical Symposium on Computer Science Education, Atlanta Georgia, 1998. pp. 267 -271

[81]   G. RoBling, M. Shuler, and B. Freisleben, "The ANIMAL Algorithm Animation Tool," Presented at Proceedings of the annual SIGCSE/SIGCUE ITiCSE on Innovation and Technology in Computer Science Education, Helsinki Finland, New York: ACM Press, 2000, pp 37- 40.

[82]   G. Robling and B. Freisleben, "Approaches for generating animations for lectures," Presented at AACE 11th International Society for Information Technology and Teacher Education (SITE), San Diego, 2000. pp. 809-814

[83]   S. P. Lahtinen, T. Lamminjoki, E. Sutinen, J. Tarhio, and A. P. Tuovinen, "Towards automated animation of algorithms," Presented at Fourth International Conference in Central Europe on Computing Graphics and Visualisation, University of West Behemnia, 1996. pp. 150-161

[84]   C. Hundhausen and S. Douglas, "Using Visualisations to Learn Algorithms: Should Students Construct their Own, Or View an Expert's ?", Presented at IEEE International Symposium on Visual Languages, 2000, pp. 21-30.

[85]   J. Stasko, "The PARADE Environment for Visualising Parallel Program Executions: A Progress Report," Georgia Institute of Technology, Atlanta, Technical Report GIT-GVU-95-03 1995.

[86]   C. Burger, K. Rothermel, and R. Mecklenburg, "Interactive Protocol Simulation Applets for Distance Education," Presented at Proceeding of the 5th International Workshop on Interactive Distributed Multimedia Systems and Telecommunication Services (IDMS), 1998, p. 7- 10.

[87]   S. Gruner, M. Mosbah, and M. Bauderon, "A New Tool for the Simulation And Visualisation of Distributed Algorithms," Technical Report, LaBRI, Universite Bordeaux 1, Talence, Cedex, Technical Report 2001.

[88]   Y. Moses, Z. Polunsky, A. Tal, and L. Ulitsky, "Algorithm Visualisation for distributed environments.," Presented at Proceedings of the IEEE Symposium on Information Visualisation, Los Alamitos, CA, 1998. pp. 71-78

[89]   B.-A. Mordechai, "Interactive Execution of Distributed Algorithms," *Journal of Educational Resources in Computing*, vol. 1, 2001.

[90]   W. Schreiner, "A Java Toolkit for Teaching Distributed Algorithms," Presented at International conference for Technology in Computer Science Education, Aarhus, Denmark, 2002. pp. 111 - 115

[91]   S. Khanvilkar and S. M. Shatz, "Tool Integration for Flexible Simulation of Distributed Algorithms," Presented at Software - Practice and Experience, 2001. pp. 1363 - 1380

[92]   R. B.-B. Levy, M. Ben-Ari, and P. A. Uronen, "The Jeliot 2000 Program Animation System," *Computers and Education*, vol. 40, pp. 1-15, 2003.

[93]   M. Lattu, J. Tarhio, and V. Meisalo, "How a visualisation tool can be used - Evaluating a tool in Research and Development," Presented at 12th Workshop of the Psychology of Programming Interest Group, Cozenza, Italy, 2000.

[94]   B. Koldehofe, M. Papatriantafilou, and P. Tsigas, "LYDIAN, An Extensible Educational Animation Environment for Distributed Algorithms," Presented at Proceedings of the 4th Annual SIGCSE/SIGCUE Conference on Innovation and Technology in Computer Science Education (ITiCSE'00), 2000. pp. 189

[95]   T. Hubscher-Younger and N. H. Narayanan, "Influence of authority on convergence in collaborative learning," Presented at Computer support for collaborative learning, 2002. pp. 481-489

[96]   S. Douglas and C. Hundhausen, "Exploring human visualisation of computer algorithms," Presented at Graphics Interface, 1996. pp. 9-16

[97]   B. Koldehofe, M. Papatriantafilou, and P. Tsigas, "Integrating a Simulation Visualisation Environment in a Basic Distributed Systems Course: A Case Study Using LYDIAN," Presented at Proceedings of the 8th Annual SIGCSE Conference on Innovation and Technology in Computer Science Education (ITiCSE'03), 2003. pp. 35-39

[98]   C. Burger and K. Rothermel, "A framework to support teaching in distributed systems," *Journal of Educational Resources in Computing (JERIC)*, vol. 1, 2001, p. 3-8.

[99]   J. Bosch, P.Molin, M. Mattson, and P. Bengtsson, "Object Oriented Frameworks - Problems and Experiences," In *Object Oriented Frameworks*, R. E. Johnson, Ed. London: Wiley & Sons, 1998.

[100]   J. V. Gurp and J. Bosch, "Design, Implementation and Evolution of Object Oriented Frameworks: Concepts and Guidelines," Presented at Software- Practice and Experience, 2001. pp. 277 - 300

[101]   A. Stewart, "The test of time: 'soft' versus 'hard skills'," in *Career Guidance Today*, vol. 9, 2001, pp. 20-24.

[102]   M. d. Raadt, R. Watson, and M. Toleman, "Language Trends in Introductory Programming Courses," Presented at InSITE, 2002. pp. 299 -337

[103] G. Coulouris, *Distributed Systems: Concepts and Designs*, 3rd ed: Addison-Wesley, 2000, p. 1 - 764.

[104] G. Booch, "Chapter 9: Frameworks: Foundation Class Library," In *Object Oriented Analysis and Design with Application*, G. Booch, Ed., 2nd ed. Santa Clara: The Benjamin/Cummings Publishing Company, Inc., 1994, p. 327 -329.

[105] G. Bernard, D. Steve, and M. Simatic, "A survey of load sharing in networks of workstations," Presented at Distributed Systems Engineering, 1993. pp. 75-86

[106] J. Gray and L. Lamport, "Consensus on Transaction Commit," Microsoft Research Institute, Technical Report MSR-TR-2003-96, January 2004.

[107] D. Mertens, *Research Methods in Education and Psychology: Integrating Diversity with Quantitative and Qualitative Approaches*. Thousand Oaks, California: SAGE Publications, 1998, p. 1 - 422

[108] J. McMillan, *Research in Education: A Conceptual Introduction*, 5th Ed. New York: Addison Wesley Longman, 2001.

[109] M. LeCompte and J. Preissle, *Ethnography and Qualitative Design in Educational Research*, 2nd ed. London: Academic Press Ltd., 1993.

[110] L. Cohen, L. Manion, and K. Morrison, *Research Methods in Education*. London: RoutledgeFalmer, Taylor & Francis Group, 2000, p. 1-438

[111] M. Langenbach, C. Vaughn, and L. Aagaard, *An Introduction to Educational Research*. Needham Heights, MA: Allyn & Bacon, 1994.

[112] K. Jennings, "Computer Graphical Interfaces, Reflection and Music Composition, A Holistic Study", Department of Computer Science, Trinity College Dublin, Phd, 2006, p. 1 - 300

[113] R. Yin, *Case Study Research: Design and Methods*, Third ed. London: Sage Publications Inc., 2003, p. 1-200.

[114] E. Costello, "The Use of a Software Enabled Scaffolding Environment to aid Novice Programmers", Department of Computer Science, Trinity College Dublin, Unpublished Master's Thesis, 2004, p. 1-156

[115] C. Wickens, S. Gordon, and Y. Liu, *An Introduction to Human Factors Engineering*. New York: Addison-Wesley Publications Inc., 1998, p.

[116] D. J. Mayhew, *Principles and Guidelines in Software User Interface Design*. Englewoods, NJ: Prentice Hall, 1992.

[117] J. Nielson, *Usability Engineering*. Cambridge, MA: AP Professional, 1993.

[118] J. Stasko and C. Hundhausen, "Algorithm Visualisation," In *Computer Science Education Research*, M. Petre, Ed. Lisse, the Netherlands: Taylor and Francis, 2004, p. 199 - 228.

[119] N. Fleming and C. Mills, "Not another inventory, rather a catalyst for reflection," *To Improve The Academy*, vol. 2, pp. 137 - 149, 1992.

[120] E. V. Glaserfield, "Constructivism in Education," in *International Encyclopedia of education*. Oxford: Pergamon Press, 1989, pp. 162-163.

[121] J. Paiget, *The science of education and the psychology of the child*. New York: Grossmon, 1970.

[122] F. O'Donnell and B. Tangney, "Toward 'Phenomenaria' in the Teaching of Distributed Systems Concepts," presented at IEEE International Conference on Advanced Learning Technologies, Athens, Greece, 2003.

[123] S. Papert, *MindStorms: Children, Computers and Powerful Ideas*. New York: Basic Books, Inc., 1980.

www.ingramcontent.com/pod-product-compliance
Lightning Source LLC
LaVergne TN
LVHW042331060326
832902LV00006B/112

* 9 7 8 3 6 3 9 1 2 2 9 8 5 *